Children of Disabled Parents

New Thinking
About Families Affected by
Disability and Illness

Tony Newman

RHP

Russell House Publishing

For Verity

First published in 2003 by:
Russell House Publishing Ltd.
4 St. George's House
Uplyme Road
Lyme Regis
Dorset DT7 3LS

Tel: 01297-443948
Fax: 01297-442722
e-mail: help@russellhouse.co.uk
www.russellhouse.co.uk

British Library Cataloguing-in-publication Data:
A catalogue record for this book is available from the British Library.

ISBN: 1-903855-20-9

Typeset by Sheaf Graphics Ltd, Sheffield

Printed by Cromwell Press, Trowbridge

About Russell House Publishing

RHP is a group of social work, probation, education and youth and community work practitioners and academics working in collaboration with a professional publishing team. Our aim is to work closely with the field to produce innovative and valuable materials to help managers, trainers, practitioners and students. We are keen to receive feedback on publications and new ideas for future projects. For details of our other publications please visit our website or ask us for a catalogue. Contact details are on this page.

Contents

Preface

Whatever the circumstances of our birth or childhood, we all have parents. Most of us will have something else in common – we will become parents ourselves in our turn. And while not all of us may initially perceive it to be the case, almost all of us who live long enough will experience disability at first hand, either as disabled people ourselves, or as the partner, son, daughter, sibling or parent of a disabled person. We might even go so far as to suggest that 'disability' – if by this term we mean a condition where our optimum functioning is compromised by physical or psychological factors – is not a deviation from the norm but the default condition of the human body. For most of our allotted three score years and ten, we are restricted first by immaturity, then by excessive maturity. Even if we are not personally affected by impairments in the intervening years, the period when we enjoy the full vigour of our bodies is remarkably short.

'Children', 'disabled' and 'parents' are individually, let alone in combination, powerful and emotive. Many years ago, as a young and inexperienced social worker, I met an elderly lady who had spent all her adult life in a mental handicap hospital. She was well dressed, a little hesitant of speech, but friendly and talkative once we got to know each other. Slowly, through what she told me and from my speaking to members of staff, the full horror of her life became apparent. She had been admitted to hospital as a young girl, under the old Mental Deficiency Act after giving birth to a child out of wedlock. As she was from a poverty stricken family, and judged to be of low intelligence, her child – a girl she later told me – was taken into care and, as far as she knew, adopted. She never saw her again. 'I wish I could remember her name', she told me. 'But I can't'.

Such stories are now the stuff of nightmares, and the ones who can tell these dreadful tales at first hand are gone. Many disabled parents, including those with learning disabilities as well as other kinds of impairments, care successfully for their children and receive help in doing so from dedicated social care and health professionals. However, for many disabled parents, the perception that confidence in their parental role is conditional, even begrudging, remains a constant reality. Children of disabled parents – like the children of any parents – rely more on their families for their health and welfare than any other source of support. Parents, whether disabled or not, can fail in their duties towards their children, and this failure may sometimes be beyond the capacity of any child welfare service, however well-resourced and intentioned, to rectify. However, as this book will argue, the gap between what disabled parents and their children experience, and what they *could* experience, is far larger than it need be, and this gap could be closed if a more effective structure of support services were to be developed. This, however, is only likely to happen once we cease to be so pre-occupied with the perceived 'danger' that parental (and indeed sibling) disability causes to 'well' others in families.

A volume about the children of disabled parents must inevitably be clear about what exactly is meant by 'disability'. The days where one could answer this question adequately by simply citing the charmless language of the 1948 National Assistance Act are long gone, though its retention in UK legislation requires us to recall that disability refers to someone who is:

> ...blind, deaf or dumb (or who suffers from mental disorder of any description) and other persons (aged 18 and over) who are substantially and permanently handicapped by illness, injury, or congenital deformity.
>
> (National Assistance Act 1948, section 29.)

Our understanding of 'disability' has been revolutionised in the past few decades. As the views of disabled people themselves have begun to penetrate the universe of public health, education and social care, a wider understanding had developed among professionals of what has become known as **the social model of disability**. According to this model, the biggest problem faced by disabled people is not the impairment that affects them, be it sensory, physical or psychological, but the failure by public bodies to make the often simple environmental or attitudinal changes that constitute the real barriers to social inclusion. However, it is also necessary to recognise that the function of any definition is to exclude as well as include. While leading organisations representing disabled parents (in the UK www.disabledparentsnetwork.org.uk and in the US www.lookingglass.org) include populations other than those defined above, notably people dependent on drugs and alcohol, this approach will not be taken here. Apart from remaining unconvinced that conditions of this nature can meaningfully be embraced under the rubric of 'disability', reasons of space, and the specialist nature of these issues, suggest that a discussion of children affected by parental drug and alcohol dependency should take place elsewhere. While eschewing the dated language of the National Assistance Act, this book will address the population this definition describes, focusing on physical, sensory and psychological impairments, including learning disabilities, and severe and chronic illness.

This book differs from much that has been written on this subject. The typically problem-focused approach of research and practice in the field of disability has led to typically problem-focused conclusions. The main preoccupation of work in this area has been to identify the negative impacts of parental disability on children, where risk factors are most likely to emerge, and how children may be protected. Similarly, the focus of research in this field has been to identify how and to what extent children have been negatively affected, both during childhood and subsequently as adults. This has contributed to the widespread perception of disability as a personal, family and social disaster, without redeeming features, which blights the lives of all those that it touches. This highly negative material has fed the universal

human tendency to ascribe explanations to events based on prior perceptions. Thus, if we believe that parental disability is a significant risk factor for children, and we encounter a child of a disabled parent who is missing school, is depressed, or is suffering from an emotional disorder, our explanation for these events is likely to include some reference to the parental condition. If on the other hand, the child of a disabled parent succeeds educationally or vocationally, or displays any other admirable trait, we will tend to ascribe this success to their overcoming adversity. Parental disability is rarely seen as a neutral factor, let alone a positive one.

This book will thus explore the impact of parental disability on children, especially where lack of support to families results in significant restrictions to children's day-to-day lives. In doing so it will:

- Review the literature on parental disability and its impact on children.
- Consider why concern for the children of disabled parents has emerged at this particular juncture of history.
- Explore whether the presence of parental disability affects the self reported health and wellbeing of children.
- Discuss how children's strengths as well as their vulnerabilities can be identified and promoted.
- Suggest how more effective social care services can be delivered to children in families affected by disability or chronic illness.

The core theme of this book is neither that parental disability is always a source of risk or suffering for children, nor that it will leave children unaffected and not in need of help or protection. It is rather that, whether disabled or not and despite their occasional failings, parents are the most important source of support for children, and that disability is a normal and essentially unremarkable aspect of the human condition. Recognising the strengths and capacities of parents, and supporting them in their parental duties, remains the single best way of guaranteeing children's present and future welfare.

Introduction

When a father helps a son, both laugh. When a
son helps a father, both cry.

(Yiddish proverb, traditional.)

Us and Them

Despite encounters with disability being such a
commonplace affair, most people, lay as well as
professional, tend to see disability as a
phenomenon affecting people other than
themselves. This observation is even more
noticeable when the subject of disabled parents is
raised. A casual conversation on the subject will
typically run as follows:

I'm writing about the children of disabled
parents.

Disabled parents. That's interesting. Yes, I
suppose it can happen when someone has an
accident or becomes seriously ill. They must need
an awful lot of help, especially where the
children are young. I guess their children must
often get taken away if they can't cope.

Is there anyone disabled in your family?

You know, now that you mention it, my
grandfather had a problem with his leg – he had
polio as a child. I always remember him as
having a very bad limp. Dad always said that he
had to run more errands than his friends
because his father couldn't walk far. And my
sister-in-law had a breakdown after her second
daughter was born. Took her ages to recover. But
I've never thought of them as **disabled**.

Terms that begin with *dis-* are generally bad
news. The Latin root simply means 'twice' or 'in two
ways'. However, its use as a prefix in English will
usually have the force of a departure from or a
reversal of a normative condition; hence
'disagreeable', 'disassociate', 'distrust', 'dishonest',
'disown' or even in the pungent jargon of youth
culture, to 'dis'. The Oxford English Dictionary
makes the negative meaning clear. Disability is
'want of ability to discharge any office or function',
'incapacity in the eye of the law', 'unable',
'incapable', 'impotent'. From Old Testament laws
barring people with physical blemishes from
priestly functions to the contemporary
disenfranchisement (that prefix again!) of people
with learning disabilities from civic obligations,
being labelled a 'dis-' anything has meant, to one
degree or another, losing a part of what makes a
person fully human.

Disability is then, literally, problematic. While its
presence may often be the occasion for compassion
and charity, the main thrust of health, education
and social care services had traditionally been
damage limitation. Disabled people have historically
been perceived as dependent, and it is this quality of
dependency that gives the phrase 'disabled parent'
its peculiarly oxymoronic flavour. Whatever else
parents are, they are not meant, in their full flush of
youth at least, to be *dependent*. It is children who
depend on parents, not just for their physical care,
but for emotional sustenance, economic support,
advice and counsel. Those readers who are parents
themselves will need no insight into what being a
parent means. Anything that threatens our status as
primary carers threatens the most important part of
our identity. Both research and practice in the field
of disability has often magnified rather than
moderated this threat by treating parental disability
as first and foremost a risk factor to children. That
disabled people *may be* less than adequate parents
is undoubtedly true. Like members of any other
social group, disabled people may be uncaring,
insensitive, selfish or cruel. They may also be poor,
uneducated, live in deprived communities, have
unreliable friends and unsupportive families.
However, disabled people, unlike other parents, may
often be judged as inadequate, or even have
questioned their right to bear children at all, on the
basis of their impairment *alone*, not because of any

personal or environmental inadequacies that affect them.

What About the Children?

> Professionals...must take positive steps to identify those families where there is a greater likelihood of children becoming carers. This includes *any* [authors' emphasis] *family, dual or lone parent, with children where sickness or disability is evident.*
>
> (Dearden and Becker, 1997.)

What, we need to ask, of the children? Children of disabled parents have achieved a somewhat more elevated role in the contemporary social care universe than disabled parents themselves. The primary concern of health and social care services, whether measured through the activities of practitioners, research, number of publications, or coverage in the popular press, has dwelt on perceived risks to the child arising from parental disability (Weir and Douglas, 1999). With infants and pre-school children, the focus of concern has tended to be potential physical harm (primarily where parents with mental health problems are involved) or neglect (most typically concerning parents with learning disabilities). With children of school age, the emotional and physical impact of parental disability, especially where associated with caregiving by children, has become the major preoccupation.

The latter issue has become widely discussed over the past decade. From a baseline of close to zero, children who have become known as 'young carers' have generated a substantial body of literature (O'Neill, 1988; Bilsborrow, 1992; Aldridge and Becker, 1993a; Jenkins and Wingate, 1994; Keith and Morris, 1995; Olsen, 1996; Becker et al., 1998; Becker et al., 2000). Such children are specifically recognised in parliamentary legislation through the 1995 Carers (Recognition and Services) Act and have been widely accepted as meeting the definition of children in need in the 1989 Children Act. In 1992, just two dedicated services existed in the UK; in 1995, this had risen to 37 projects (Dearden and Becker, 1995); by 1998, this had risen to 110 (Aldridge and Becker, 1998).

Local authority Children's Services Plans typically contain a discrete section addressing their needs, and their circumstances have been the subject of many publicity campaigns by such diverse organisations as the Princess Royal Trust for Carers, NCH Action for Children, St. John Ambulance, Crossroads, the Children's Society, Barnardo's and the Women's Institute. Extensive media coverage in the popular press has brought the issue to the attention of the wider public. The government's National Strategy on Carers, published in 1999, contains a separate chapter on children who provide care.

Young carers or children of disabled parents?

What is the difference between a 'young carer' and any child with a disabled parent? The formal government understanding of a young carer is based on a letter from the Chief Inspector of Social Services in April 1995. This is 'a child or young person who is carrying out significant caring tasks and assuming a level of responsibility for another person which would usually be taken by an adult', usually for a parent but occasionally for siblings and other family members. The guidance notes to the Carers (Recognition and Services) Act 1995 define young carers as 'children and young people (under 18) who provide or intend to provide a substantial amount of care on a regular basis' (Department of Health, 1996: p2). 'Young carers' are thus defined – formally – by the *volume* of the duties they undertake, not primarily on the *impact* these duties may have on them, However, an alternative definition has been widely adopted, in slightly differing versions, by many services in the UK (Becker et al., 1998). This rejects the core notion of classification by tasks or duties, and proposes instead that the restrictions placed on children's lives, and thus the impact, rather than the content, of the caring role, should be the defining criterion. While versions of this definition vary, the following example is typical:

> A 'young carer' is a child or young person under the age of 18 whose life is in some way restricted

because of the need to take responsibility for a person who is ill, has a disability, is elderly, is experiencing mental distress or is affected by substance misuse.

While this, and other even broader definitions, rightly recognises that observable activities are not the only important component of a caring task, it is difficult to see how this approach does not render any child of a disabled parent, at least potentially, a 'young carer'. In trying to differentiate between these overlapping groups we have two options. We can tighten our definitional boundaries and regard young carers as a small subset of children of disabled parents in general. The other option is to dispense with the notion of 'young carers' all together, and consider them children of disabled parents whose family is suffering from a significant deficit of support from statutory, voluntary and informal sources. This book will argue for the latter course. By relinquishing the concept of 'young carers' (though most certainly not the children themselves), we can emphasise their proper role as dependants of adults whom, in the vast majority of cases, wish to discharge – with help if necessary – their role as primary carers. This course of action avoids both the distasteful necessity of a child having to 'qualify' for a support service by crossing a welfare threshold. It also prevents our implying that disabled parents are the passive recipients of care by their children, or even worse, active participants in the subversion of 'normal' parent-child relationships. In short, it ensures that parents remain in the frame, that the potentially vulnerable status of disabled parents is not put at further risk and that children, as well as their parents, receive the help they need.

When services fail

Historically, concern for the situation of disabled parents' children is based on a number of beliefs, some more supported by evidence than others. These can be summarised briefly as follows. Excessive responsibility for, or need to worry about the welfare of other family members at too early an age is injurious to a child's psychosocial health. Negative consequences may include impaired educational careers due to missing school, physical harm (due to, for example, having to lift a disabled sibling or parent), mental health problems, low self-esteem and restricted social networks. Within the psychoanalytical tradition, the reversal of the caring role, when associated with parental psychopathology, is believed to render the child vulnerable to personality disorders characterised by compulsive care giving and a corresponding inability to receive care. The consequences, it is suggested, often extend into adult life, not just though distorted family dynamics and future relationship difficulties, but also in terms of damaged career trajectories and an increased vulnerability to depressive illnesses and other psychological disorders. Our knowledge of these long term effects depends largely on the post hoc accounts of adults. While these may be very illuminating and often very moving, it is difficult to know how representative these are of the wider population. Nonetheless, a wide range of studies and reports have argued strongly that, whether arising from exposure to psychiatric disorder, learning disability, sensory or physical impairment, and whether or not substantial care giving is a feature of the family context, parental disability is associated with negative long term effects on children.

A widespread consensus has thus emerged from recent research studies, accompanied by professional and media accounts and accounts from children themselves, that children of disabled parents may have their health, educational careers and social relationships affected in the following ways:

Impact on emotional and physical health

- Children will typically resist telling others about their situation, as they are afraid of the consequences, particularly interventions by child protection services and consequent separation from their parents.
- The traditional parent-child relationship may be

inverted. The long term effects are assumed to be negative.

- Unacceptable levels of stress may be experienced, both arising from the atypical levels of responsibility children may carry and through lack of information regarding the aetiology of their parent's illness.
- Physical damage may occur to children who undertake tasks involving, for example, heavy lifting, either of people or of objects, such as shopping.
- Children's sense of duty, or anxiety about the consequences of, for example, leaving parents unattended, will have negative psychosocial consequences.
- Infants will be at risk because their parent is unable to deliver an adequate level of physical care.

Impact on education

- Children will miss school, be persistently late, or have aspects of their curriculum impeded.
- Vocational careers will be damaged.

Impact on social relationships

- Children will find it more difficult to make and maintain friendships, as their domestic situations will affect the way in which peer relationships are formed.
- Parents will consciously or unconsciously pressure children into sacrificing social contacts for presence at home, whether to care for themselves or for siblings.

Despite being widely believed, few of these propositions have been tested empirically. We do have a substantial body of evidence which points to a range of associations, albeit of varying strengths, between parental disability and child illness and dysfunction, especially where the family situation is compounded by poverty, and parenting style is unrewarding, hostile and critical. Conversely, exposure to different aspects of disability, even in cases where additional domestic responsibilities are necessary, has been associated with *positive* benefits for children,

including increased maturity and competencies. We also know that children, contrary to the beliefs of many health and social welfare practitioners, possess a powerful capacity to recover from adversities. Many children who encounter major stress-inducing events – seemingly between one half and two thirds – show few observable long term effects in adult life (Fraser, 1998).

Dissenting voices

The rapid rise to prominence, largely over the decade 1989-1999, of the situation of disabled parents, and especially that of 'young carers', has generated a number of questions and not a few controversies. First, the perceived focus on supporting children rather than supporting parents has been criticised as further pathologising disabled people (Keith and Morris, 1995; Morris, 1997). Second, a concern has been expressed that the expansion of services to the children of disabled parents has run ahead of any robust research about their circumstances (Parker and Olsen, 1995; Olsen, 1996). Third, disputes concerning prevalence have also rumbled through the debate, with estimates of the numbers of affected children in the UK varying wildly from a low of 10,000 to a high of 212,000, and are capable of even greater inflation where weaker criteria are adopted. The only general population sample surveyed to date (Walker, 1996) located 18 young people from 12,000 households who could be described as 'young carers' (using the Chief Inspector's definition above), generating a UK estimate of between 19,000 and 51,000. Data from the 1996 General Household survey, which included questions on child caregivers remain unpublished as the numbers located were considered too low for statistical analysis (personal communication, 1998). Finally, it is not clear how widely the commonly used label of 'young carer' is recognised by children, or if it is an identity constructed by adults and offered to children whose lives are affected by parental disability and illness.

While this book draws on a substantial body of literature emanating from outside the UK, particularly that relating to parental disability and its consequences, it is notable that the issue of 'young carers' is predominantly a UK phenomenon. Many other European countries show little interest in this aspect of children's welfare. In Sweden, it is suggested, the welfare state is so supportive of families that children's needs are covered by normal family services. In France, the family is the primary target of support; in Germany adult children are expected to be responsible for their parents (Hantrais and Becker, 1995). Even in the USA, where, in relation to published literature at least, one might expect to find a substantial body of work, the issue of young carers, termed 'child caregivers', has resulted in only a small number of exploratory studies (Lackey and Gates, 1997; Gates and Lackey, 1998). Brief accounts have been published of initiatives in Malta (Cachia et al., 1998) and Australia (Fisher, 1998). Home based health care by children in Southern Africa (primarily associated with the AIDS pandemic), has been explored by authors, and speculative comparisons drawn between Zimbabwean children and children in developed countries (Robson, 1999; Robson and Ansell, 2000). However, this material remains, to date, highly limited and renders any but the most general international comparisons unsatisfactory.

Existing research on young carers, while providing many illuminating case studies of young people with often distressing family circumstances, has suffered from numerous flaws. Much work has been carried out by or on behalf of child care charities or national pressure groups who typically wish to highlight the most extreme forms of adversity affecting children and to stress their vulnerability to adversities, often as part of promotional campaigns. Second, while many studies have examined different dimensions of children's health and wellbeing, almost all accounts have been either retrospective, have arisen from opportunistic sampling or have had no controls. Third, it is rare for any kind of quantitative study to be undertaken. Research to date has relied heavily on adult retrospective accounts, narrative accounts from children currently known to services, and to a lesser extent, their parents. While such accounts are essential to any overall understanding of the situation of children affected by parental disability, they are insufficient in themselves to sustain an increasingly important dimension of child care practice.

Those working and researching in the field have long recognised the need to consider the welfare of the whole family, not just that of the children and young people. However, supporting disabled parents is a rather harder concept to sell to both professional media and lay constituencies than that of helping children. The extent to which investment in dedicated services for children has been at the expense of supporting families is unknown, but was a major source of concern in the 2000 Social Service Inspectorate inspections, as was the possibility that support could be diverted from secure mainstream services towards often precariously funded young carer services (Goodinge, 2000). It is not necessary to dispute the primacy of the child's welfare to argue that the child's wellbeing is best secured by ensuring their parents are able to carry out their duties adequately. Despite the best intentions of those who support and advocate for 'young carers', the continuing emphasis on the needs of children is perceived by many disabled people as an accusation that they are failing in their duty as parents. Many disabled parents – some ten per cent of the population of UK parents – are growing increasingly impatient with this trend, and are beginning to demand a substantial policy and practice re-alignment that does not begin from a default assumption that disability or illness is an impediment to good parenting (Wates, 2002).

They **** You up, Your Mum and Dad

Families have often been represented as a toxic reservoir of adult insecurities and the main source of children's problems. In the realm of popular literature, the public have developed a remarkable appetite for books by authors who survived seemingly appalling childhoods where parental, or sometimes sibling disability, was a defining feature of family life. From Philip Larkin's gloomy rhyme to the best selling biographies of Frank McCourt, Elizabeth Wurtzel, Jennifer Lauck and Dave Peltzer, parents have not had a good press. A generation of child care practitioners, myself included, was raised on the false belief that childhood as a distinct phase of life did not exist before the early modern era.

One of the most widely read and quoted histories of childhood opens with the sentence 'the history of childhood is a nightmare from which we have only recently begun to awaken' (De Mause 1976). A new paradigm of adult-child relationships, based on the paramountcy of the child's welfare, recognition of the rights of children and the placing of children's interests at the heart of the social and political agenda would ensure, again in the words of De Mause, that children would become 'gentle, sincere and never depressed' (ibid.).

This epiphany formed the platform for the first generation of children's rights activists, who shared De Mause's belief that a new era was dawning. Unfortunately, this confident chronology of childhood is rather undermined by convincing evidence that the exact opposite has occurred, and that children's mental health (including the prevalence of depressive disorders) has deteriorated in all developed countries over the very period that our 'new' attitudes towards children were supposed to vanquish the demons of the past. This has occurred despite the increasing presence of factors that have been theorised to improve child welfare: more educational opportunities, smaller family size, greater sensitivity to abusive behaviour by adults, greater affect by parents, more say by children in events that shape their lives, easier access to contraception, 24 hour help lines, less punitive legal sanctions, child impact statements on parliamentary legislation, children's commissioners, the European Convention on Human Rights and the United Nations Convention on the Rights of the Child. Western Europe and North American societies, on almost every possible measurement of child-centredness, can claim to have promoted the paramountcy of children to a degree never previously attained in history (Dekker, 2000).

However, despite the setting of children's welfare at the heart of the political and social agenda, children in developed countries are cutting and killing themselves, suffering from eating disorders and depressive illnesses, misusing drugs and alcohol, being excluded from school, having emotional and behavioural problems and committing crimes at record levels (Rutter and Smith, 1995; Mental Health Foundation, 1999). Children, despite being increasingly prominent in policy terms, are less visible in physical terms: the average family in the UK now contains fewer than 1.7 children, well below the natural replacement rate for a population. In middle class families, this average is even lower.

Children of disabled parents are as affected by these social trends as much, if not more than other children, which is to say that the child of a disabled parent is, on average, likely to suffer from more psychosocial disorders than a similar child of a generation ago. Adults have also been affected by this increase in psychological morbidity, with self reports of long term limiting illness rising substantially for both adults and children over the period 1975–98 (Office for National Statistics, 2000c). There are, simply, far more children living in households with disabled parents than there were 30 years ago and, given the substantial rise in parental separation and single parenthood over the same period, a corresponding decrease in the proportion of children in households where a second, and non-disabled, primary carer is present. This is particularly pertinent given the strong association between poverty, lone female parenthood and psychological disorders, most commonly depressive illnesses. This trend has been compounded by policy decisions which have de-institutionalised many adults of child bearing age whom in previous generations would have been discouraged, or actively prevented, from bearing children. The result of these trends has been to elevate a field of child care practice from the province of a small number of clinical specialists to one that requires the active engagement of most practitioners in both child and adult social care services.

Disabled parents, their children, and the responsibilities that child welfare services have towards them can thus justifiably claim to be an issue of growing importance. However, disabled parents may be wise to view this development with both optimism and trepidation. In a world of competing child welfare priorities, numbers matter. The extent of public investment depends on how a social problem is perceived, with the two most important factors being how seriously, and how many, children are affected. Inflating the magnitude and intensity of a child care 'problem' is the usual method of raising public consciousness. In achieving this, the claims of child welfare advocates are generally treated far more tolerantly by both the professional and popular media than similar claims made by for-profit organisations. How, for example, would we respond to a claim by a drug manufacturer that a new product, if universally distributed, would eliminate youth crime? Compare the probable response (almost inevitably one consisting of extreme scepticism and accusations of self-promotion) with the claim made that 'More than three million children aged 10-14 are being tempted into a life of crime, drug-taking, smoking and drinking because of a failure to provide out-of-school clubs' (The Independent, 6/1/02).

Leaving aside the fact that the alleged number of three million includes every child between these ages in the United Kingdom, we all know that this claim, whatever the undoubted merits of out-of-school clubs, is false. However, we are less likely to take issue with it (publicly, at least) because of an innate sympathy for the cause and a belief that, even if it is a bit over the top, some good may arise from it. However, dangers can arise from the well-meaning exaggeration of problems (and the efficacy of suggested solutions) for people on the receiving end of child welfare services. Rather like comets pulling a long trail of debris behind their solid core, family support services cannot be disassociated from child protection concerns. The dual relief and anxiety that many disabled parents feel at the prospect of their circumstances

achieving greater prominence in the child welfare universe can be attributed to their fear that such prominence may not come without a price.

Problems, Problems

When we go looking for problems, we tend to find them, especially when we are rewarded more when we find them than when we don't. For example, we might ask, 'Are children of disabled parents more or less likely than those of non-disabled parents to receive adequate health care?' This is a reasonable question, and one that can be investigated by, for example, exploring whether parental disability is associated with lower or higher rates of primary child immunisations. A recent American study did just this.

The US Census Bureau reports that 20 per cent of Americans are affected by a disability and that just over 20 million families with dependent children have at least one family member with a functional limitation. Is a child, the study asked, 'disabled' by living in a household with a disabled adult? Examining data for almost 4,000 children from the 1995 US National Health Interview Surveys, the study concluded that parental disability status did indeed make child immunisation less likely. However, this was only true of the very small number of parents in the most severe disability classification used. Overall, children of disabled parents were *more* likely to be inoculated than children of non-disabled parents. This, however, was not the primary conclusion, which was 'parental disability threatens child health'. The question as to why most children of disabled parents received *better* health care was not explored. What might harm children, in contrast to what might protect children, continues to preoccupy our practice and policy responses.

It is significant that, as part of a process replicated by many marginalised groups, challenges to the 'problematic' nature of disability and parenthood have not emerged primarily as a result of heightened professional sensitivity, but through increasing demands by disabled people themselves for their voices to be heard.

Partnership, empowerment and participation have become such familiar terms to those of us who work in social care services that we occasionally need to remind ourselves of why these concepts are so important. Historically, the exclusion of vulnerable social groups from decision making processes has always resulted in their welfare being compromised. Professionals, however well meaning they might be, tend to respond differently to an issue when the target of their intervention is inarticulate, powerless or unrepresented. Stressing the ethical imperative of participation can cause us to miss the main reason why we must listen closely to the voices of those in whose lives we wish to intervene. Professionals *need* the involvement of parents and children in order to function effectively. 'Empowerment', which is often perceived as a gift bestowed on the powerless by the powerful, is perhaps better construed as a two way process. Who benefits more is a moot point.

Structure of the Book

Chapter 2 discusses how and why illness and disability have become a more prominent part of children's lives over the past few decades.

Chapter 3 describes the emergence of the 'young carer' phenomenon, and how the issue has come to dominate the broader social policy and practice perspective at the expense of disabled parents themselves.

Chapter 4 reviews the literature on the impact of parental illness and disability on children, and argues that a disproportionate emphasis on negative outcomes has distorted both professional and lay perspectives.

Chapter 5 is an account of two large surveys, one of a general child population, the other of children of disabled parents known to child welfare services. The effects of parental illness and disability on the health and wellbeing of children are discussed and areas of concern, as well as areas where no evidence of concern emerges, are identified.

Chapter 6 summarises how children and families may be supported more effectively, and how an emphasis on strengths, rather than deficits, can result in better outcomes for children and their families. Much severe illness and many disabling conditions can cause severe distress to both adults and children, both temporarily and in the long term. In the not so distant past, children's distress at their parents' premature infirmity was rarely acknowledged by health and social care workers. No-one, professionals and disabled parents alike, wishes to roll back the clock to a time where parents remained the sole focus of attention and children's feelings were ignored. However, helping children cope with parental illness and disability also means demystifying and de-stigmatising impairment, both physical and psychological. When we are finally able to discard the notion that some people have 'special' needs, and recognise that most 'special' needs are actually rather ordinary needs, the differences between children with or without disabled parents will become less significant. This book seeks to make a contribution to this process.

2 The Health of the Nation

Social Services seem to be evolving exactly in the same unfortunate way as medicine by suggesting that wherever there is a social 'need' a social worker must be appointed whether or not there is any evidence that the social worker can alter the natural history of the social problem.

(Cochrane, 1972.)

Key Points

- Despite substantial improvements in many dimensions of health status, the proportion of both adults and children in the population with limiting illnesses has substantially increased since 1970.
- The proportion of adults, and especially parents, who may be defined as disabled, has also increased over the same period. Both these factors may be associated with greater expectations of better health.
- More awareness of children's rights and the requirement to consider children separately from their family has entered the consciousness of legislators, professionals, parents and children themselves.
- Family structures have undergone a seismic change over the past quarter century, with parental separation, family re-constitution, and lone parenthood being key features.
- Social groups characterised by a shared experience of perceived suffering have become more prominent, and have displaced other more traditional constituencies.
- There has been a substantial rise in our preoccupation with risk. This has been accompanied by an increased emphasis on the vulnerability of children and a corresponding pressure on health and social care services to develop protective strategies.

At the turn of the century, both health and social welfare services in developed countries are confronted with a similar problem, indeed a paradox. While many physical illnesses and disorders are in decline, psychological illnesses are increasing (Smith and Rutter, 1995; Robins, 1995; Wilkinson, 1996; Mental Health Foundation, 1999). Furthermore, both social care and primary health care services are under considerable pressure to identify, quantify, and treat increasingly diverse forms of human suffering, including some previously unrecognised psychological disorders (Showalter, 1998). In what ways has the health of the nation changed, and how has this affected our perception of what factors threaten, and which protect, children's health?

The Health of the Nation

During the twentieth century in Western Europe and North America, in what was until recently known as the First World, the physical health of both children and adults has undergone a considerable improvement. Infant mortality rates in the UK have declined from around 85 per thousand live births in 1921 to under two per thousand today. Mass immunisation has reduced annual deaths in the UK caused by tuberculosis from 10,590 in 1939 to 420 in 1996, deaths from diphtheria from over 2000 in 1939 to zero today. Even over a much shorter time scale – 1967 to 1996 – annual deaths from measles in the UK have declined from 99 to zero (Bedford and Elliman, 2000). Deaths from infectious diseases have declined from 25 per cent of all deaths in 1900 to one per cent of all deaths today (Department of Health, 1999b). Height is a powerful indicator of health and a substantial increase has taken place over this period with the average height of seven year old boys and girls increasing by 1.1 and 1.6 centimetres respectively. We are thus, on many important measurements, a much healthier nation.

However, despite this substantial improvement many common indicators of physical health, self-reported sickness and restrictive illnesses have substantially increased in the past generation. Figure 2.1 illustrates the changes in long-standing illness, limiting long-standing illness, and restricted activity (in a 14 day period before interview) from 1975 to 1998, for adults aged 16–44 years.

As we can see, substantial rises in all categories, long-standing illness, limiting long-

standing illness and restricted activity, have taken place. The largest increases took place during the 1970s, with the pattern since 1990 being more stable. In this age band, where dependent children are most likely to be found, the proportion of people reporting a long-standing illness increased from 13 per cent to 24 per cent, a limiting long-standing illness from nine per cent to 13 per cent and restricted activity from eight per cent to 12 per cent. Female and male reporting rates are roughly similar.

Children, of course, encounter illness and disability in adults other than their parents, especially older relatives. In 1995, 42 per cent of men and 41 per cent of women in England reported having at least one long-standing illness (Department of Health, 1997). Acute illness (experienced in the previous two weeks before interview) was reported by 13 per cent of men and 17 per cent of women. Twenty one per cent of men and 22 per cent of women aged 16–44 years reported having one or more moderate or serious disability.

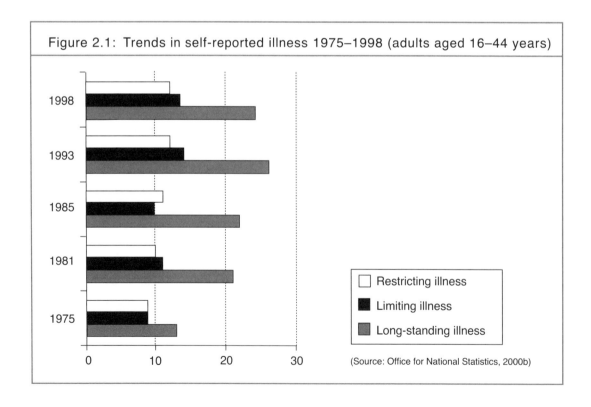

Figure 2.1: Trends in self-reported illness 1975–1998 (adults aged 16–44 years)

Restricting illness

Limiting illness

Long-standing illness

(Source: Office for National Statistics, 2000b)

Parents and morbidity

The same study also reported that some 16 per cent of adults suffered a neurotic disorder in the week before interview, with this event being significantly more common for women. As with England, self-reported physical and mental illnesses in Wales (as measured by the SF-36 instrument) increased across almost all dimensions between the years 1995-98 (National Assembly of Wales, 1999).

Nationally, around 16 per cent of parents can be described as suffering from psychiatric morbidity of varying degrees of intensity (Meltzer et al., 1995). In a study of referrals to the NSPCC child protection helpline, some ten per cent of referrals were made on the basis of concerns for the parent's (usually the mother's) mental health (Lewis and Creighton, 1999).

Up to half of all patients receiving treatment for mental illness are parents with dependent children (Gopfert et al., 1996). Clinical depression affects primary caregivers, women, twice as often as it does men, and prevalence among lone parents, again overwhelmingly women, is notably high. The proportion of lone parents as a percentage of all households with children has risen over the past quarter century to around 20 per cent. Lone parents are disproportionately affected by poverty which is in turn strongly associated with increased levels of ill health, both physical and mental. Compared to a generation ago, children, even without considering other precipitating factors, are more likely to grow up in a household where a parent, who will much more frequently be a lone parent, suffers from a debilitating illness. This situation is compounded by the greater likelihood that support from extended family members, due to smaller families, increased participation of women in the workforce, and greater mobility will be less readily available. Social capital, the accumulation of formal and informal community assets available to families, is closely linked to emotional health. Less stable communities and more transient populations weaken social capital, putting more pressure on families with the least personal assets.

Children's health

Similar increases to those noted in adults are found in reports of child illness.

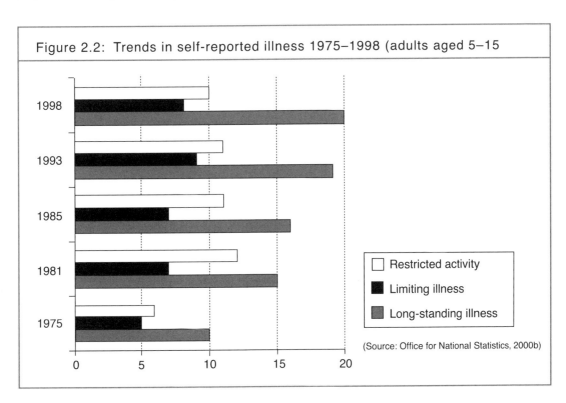

Figure 2.2: Trends in self-reported illness 1975–1998 (adults aged 5–15

Restricted activity

Limiting illness

Long-standing illness

(Source: Office for National Statistics, 2000b)

As we can see, Figure 2.2 is an analogue of child reports of illness. Long-standing illnesses of children have increased over this quarter century from eight per cent to 20 per cent, limiting long-standing illnesses from five per cent to eight per cent, and restricted activity from six per cent to ten per cent. The most comprehensive picture we have of children's current health profile in England is from the Department of Health surveys, conducted in 1995-97 (Prescott-Clarke and Primatesta, 1998). Just over a quarter of boys, and just under a quarter of girls aged two-15 years reported a long-standing illness, with 10 per cent indicating that it limited their activities in some way. Respiratory illnesses, followed by skin and musculo-skeletal conditions were the most commonly reported problems. While parents spoke for children aged 2-12, children 13 and over spoke for themselves. This seemingly high rate of illness was not matched by children's self or proxy description of their general health, with 90 per cent of 2-15 year olds describing their general health as 'good' or 'very good'. The likelihood of long-standing illness in children was increased when a parent smoked or had a long-standing illness themselves. Across both age bands and genders, the prevalence of reported ill health increased from social class I to V. Reporting patterns vary by social class; children from poorer families consult their GPs more than children from richer ones for a wide range of illnesses. For *preventive* treatments, however, they consult less (Saxena et al., 1999).

Expectations of health

Changes in self reports of illness, of course, reflect *expectations* of health as well as changes in prevalence. Clinicians, for example, are increasingly willing to factor cultural and historical variables into explanations of increases or decreases in the prevalence of illnesses (for example, Shorter, 1992; Harrington, 1996). Reports of restrictions may increase when, for example, expectations of a particular quality of life similarly increases, or a changed lifestyle requires access to a wider range of resources. Furthermore, the proportion of people in manual social classes has declined from 1972-1996.

Since non-manual social classes are more likely to report chronic conditions, even when they are not troublesome or accompanied by symptoms (Office of National Statistics, 2000b), the changing class profile of the UK population over this period may have affected the level of self reported illnesses.

The relationship between expectations of health, actual health and self reported illness is a highly contentious one. However, regardless of the 'true' rate of ill health and disability in the population, these figures illustrate that *perceived* sickness and disability are not an unusual event for adults, and hence a normative part of the lives of a very high proportion of children.

Disability, Impairment and Health

Twenty-five thousand of the 76,000 impaired women* housewives in Great Britain with dependent children under 12 have some special difficulty looking after them because of their disability. The most common problems are of an emotional or mental nature, and it is difficult to see what provision, if any, could be made to help them.

(Harris et al., 1971.)

(*Note: here the term 'women' is not a redundant one. In 1971, the OPCS definition of a housewife was 'the person, other than a domestic servant, who is responsible for most of the domestic duties'. A 'housewife' could thus be male or female, or, indeed, work outside the home.)

A major survey carried out a little over one generation ago illustrates the changes that have taken place in the profile of disability in the UK, the structure and distribution of labour within families and the role of children in families where disabled and sick parents are present. The 1971 OPCS survey of disability (Harris et al., 1971) contains a wealth of information about the numbers, situations and needs of people with impairments in Great Britain (see Table 2.1).

Part 1 of the 1971 survey devoted a short section specifically to the situation of impaired mothers with dependent children under 12 years, and apologised for not exploring the situations of impaired fathers. Only four per cent of the women in the sample

Table 2.1: Profile of disability 1971	
Very severely handicapped, needing special care	157,000
Severely handicapped, needing considerable support	356,000
Appreciably handicapped, needing some support	616,000
Impaired, but needing little support with everyday tasks	1,942,000
Total	**3,071,000**
	(From Harris et al., 1971)

Table 2.2: Problems reported by disabled mothers in 1971	
Playing with children	22%
Washing and bathing children	18%
Preparing and serving food	14%
Getting children ready for school	9%
Other problems than above	22%

(n=76,000), three-quarters of whom were aged 30-49, had dependent children under 12. Of these, a third said they had difficulty looking after their children. Of the 25,000 experiencing difficulties, the most challenging aspects are set out in Table 2.2.

The largest single difficulty reported by parents was an inability to play with their children, a statistic illuminated by supplementary interviews, which highlighted the distress caused to parents when they were unable to share their children's play, though this situation was remedied in several reported cases by big sisters. The large majority of women whose impairment caused them difficulty in caring for their children were living with their husbands. Only ten of the 105 interviewed (nine per cent) were not. Of these, two had husbands working away from home, one was single and the other seven were widowed, divorced or separated (though in two of these cases there was another adult in the household). It can be thus seen that in 94 per cent of households where a child might be most severely affected by a maternal disability, another adult was a member of the household. Using this figure to project a national total, there would have only been, in 1971, around 1,500 disabled women who expressed difficulty caring for children under 12 years living in households where no other adult was available to help.

Then and now

The 1971 survey identified shopping as the domestic task most affected by disability, an aspect of life transformed since 1971 by the development of supermarkets, better disabled access, and for increasing numbers of people, internet shopping. Another major need was more help with housework, OPCS estimating that a doubling of the home help service would be required to satisfy demand. The only specific 'helping' activity attributed to children was laundry, where sons and daughters were the main source of help for women who were unable to manage this task themselves, again, a task reduced in magnitude over the last 30 years by the widespread ownership of automatic washing machines, disposable nappies, and fewer soiled clothes due to the decline of industrial occupations. The contribution of children to the household of the disabled parent was not the focus of this survey, nor was the emotional or psychological impact of parental illness and disability on the child.

However, the demography of disability in the early 1970s had a number of features which were likely to reduce the concern of child welfare services for the wellbeing of children of disabled parents. There were few disabled lone parents. The total number of people within the general population defined as impaired was substantially fewer than in 1996. Some four fifths of the 488,000 housewives prevented by impairment from undertaking household chores had family support. Where lone parents were located, they were more likely to live with other adult family members, primarily their own parents. In addition, the routine contribution of children to household tasks, especially washing, playing with younger siblings and babysitting was regarded as normative, with the authors of the survey regretfully observing that 60 per cent of women with dependent children under 12 years had no older children (that is, over 12 years) on whom they could rely for help.

Caring and the prevalence of disability

Estimates of the number of disabled people living in the community in the UK and the number of carers have been subject to considerable change. One factor is common to almost all estimates over the last 30 years – numbers have increased substantially. The 1968/9 OPCS national survey of handicap and impairment estimated that there were around 1.1 million handicapped people (the term then used) (16 years and over) in the UK (Harris, 1971). Using data from this survey and government population projections (1978-2018) it was calculated in 1980, that the total number of handicapped people aged 16 and over would, in 2001, be 1,378,000 (Wilson, 1980). These estimates did not include adults affected by mental illnesses. Ambiguity over figures remains; a recent series of inspections by the Department of Health of local authority services for disabled adults suggested a UK estimate of between 1.2 and 4 million disabled *parents*, substantially more than the entire predicted UK disabled population only two decades earlier, with numbers 'thought to be increasing', and these figures excluded parents affected by mental illnesses or dependent on drugs and alcohol (Goodinge, 2000). On the basis of figures from the 1996/7 Family Resources Survey, the Department of Social Security updated their estimate of the numbers of disabled people living in private households in the UK from 5.8 to 8.6 million. In terms of care provision, it is suggested that one in eight adults gives informal care and one in six homes has a carer (Fruin, 1998).

The numbers of disabled children are relevant also and give concern over the impact of sibling disability on children. In 1969 this was estimated as some 150,000; the 1989 surveys suggested 355,000 in private households. The most dramatic rise in self-reported illness has taken place among pre-school children, where the proportion with a long-standing illness has increased by 300 per cent since 1972, to 13 per cent of all children (Office of National Statistics, 1998a). The largest increases have taken place in illness and disability categories with contentious diagnostic procedures, such as asthma, chronic fatigue syndrome, autistic spectrum disorders and attention deficit disorders. The extent to which this reflects an *actual* increase in these illnesses, improvements in diagnostic techniques, greater scrutiny of populations, changing expectations of health or, as some commentators have suggested, a modern equivalent of late Victorian hysterical disorders (Showalter,1998) or indeed, a combination of all these, is open to question.

For adults, both prevalence and degree of impairment, as one might expect, increase with age. Age has a strong effect on prevalence. The disability profile of adults is pyramid shaped, while that of children more like a rectangle. That is, a large number of adults have moderate disabilities; fewer have severe disabilities and a small number very severe. Severity of disability in children is more equally distributed, with relatively similar numbers of children in the very severe, severe, and moderate categories. Weakening or strengthening diagnostic criteria or disability definitions will thus have a large effect on adult prevalence, by including or excluding large numbers of people at the 'moderate' end of the spectrum, but will have a less powerful effect on child disability prevalence. Clearly, this factor is of some importance, as the number of children potentially in need of support will be primarily related to the numbers of disabled adults, and less to the numbers of disabled children.

The Changing Family

In addition to health status and disability profile, major demographic changes have taken place in the social environment of children over the last three decades, arguably a more rapid change in modern history in a single generation than any outside wartime. Most importantly, these have included the rise in divorce and the increased participation of mothers in the labour market (Kiernan, 1996). In one generation, the number of first time marriages has halved, the number of divorces has trebled and the number of children born outside marriage has increased by a multiple of four.

Gender, marital status, social class and family structure are all variables that are significantly associated with levels of psychiatric morbidity. Women are more likely than men to have scores of 12 or greater on the Clinical Interview Schedule – Revised (CIS-R), which assesses neurotic psychopathology, for example, depressive and phobic disorders. The highest CIS-R scores are for divorced and separated women, and men separated from their wives. Over a quarter of all lone parents had CIS-R scores of 12 or more, compared to 14 per cent of couples with children. The prevalence of psycho-neurotic symptoms declines as social class increases (Meltzer et al., 1995). Children too, in both one-parent and reconstituted families, have a higher prevalence of mental disorders compared to two-parent families: 16 per cent v. eight per cent; and 15 per cent v. nine per cent respectively. Like adults, children will experience more mental disorders where parents live in poverty and report no educational qualifications (Office for National Statistics, 2000c). In only one respect does higher social class result in a greater likelihood of vulnerability to morbid symptomatology: levels of self reported stress and pressure are the highest in social classes I and II and the lowest in classes III and IV (Hansbro et al., 1997).

The number of families with dependent children headed by a lone parent doubled between 1976 and 1996 from 0.75 million to 1.6 million, as have the numbers of children in lone parent families, from 1.3 to 2.8 million (Office for National Statistics, 2000a). Over 4.3 million children, around a third of all children, live in poverty, that is in households with below half the average income, a threefold increase from 1968. This includes 43 per cent of children in lone-parent families (Gregg et al., 1999). In 1999, a thousand children under five in England and Wales were affected by divorce each week, 1,400 between the ages of five and 10 and 1,000 more aged 11–15. One in 65 of all children each year in England and Wales are affected by their parents' separation, some 160,000 children in England and Wales per annum. Between a third and a half of all UK children will spend some of their childhood in a single-parent household (Barnes et al., 1998). If the estimation that approximately 43 per cent of males lose touch with their children within five years of parental separation is correct (Bradshaw and Miller, 1991), more children in England and Wales have lost contact with fathers through divorce since 1970 than through death in both World Wars combined.

Healthier Bodies, Unhealthier Minds

As noted above, children are less likely to die in the neo-natal period, or through lethal illnesses later in life. However, psychological disorders have not diminished in the same way:

> *Psychosocial disorders have shown no such fall in frequency...the evidence suggests that many have become substantially more prevalent.*
> (Smith and Rutter,1995.)

Smith and Rutter base this observation on their examination of five types of disorders; depression, eating disorders, suicide and suicidal behaviour, substance misuse, youth crime and conduct disorders. The prevalence of clinical depression increased tenfold during the years 1950-80. The lifetime prevalence of depression for a person born in 1905 was one per cent. Current lifetime prevalence of major depressive disorder (MDD) is 17.1 per cent (Roth and Fonagy, 1996). Even over a short time scale, major changes in rates of adolescent depression have been noted, with the proportion of adolescents experiencing severe depression increasing from 4.5 per cent to 7.5 per cent over the period 1968–71 to 1972–74 (Lewinsohn et al., 1994). World-wide, depressive disorders now constitute the biggest cause of life years lost to any one dimension of disability.

A dramatic rise in male suicide rates has taken place among the under 24s, with over half this increase likely to be explained by parental divorce (Office for National Statistics, 1998b). A huge increase in illegal drug use has taken place over this period, with almost half of 16–19 year olds reporting that they have used illegal drugs. In the last decade alone, the proportion of 11–15 year old children in England who drink alcohol has increased from 21 per cent to 27 per cent and in Scotland, over the same period, from 14 per cent to 23 per cent (Office for National Statistics, 1997). While a steep decline in fertility rates has taken place over this period, teenage conceptions in the UK have remained stable (and the highest in Europe).

Psychological disorders are real, distressing and frequently need treatment. However, one way in which their prevalence may be inflated is through the problematising of normative psychological processes. For example, a study of the prevalence of depression and anxiety in patients attending a GP practice, using the General Health Questionnaire (n=305), suggested that over half of patients were suffering from measurable depression, despite the GPs themselves making this diagnosis in less than a quarter of cases (Kessler et al., 1999). The study concluded that physicians colluded with patients, mostly young and male, with a 'normalising attribution' style (i.e. they said they could cope) by refraining from diagnosing depression. This proposition – that large amounts of avoidable suffering are hidden – is a common proposition in child welfare practice. A response to this study makes a point of equal validity for both disciplines:

> *Human beings struggle to make sense of suffering and illness by finding meaning for it in the very particular context of each individual life. Patients who normalise their experience may have already begun this process of finding meaning, making sense and learning to cope.*
>
> (Heath, 1999.)

Risk

The dominant paradigm of child welfare that has developed within both health and social care over the last century has increasingly emphasised the vulnerability of children, the need to protect them against early entry to the adult world, and the long term damaging effects of premature exposure to mature roles. Ferenczi's observation, that 'if, near the beginning of life, you do only a little harm to a child, it may cast a shadow over its whole life' (1928), is unlikely to be challenged in principle by many social care practitioners, nor indeed by the lay public. Nonetheless, as noted above, the increased emphasis on children's vulnerability has not been accompanied by a corresponding rise in measurable levels of children's psychosocial wellbeing, at least in the industrialised countries of the western world. Risks are frequently seen as arising from the perceived deficiencies of the people under scrutiny; unlike health care, social care interventions are normally perceived to be beneficial or at worst neutral.

> *Approaches to risk tend to pathologise individuals and locate risk factors intrinsic to them or to their immediate environment. It often avoids considering risks arising from the protective intervention itself.*
>
> (Calder, 2002.)

A major function of child welfare services, indeed any service with a preventive function, is to analyse a phenomenon, make any patterns explicit, and to use this information to construct a predictive framework. Child care services, for example, are under continual pressure to prevent serious injury and death by perfecting a method of accurately predicting which children are in the highest categories of risk. Much influential work is based on the proposition that strong linear associations exist between stimulus and outcome; for example, poverty mediated by early loss and absence of supportive relationships plus several children is associated with depression (Brown and Harris, 1978). Similarly, it is suggested that children in one-parent families appear more likely than those in two-parent families, to undertake caregiving or substitute in other ways for normative parental roles (Goglia et al., 1992). Once a pattern, however tenuous, has been established, a tendency exists for observed behaviour to be attributed to these patterns. This, however, fails to recognise the possibility of false positives – diagnosing a phenomenon where none exists.

Diagnostic accuracy

The diagnosis of child welfare problems is often fraught with difficulties, even where the phenomenon is a specific and recognised disorder and the evaluation takes place under clinical conditions. The lower the prevalence of the phenomenon and the less pre-screened the survey population, the higher the risk of error, even where the screening procedure is operating at a high level of sensitivity. This is not a difficulty confined to child welfare practice:

> *Studies of the ways that other professional groups diagnose disorders have shown that they attach too little weight to base rates of disorder when interpreting the results of diagnostic tests.*
> (Clark and Harrington, 1999.)

While the procedures used to estimate numbers of children in a social care welfare category rely less on statistical models, the broad principle applies that drawing conclusions based on statistics from the primarily disadvantaged populations that child welfare services encounter, rather than from the *general* population, may result in excessive estimates of prevalence. The frequent failure of social welfare services to fully consider the relationship between risk, probability and false positives may be illustrated by Table 2.3 from a social work journal, which suggests a scale by which potential risks can be judged.

Table 2.3: Risk	
Probability	Chance of risk occurring
Unlikely	Less than 20%
Likely	20–50%
Highly likely	Over 50%
	(Twyford, 1999)

Clearly, any threshold of intervention which is triggered by a 51 per cent probability that an event will occur is only marginally more reliable than tossing a coin. The danger of failing to consider error can be illustrated by a statistical example. A risk assessment instrument, designed to predict the suicide risk of discharged psychiatric patients, which has 80 per cent sensitivity (ability to locate true positives) and 80 per cent specificity (ability to locate true negatives) would identify, given the known rate of suicides in the period after discharge, 32 true positives and almost 4000 false ones (Geddes, 1999). Although predictability is less fragile where a phenomenon is more common and confined to very specific and easily identifiable population groups, child welfare interventions are often concerned with comparatively rare events. Even where the prevalence of a problem is relatively high, say 10 per cent, a screening instrument of 80 per cent specificity and sensitivity will misdiagnose twice as many people as it diagnoses correctly (Clark and Harrington, 1999).

Screening procedures in health services are based on a concordance between the importance of the problem, population prevalence and the reliability of the screening method. One would not, for example, expect the entire UK population to be screened, at enormous expense, for illnesses that are very rare or primarily confined to identifiable social groups or geographical areas. An example of this is testing for HIV status. Even where diagnostic tests are highly accurate, large numbers of people may be affected by errors. For example, only a 0.1 per cent error rate for the 4.5 million cervical smears performed in England and Wales annually is necessary for almost 4,500 misdiagnoses to be made. Primary care services are rightly seen as having a vital preventive function and the identification of health and social welfare problems at an early stage are essential. However, the same principles of relativity apply. In relation to children of disabled parents, it has been suggested by a consultant paediatrician, that all GPs ensure:

> *Every health record includes an up to date family tree, that individuals with disabilities are identified and the question asked, 'who is the carer?'*
> (Dearden et al., 1994.)

Given that there are some 3 million disabled parents in the UK, depending on the definition used, and 19–51,000 children meeting the Department of Health definition of a 'young carer', this would result in around one per cent of disabled parents' health records containing any pertinent information. Even with diagnostic tests of 95 per cent accuracy (much higher than any applicable to most child welfare problems), the number of false positives generated, i.e. children falling outside the official definition, would be much greater than those falling within. Even assuming that no negative consequences arise from the unnecessary involvement of child welfare services, the cost of such an exercise would be likely to outweigh any conceivable benefit.

The conclusion we must reach is not one of our liking, which is that our capacity to identify children at risk, particularly where there are confusing and compromising social circumstances and however robust our assessment procedures, is subject to considerable limitations.

Our growing concern with risk

The Government, many children's charities and local authorities are unfortunately promoting the idea that children are constantly 'at risk' and appear to have as an organising principle the concept of 'child safety'. Little else matters, as long as children are seen to be safe.

(Waiton, 2000.)

How risky is being a child and how much do children depend on the personal social services (PSS) for their safety? In the years following the war, not a lot, on both counts, it appears. In 1955, direct government spending on the health and welfare of children in the form of school meals, milk and welfare foods was double that of the PSS as a proportion of all public spending (Webb and Wistow, 1987). The physical, rather than the emotional sustenance of children was the main aim of social policy. In the past quarter century, the emotional wellbeing of children and concern over potential threats to their health have achieved greater prominence. However, as we have noted above, the success of the state in improving

children's physical health has not been matched by similar successes in terms of improving children's psychological and emotional health. If we measure the level of concern for children's safety by the proportion of scientific articles addressing the subject, then there is little doubt that risk and safety is a growth area.

Figure 2.3 represents the proportion of MEDLINE records, the worlds largest data base of bio-medical research abstracts, that contain both the words 'child' and 'risk' over a thirty year period. As can be seen, in 1966–74, the words appeared together in the same abstract in only 0.2 per cent of cases. By 1996–2000 (by which time, it should be noted, the total number of records was substantially larger) the proportion had grown to over 15 per cent. The steady growth over this period illustrates the corresponding growth in concern by both medical and social care agencies in the range of risk factors believed to be facing children as they negotiate their path to adulthood.

The increased emphasis on the potential risks confronting children has manifested itself in a number of ways. The summer of 1999 saw one of the UK's largest child care charities, the NSPCC, campaigning for all play areas in Britain's parks to be supervised, having found only 19 per cent are, and citing in support a 1999 MORI poll which found over 75 per cent of parents unwilling to allow their children to play in unsupervised parks (*Community Care*, 2–8 September). 'Stranger danger' is reported as being the greatest single fear for 98 per cent of parents, despite there being fewer than six children under 14 years killed by strangers each year in the decade 1984–94, compared to over 600 per annum who die in accidents (Harden et al., 2000). Child impact statements are now commonly constructed to explore any unintended effects of government legislation (Hodgkin and Newell, 1996). These phenomena represent a recent transformation in the way in which both parents and children are invited to perceive the child's relationship to the adult world. Social policy, local and national government, indeed, the adult world itself, is considered, *a priori*, to be potentially abusive, either by acts of omission or commission. Instead of being

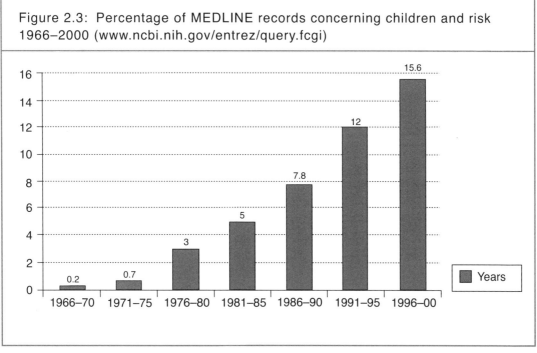

Figure 2.3: Percentage of MEDLINE records concerning children and risk 1966–2000 (www.ncbi.nih.gov/entrez/query.fcgi)

seen as the child's main refuge, adults have become perceived as their primary source of danger.

There is an inverse relationship between how much we worry about the unwanted side-effects of an intervention and the perceived size of the problem the intervention is designed to address. For example, outbreaks of meningococcal infection are typically received by demands from the public for mass vaccination programmes, despite the inability of the currently available polysaccharide vaccines to provide adequate protection to the group most at risk – young children (Begg and Gregor, 1999). Where fear of harm and perceived prevalence is high, concern about the safety of interventions, such as, in this case, the side effects of immunisation, is low. When the phenomenon is perceived to be of low prevalence, concern about unintended consequences is high. This can be represented graphically as in Figure 2.4.

Demand for intervention increases as a high fear of harm and a low fear of error coincide. While the same principle may be applied to child welfare services, there is less concern about diagnostic accuracy as the assumption is typically made that either good or no harm will result. In cases where

the possibility of harm is recognised (for example, a concern for 'net widening' in youth justice services, or compulsory treatment under mental health legislation) fear of harm is inversely related to fear of error. Thus, we care little about restrictions on children's freedom to work or roam when they are perceived to be at serious physical risk from accidental injuries, or we defend restrictive legislation if we believe it is essential to protect children from paedophiles. Those campaigning for more child welfare interventions are affected by this rule and will typically inflate fear of harm while diminishing fear of error. Where no apparent 'side effects' are anticipated from an intervention – or thought to be possible – inhibitions to the expansion of welfare categories are diminished.

Victims

It has been suggested that a culture of victimhood has developed which has promoted the construction of identities around the experience of stressful events (Hughes, 1993; Dineen, 2000), illustrated, for example, by the use of the term 'survivor' to describe someone

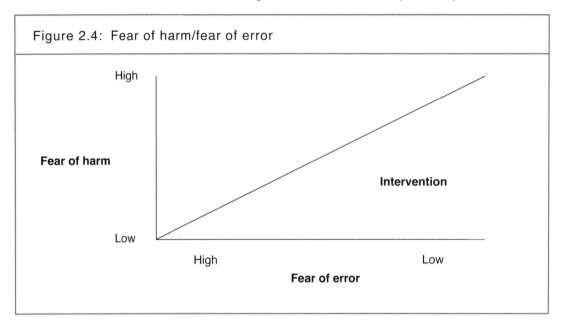

Figure 2.4: Fear of harm/fear of error

who has experienced a variety of traumatic events from sexual abuse and eating disorders, to mental health treatment by the NHS. Identification with oppressed groups has displaced, for increasingly large numbers of people, prior social attachments such as families, communities or trade unions (Beck, 1992). A social history of shared suffering has become an important ingredient in the construction and maintenance of communal identities, and has reversed the polarity of group identification. Instead of actively avoiding negative labels for fear of incurring stigma, claiming membership of an oppressed group may now have a range of significant benefits.

Risk inflation and the consequences for children

The regulatory regime that has emerged as a result of these factors contrasts markedly with the growing emphasis on children's rights. As children's rights have increasingly become a justification for child care agency interventions, the liberty of children, in terms of where they may play, who may care for them, what activities they may undertake unsupervised or unadvised, has become progressively curtailed. While promoting a vision of children as autonomous beings, in terms of their

choices, volition and rights, children's lives have been simultaneously constrained with more surveillance, regulations and restrictions that ever before in history (James et al., 1998). Parents have been persuaded that the environment outside the home is one of constant danger from which their children must be protected, a phenomenon which, it has been argued, has contributed to a rise in the prevalence in adolescent anti-social behaviours (Ward, 1994).

Furthermore, despite the increased emphasis on listening to the voices of children, the presumption of incompetence inherent in theories of risk has led to the assessment and management of risk being seen primarily as an adult activity, and has led to children's own capacity to estimate risk being undervalued (Harden, 2000). An increased pre-occupation with risk has not, it seems, resulted in healthier children. A report reviewing a wide range of evidence on the contemporary state of children's psychological health (Mental Health Foundation, 1999) reported that 20 per cent of children suffer from a range of diagnosable problems, from bed-wetting to eating disorders, and concluded that children are becoming less resilient and less able to cope with the ups and downs of life.

The way in which we assess risk has been strongly influenced by this new view of relationships between adult and child. This has resulted in a number of consequences:

- The threshold of risk has been lowered to include an inflated range of situations now considered to be potentially threatening to children.

- The extent to which children may be damaged by these adversities has been revised upwards.

- A diminution has occurred in our belief that children may resist such damage and consequently a widespread conviction in the inevitability of long-term harm has emerged.

- Child care practice has encouraged the belief that children's interests are best served by magnifying the range of potential threats and the extent of their impact on children, in order to galvanise public opinion into preventive action.

While there have been some dissenting voices (Freeman-Longo, 1996; Minty, 2000; Moore and Parsons, 2000), the consequences have been a peculiar kind of moral extortion which has often rendered any opposition to child welfare expansionism – or even the expression of a note of caution about its unintended effects – as akin to child abuse itself. For example, while reluctantly voicing its disapproval of the Child Protection Bill on civil liberties grounds, a national newspaper editorial illustrated the moral dilemma that emerges, where children are concerned, when attempting to balance the equation of risk and protection more rationally:

> *Children can never be made completely safe, **and there is little evidence that the dangers they face are any greater than they have ever been** [my emphasis] ...it takes enormous courage to make these arguments and risk being portrayed as a friend of the paedophile. It is a wretched choice; no one could easily oppose a measure that just might prevent one case of child abuse.*
>
> (*Observer*, 21.2.99.)

Children of Disabled Parents as Children in Need?

Since the passage of the 1989 Children Act, categories of need have become a crucial passport to personal social services entry. A child is regarded as being in need in England, Wales and Northern Ireland if:

- Services are required in order for the child to achieve or maintain a reasonable standard of health or development.

- The health and development of the child would be significantly impaired without such services.

- The child is disabled.

In Scotland, the Children (Scotland) Act 1995 adds another category, children who are 'adversely affected by the disability of any other person in their family' [section 94, 4 (a)]. Regardless of intellectual, physical or psychological limitations, if the standard of care provided by a parent is insufficient for an adequate standard of health and development to be attained or maintained by the child, the parent will be acting unreasonably if help is not sought. Both parties thus have obligations; parents to acknowledge their incapacity and to seek help if needed, the local authority to carry out assessments of need within their jurisdiction and provide services based on their legislative responsibilities.

Do need thresholds, like clinical diagnoses, change over time? For example, the point at which an adversity becomes abusive has been in steady decline for a century (Department of Health, 1995). An *a priori* assumption of need based on personal, environmental or familial factors associated with the child is clearly the easiest way to classify any child population as being 'in need'. The Framework for the Assessment of Children in Need and their Families (www.doh.gov.uk/cmo/frass.pdf) suggests that there are some 3–400,000 in England and Wales. A further four million children (one in three of the child population) are described as 'vulnerable', on the basis that this proportion live in families with less than half average income. A high proportion of these children are claimed to be in need because of parental disability. A survey sponsored by the Department of Health into children's needs categories in England (Rowlands, 1997) found 16.1 per cent of the children were reported as being in need as a result of parents' or carers' disability, illness, mental illness or addictions, the latter being second highest need category. This category aggregates parental disability resulting from congenital impairment, impairment through trauma or illness, both chronic and acute mental illness, including affective and bipolar disorders, psychotic and neurotic illnesses and all manifestations of depression, pharmacological dependency (legal and illegal), and all forms of restrictive illnesses. The Framework for Assessment makes clear that, as well as direct contact with the young person for assessment purposes, 'services should be provided to parents to enhance their ability to fulfil their parenting responsibilities' (Section 3.62).

In the case of parental disability or illness, a formal assessment of the needs of any children affected is possible (in England and Wales) on two bases; under section 1(1) of the Carers (Recognition and Services) Act 1995 where 'inappropriate levels of caring which have an adverse impact on their development and life chances' are being carried out, or under the 1989 Children Act in cases where 'a child's welfare or development might suffer if support is not provided to the child or family' (Department of Health, 1999c). As we can see, under both pieces of legislation, it is the potential *outcome*, impeded health or development, rather than *tasks* undertaken, that legitimates the entitlement. The problems with definitional 'fit' are likely to become more contentious as social service performance indicators become operational.

Being 'in need', of course, may be regarded as a positive or negative attribute by different parties. The position of children of disabled parents and their families is ambiguous in this respect. For the child, 'in need' status may bring physical and emotional help; it may also bring fear of reception into care. Parents may experience the same conflict, with the additional possibility of the degradation of their autonomy and self-esteem. The stress in the 1989 Children Act on the primacy of the child's welfare makes clear, to ill or disabled parents, that their welfare (like that of all parents) is secondary to that of their child. Practitioners too experience ambiguity, simultaneously seeking to support the child and assess the parent's caring capacity. Where the situation of the children of disabled parents differs from that of many other children is the potential added ingredient of caregiving. As we have seen, the provision of some elements of caregiving a generation ago was regarded with less alarm than it is today. Where 'excessive', inevitably a subjective judgement, it will lead, *inter alia*, in the words of the 1989 Children Act, to a child not achieving or maintaining a reasonable standard of health without the provision of social welfare services. The assertion, that care giving damages health, is thus crucial to the campaign for dedicated services to children of disabled parents. By proving, or persuading, that caregiving impedes development, the child will be in need and the local authority will consequently be under an obligation to act. However, even where specific actions are taken to identify and meet need, the result is not necessarily an increase in perceived wellbeing. We have no corresponding data for children, but according to a poll commissioned by BT and St. John Ambulance, the proportion of adult carers reporting depression *increased* from 24 per cent to 28 per cent in the three years following the introduction of the Carers Act (*Community Care*, 16-22 March 2000). As we have noted in relation to health status, expectations of health can outpace actual improvements in health.

How consistent are needs?

Judgements about risk and whether children are in need are clearly co-dependent. Has the changing threshold of risk, which we have argued has weakened, affected children of disabled parents? That needs have at least an element of social and political construction is widely recognised; needs are demands that are seen by government as important enough to be met by goods or services (Nevitt, 1977; Doyal and Gough, 1991). The extent to which children are in need partly depends on judgements made by adults as to what extent their health and wellbeing is threatened by factors in their immediate environment. Increasingly, risk assessment, and the promotion of risk awareness, has, as noted above, become a core business of child care organisations. The volume of needs in a given population may, however, increase or decrease with surprising ease. A study into children on waiting lists for mental health services illustrates this. When North East Essex Mental Health Trust were unable to serve all the child patients on their waiting list, they wrote to all parents (n=143) asking them to confirm whether they wished their child to remain on the list. Failure to reply was regarded as a negative response. Only 30 per cent of parents replied. In a follow-up study over three years, only 10 per cent of the children removed from the waiting list were re-referred (Walker, 1998).

Conclusion

The changing health profile of the nation has resulted in children experiencing an increasingly pathogenic environment, where illness and incapacity in general has become a normative part of many children's daily experiences. The prevalence of illness, the substantial rise in lone parenthood, the emphasis on children's rights, our fear of risk, the belief that children are fragile and easily damaged organisms and the benefits that are perceived to accrue from membership of oppressed groups are all factors that have driven concerns for children of disabled parents, particularly where they are believed to be vulnerable to undertaking caregiving responsibilities.

A century ago, children, despite the many hardships they encountered, possessed important economic roles both within and outside the household (Olsen, 2000; Newman, 2000). Girls, and not infrequently boys, made substantial contributions to family care, especially where one or both parents were incapacitated, earning themselves the title of 'little mothers'. Childhood historians, while not over-romanticising their situations, have pointed out the pride that children took in these roles, and the skills they learnt in order to fulfil them (Pollock 1983; Davin, 1996). Over the next few decades, the concept of the child-as-contributor was replaced by the concept of the child-as-dependant and the history of their role as important social agents replaced by a history of exploitation and oppression (De Mause, 1976). As we have noted, children have been allocated 'adult' rights but have also had their liberty subjected to unprecedented

restrictions. Their capabilities and vulnerabilities are simultaneously stressed. The rise in lone parenthood over the last three decades, and the simultaneous entry of mothers of dependent children into the workforce in greater numbers has inflated the value of children's contribution to the household economy during a period where increasing concern has been expressed as to its harmful potential (Zelizer, 1994). Nonetheless, we are still presented by a range of highly contradictory narratives about the value of children's agency and its impact on children. Should we be convinced by the proposition (Rheingold, 1982) that even pre-school children should be given opportunities to help adults in order to encourage pro-social behaviours? Or should we take note of the assertion (McClelland, 1961) that making children do regular chores will inhibit children's social and educational achievements? However, regardless whether its purpose is income generation or pastoral care for family members, our model of what constitutes legitimate and non-legitimate 'work' by young people, within and outside the domestic domain has become fundamentally restrictive. In the economic realm, work by children may be reluctantly tolerated but it continues to be a cause for concern and its diminution remains the aim of public welfare policy. In the domestic realm, children's labour is perceived as resulting from a failure of parent or state and evokes a similar response. Yet despite public disapproval of 'premature' responsibilities within household economies, many children continue to function as important actors possessing real agency; working outside the home, looking after siblings, babysitting and caring for ill or aged relatives.

The lack of congruity between our social construction of childhood and the reality of children's lives is replicated in our responses to children undertaking 'adult' roles. Morrow (1994) reports the comments of two Birmingham head teachers on pupils who were responsible for taking younger siblings to school. One head teacher condemned the practice as interfering with the children's studies. The other regarded the task as a positive achievement that should be recorded on children's record of performance.

3 'Young Carers': The Emergence of a Child Welfare Issue

Research evidence over the past ten years has suggested that when children take on care-giving roles in the family their educational, social and emotional experiences and health can often be seriously jeopardized. Such role adoption can occur as a consequence of long or short-term parental illness or disability.

(Aldridge and Becker, 1999.)

Key Points

- There is tension between concern for the welfare of children and the pathologising of families where disability is present.
- A children's rights approach has considerable limitations when applied to kinship relationships.
- The extent to which a 'young carer' label is either beneficial to, or accepted by, children, is unresolved, as is the long-term effect of encouraging the internalisation of a social identity of this kind.
- Existing survey data are rarely drawn from representative populations, leaving such data vulnerable to accusations of skewed findings.
- No cohort data from longitudinal studies are available, which raises significant problems in attributing later outcomes to early experiences.
- The reluctance of social care organisations to develop robust entry criteria has resulted in there being little distinction between a 'young carer' and any child with a disabled parent.

In the late 1980s, and especially in the first half of the 1990s, a new child welfare category emerged. Substantial numbers of children, it was argued, were undertaking roles within their households, occasioned by family illness of disability, which were damaging and inappropriate. These children were to become known as 'young carers'. As noted in the previous chapter, 'little mothers' were well known to Victorian society, and pre-naturally young caregivers have long been a staple of both fiction and biography, from Dicken's *Little Dorrit* and Zangwill's Esther Ansell, to the older sister of Laurie Lee in *Cider with Rosie*. It is important to recognise that children's contribution to the household economy, including caring roles for other family members whether or not driven by parental disability, has been culturally normative throughout most of our history and remains so in all developing countries, and even in much of the developed world. Why then has this issue emerged at this juncture, to what extent have the services that have accompanied it been justified, and how has the situation of disabled parents and their families been affected?

Caring, Carers and the Cared for

The literature on 'young carers' primarily, though not exclusively, concerns care delivered by a son or daughter for a mother or a father. Emotionally, as well as physically, the inversion of care for the older by the younger has a mythic quality which transcends the simple negotiation of a welfare bond. That we should care for our infirm relatives, as we may hope to be cared for ourselves in our turn, is an understanding that is shared, though not necessarily equally observed, across cultures and generations (Albert, 1990). It is embedded in our social customs, our literature and our morality.

However, the provision of care for a parent by a person who has yet to reach their majority breaches our understanding, in a fundamental way, of what a parent-child relationship is about. It *feels* wrong, and such wrongness is evident even before any analytical approach to the phenomenon begins. When discussing the direction of caregiving between parent and child, we are dealing with a complex brew of instinct, ritual and social bonds, none of which are easily deconstructed and disentangled. In short, the issue of 'young carers' has a hinterland greater than the sum of its parts; we cannot comprehend its totality merely by measuring impacts, describing interventions and reviewing legislative responses. While parents are the primary recipients of care, they may not be the *only* recipients of care, though they comprise by far the largest group. Siblings also feature prominently as care receivers in accounts of young carers, especially younger, disabled or chronically ill siblings. Less frequently, other family members, notably grandparents, and more rarely, adults outside the immediate family are reported as receiving care from children. The circumstances that appear to propel a child into an inappropriate caring role are various. Most commonly, the chronic illness or impairment of a parent or other family member, most often a sibling, is reported. Disabilities may be somatic, psychological, sensory, or behavioural. Within the psychoanalytical tradition it is proposed that children may be coerced into taking on parenting roles to compensate for their mothers or fathers' failing to receive sufficient care from their own parents, a form of child maltreatment known as 'parentification' (Jurkovic, 1997). Whatever the causality involved, the focus remains the same: the child's assumption of a role held to be premature as a result of a parent's incapacity, or the parent's inability to provide sufficient care for other dependants without the child's help.

What exactly constitutes an act of care? The potential impact on the caregiver is implicit in the term itself; while 'an oversight with a view to protection' provides one definition, the dictionary also tells us that 'mental suffering', 'sorrow' and 'a burdened state of mind' are inseparable dimensions of meaning. We cannot construct a taxonomy of caring solely by defining the breadth or magnitude of observable tasks, such as shopping, washing the dishes, changing the dressing on a wound, looking after a younger sibling. As with adult carers, less tangible but no less important tasks, providing reassurance when panic attacks strike, extinguishing naked flames where alcoholism has impaired a sense of safety, being a source of optimism in the face of chronic depression, may come to penetrate far more deeply into daily routines than more easily definable domestic duties. However, with adult carers, such tasks and their emotional consequences, while often distressing, are comprehensible within families as part of the shifting balances of caregiving and care receiving that alter with the lifecycle. We expect to be cared for when we are young, we expect to deliver care when we are mature, and we expect, albeit reluctantly, to receive care again when we become infirm. The apparent disruption of this cycle is a key feature of the 'young carer' debate.

One further complication emerges as a result of the difficulty in defining 'care'. It is difficult to explain, for example, why a child who may run regular shopping errands for a wheelchair-using mother in a loving family would be more in need of a welfare response than a child with no observable caring duties living with a parent suffering from a severe and unpredictable personality disorder; or indeed, why the former might be 'in need' at all. The *impact* on children of parental disability may not, therefore, always be closely correlated with the frequency or extent to which children carry out caring tasks. In addition, the same task may have positive or negative potential in terms of a child's psychosocial development, depending on the context in which it is undertaken. A helping role which, while demanding, is valued and rewarded with praise and recognition may have a very different impact than if the same role results in the child experiencing ingratitude and complaints. Similarly, while a role for which the child is chronologically and temperamentally equipped may promote competencies, the opposite may be true if there is no congruence between the child's developmental phase and the tasks required.

Young Carers: Who are They?

A young carer may be a child in need under the Children Act. The key issue is whether the child's welfare or development might suffer if support is not provided to the child or family.

(Department of Health, 2000.)

As we have noted, 'young carers' have become difficult to distinguish from any child living in a household with a disabled parent. However, while not all children of disabled parents can be considered 'young carers', these are undoubtedly the group that have, understandably, become the focus of child welfare services. Who are they? The policy guidance for the Carers (Recognition and Services) Act 1995 describes young carers as:

Children and young people (under 18) who provide or intend to provide a substantial amount of care on a regular basis.

(Department of Health, 1996.)

While the term 'young carer' has entered common currency, it should be noted that the extent to which children themselves see being a young carer as their primary identity may vary widely. Providing a label for children who share certain commonalities may, in some circumstances, help children understand their situation by relieving their sense of isolation. Knowing other children are like you and have the same feelings and worries may, in itself, make a large contribution to a child's wellbeing. However, children also have other identities, as sons, daughters, brothers, sisters, students, and friends among many more. Ultimately, the term is a professionally generated label and may not be necessarily accepted or considered meaningful by children themselves; indeed, it may be seen as stigmatising and unhelpful (Falkov, 1998).

Why should the situation of these children be of concern to child welfare services? While the study of young carers and their circumstances has a relatively short pedigree, the impact on children of parental illness and disability in general has accumulated a rather larger body of knowledge.

Given the current direction of young carer services, which places less emphasis on the actual tasks undertaken than their impact on the psycho-social development of the child (Becker et al., 1998), it is necessary to locate the situation of young carers in the wider context of family illness and disability. Whatever the breadth and penetration of child welfare services, the vast majority of children will remain largely dependent on their parent or parents for both their physical and emotional growth. The caring role in itself may be of less importance to a child than an illness or impairment that impedes an adult's ability to offer consistent and effective parenting. This position has always been implicitly accepted by young carer services, as 'emotional' support has been consistently cited as a role deserving of as much concern as the carrying out of physical caring tasks. Indeed, a specific caring or supportive role, when adequately recognised and rewarded, may, in some circumstances, have a protective rather than a damaging effect.

Nonetheless, a compelling body of evidence exists as to the potentially damaging impact on children who live in families where one, and especially where both, parents are incapacitated by a chronic illness or disability. This statement, however, needs several very substantial qualifications. A large number of studies have found that parental illness or disability *per se* is not closely correlated with child psychopathology. The main precipitating conditions appear to be degradation in the quality of the parent-child relationship, poverty, a paucity of other sources of family support and an absence of external contacts, both lay and professional. These issues will be discussed more fully in Chapter 4. Similarly, we can expect any psychosocial damage arising from child caregiving to be compounded by the child's wider circumstances, which may be of greater importance than the actual caring tasks undertaken. Furthermore, there is extensive evidence that whatever the nature and intensity of the adversities faced by children, a large number will grow into adulthood having suffered no discernible long term damage to their physical and emotional health. This is not, it should be emphasised, a reason to respond to the needs of children with any less alacrity.

Relieving a child's distress (as any parent knows) does not need to be justified by reference to the presence or absence of long term effects. However, unlike both health and social care interventions for adults, the *future* trajectory of the child's wellbeing is a predominant concern when serious adversities appear to be present.

A brief history of young carers, 1990-2002

Becker et al. (1998), place the modern genesis of concern for children with domestic caring responsibilities in the mid 1980s, specifically to a BBC television programme concerning disabled mothers, broadcast in 1985. The substantial publicity generated by the programme enabled Carers National Association (until 1988, the Association of Carers, now Carers UK) to appoint a dedicated worker to develop this area of work. The earliest studies, in Manchester and Sandwell were primarily school based surveys which sought to estimate the extent of the problem (O'Neill, 1988; Page, 1988). These were followed by more descriptive studies (Meredith, 1991a; 1991b; Grimshaw, 1991; Bilsborrow, 1992; Segal and Simpkins, 1993) which primarily comprised of interviews with children and discussions of their circumstances. The subject began to enter the arena of academic discourse primarily through the work of Saul Becker and his colleagues at Loughborough University (Aldridge and Becker, 1993a; 1993b; Aldridge and Becker, 1994a; Dearden et al., 1994; Dearden and Becker, 1996; Aldridge and Becker, 1996a; Newton and Becker, 1996) who have been the primary source of material on children who have become known as 'young carers'.

By 1995, the subject was sufficiently established as a discrete dimension of child care practice to merit a summary in the NCB/Barnardo's *Highlight* series (Reed, 1995). While only one book to date solely addressing the issue of young carers has been published (Becker et al., 1998), dedicated chapters addressing this population have become commonplace in generic social care texts (for example, Garratt et al., 1997; Blyth and Milner, 1997) and the subject is routinely included as a

separate chapter in texts concerning carers in general (for example, Tucker and Liddiard, 1998; Heron, 1998).

Caring and carers

The emergence of young carers, both as a welfare category and as a social identity, has thus been largely accomplished during the 1990s. Much of the debate concerning the aetiology of young carers – the aptness of the term, the content of their tasks, their 'concealed' nature, the need to develop the conscious recognition by children of their identity as carers, the raising of practitioner awareness – has replicated earlier discussions on adult carers, largely in relation to the care of the elderly by adult children. Caring by adults has been described as a sociology of gender (Lewis and Meredith, 1988; Finch, 1989). This dimension, however, is less evident in the literature on young carers, where gender differences are somewhat less dramatic. The term 'carer' itself defies easy classification. The role replicates some of the components of a paid task. It may be quantified in terms of number of hours worked and type of work performed, but it may also be difficult to disentangle from unexceptional tasks that family members do for each other on a routine basis.

However, caring roles involve a degree of emotional investment, and often a distortion of normative dependency relationships, the consideration of which is essential for a fuller understanding of what caring means for all parties involved. The similar development of adult carer and young carer concepts can be illustrated by the following passages from a major review on adult carer research, conducted a decade ago, which could equally serve as a summary of young carer research at the turn of the century:

> The use of the term 'carer' has grown in the last decade. In its origins, it is an essentially professionally-oriented term. The word itself was developed within social care agencies and it bears the mark of that origin. The point is frequently made that many carers do not recognise themselves as such; the term is unfamiliar to them and, some would argue, at

odds with how they perceive their actions, which they would regard as an extension of family or personal relations rather than in terms of being a carer, with its formal, quasi-employment overtones. Despite this, the currency of the term has grown. It is now widely used in government statements and has entered the political debate. Most importantly, it shows signs of translating easily into the language of everyday life.

(Twigg et al., 1990.)

This passage contains all the main propositions that have subsequently driven the young carer debate; the professional labelling process, the inability of carers to see themselves as such, the gradual acceptance of the concept in formal circles and the entry of the term into common parlance. The passage continues:

At least as onerous, however, can be the restriction imposed on carers by their need to oversee their dependants' well being on a day-to-day and, sometimes, on a moment-to-moment basis. Physical tasks performed for the person may not necessarily be the most important feature of the caregiving; 'being responsible' for the person achieves greater significance.

(ibid.)

The proposition that the emotional investment in the caring role rather than the performance of specific physical tasks may be the primary feature of the caring paradigm also features strongly in young carer research; indeed, it can be said to be the defining feature of children's 'caring' roles.

Legislation

A carer, young or old, is clearly dependent, for their definitional status, on the presence of a person for whom they care. The status of both parties is thus relevant. A child may undertake limited caring tasks for a very severely restricted adult; equally they may undertake extensive duties in households where the degree of impairment is moderate or slight. The status of the cared-for person is defined in legislation dating back to the establishment of the welfare state, and retained for definitional purposes in all successive legislation that relates to disablement. Disability in the UK refers to a person who is:

Blind, deaf or dumb (or who suffers from mental disorder of any description) and other persons (aged 18 and over) who are substantially and permanently handicapped by illness, injury, or congenital deformity.

(National Assistance Act 1948, section 29.)

The Carers (Recognition and Services) Act 1995, which came into force in April 1996, is the first piece of legislation in the UK to specifically address, in part, the situation of young carers. Prior to this act, the key legislation relating to care in the community, the NHS and Community Care Act 1990 was entirely adult-focused. Before April 1996, in England and Wales, support for young carers could only be justified from a legislative perspective if the local authority in which they lived regarded them as a child in need, under section 17 of the Children Act 1989, and subsequently in Northern Ireland under article 18 of the Children (Northern Ireland) Order 1995. While this interpretation has since received the support of the Department of Health, in the early part of the 1990s such an understanding was discretionary. The same entry definition to the provisions of the Carers Act applies to both children and adults: a carer is a person who provides, or intends to provide, 'a substantial amount of care on a regular basis' (Section 1). Such a person is entitled to have their needs assessed at the same time as a dependent person is having their needs met for community care support. In Scotland, the Carers Act refers only to carers aged 16 years and over. However, unlike its counterpart in England and Wales, the Children (Scotland) Act 1995 includes, among the four categories of children considered 'in need', a child in need of care and attention because:

...he or she is affected adversely by the disability of any other person in his or her family.

(Scotland's Children, Scottish Office, 1997.)

Section 23 of this Act enables a local authority to support children affected by the disability of another in their family to receive support in order to minimise any negative effects on the child.

The obligations of social service departments to provide assistance to families affected by parental illness or disability are primarily met through two routes; Part 3 of the 1989 Children Act which obliges social services departments to assist children in need and the 1990 NHS and Community Care Act which involves the discharge of duties towards a child's parents. The former route is specifically recommended, should circumstances justify it, in the policy and practice guide issued by the Department of Health for the Carers Act (Department of Health, 1996). Both routes, well co-ordinated, are held to be necessary for the optimum provision of support (Social Services Inspectorate, 1999). *Quality Protects: Transforming Children's Services* directs social service departments:

> ...to ensure that children whose parents have specific needs arising out of disability or health conditions enjoy the same life chances as all other children in the locality.
>
> (para. 3.4.)

Children of disabled parents are thus firmly established as part of the social welfare universe, with local authorities being both able and obliged to respond to their circumstances in several legislative dimensions. The specific issue of recognising, assessing and treating children in caring situations as actors separate from their parents has been the single most important judicial development in this field. In the first case of its kind, less than 12 months after the Carers Act came into force, the London Borough of Newham was found to have behaved unlawfully in failing to assess the needs of a 14 year old girl, who was helping her mother care for a disabled younger sibling (Carers National Association, 1st February, 1997).

Young carers: what do dedicated services do?

The largest survey to date carried out on dedicated young carer services (Aldridge and Becker, 1998) provided information on 110 projects in the UK. Most provided information on the services offered, which illustrated a high degree of homogeneity. Apart from a very small number of anomalous categories, all reported services fell into the eight classifications shown in Table 3.1.

All projects delivering these services were very small. It is not possible to calculate mean size from the survey as whole time equivalent (WTE) hours are not reported. However, many services function with only one WTE, sometimes complimented by volunteers. Larger staff establishments are the exception rather than the rule, as are funding arrangements longer than three years. While this table is of limited utility, a notable feature is the very low number of services specifically reporting that they address educational disadvantage, a peculiar deficit given the constant association of child caregiving with reports of educational problems.

Table 3.1: Services reported in 1998 national survey of young carer projects

Service	Number providing (n)
Practical support or access to support	94
Provision of information	86
Leisure activities and holidays	82
Advocacy	80
Befriending	71
Counselling	63
Arranging respite care	47
Educational support	9

Education

The apparently low level of emphasis on educational support by young carer projects is surprising given that school absenteeism is one of the causes for concern most often cited by professionals. Some of the earliest contemporary discussion of children who were subsequently to be known as young carers can be found in educational literature (for example, Galloway, 1980). Absences from school by children undertaking domestic duties are both a historically familiar and socially comprehensible phenomenon to teachers. Typically, the source of a school's concern for absences of this kind is the potential damage to a child's educational career. Alternative discourses, which located the focus of concern in possible damage to children's emotional or physical health, as opposed to their educational careers, emerged at a much later date. Instances of child caregiving encountered in the course of government surveys (for example, Hunt et al., 1973), were noted in passing, but not considered worthy of more detailed analysis or concern.

However, professional groups have very different views on where the focus of a child caregiver's problems lie. Fox (1995) suggests that 10 per cent of all school absences are caused by children's domestic duties in the home. Teachers, he proposed, typically believe that absences are explained by a lack of parental appreciation of the importance of education, education welfare officers attribute absences to environmental deficits and social workers believe that underlying psychodynamic issues are at the root of the problem. The primacy of education, or social justice, or positive mental health, depending on the value base of the respective profession, is clearly a movable feast, in that professional and policy responses will vary depending on which discourse dominates.

What is missing in the literature is any empirical evidence that young carers' absences from school are higher than average, or that where more absences do occur, they can be attributed to 'caring'. No study has identified numbers of absences from independent sources such as school

registers and sought to examine whether caring duties are associated with any observed higher rates. We know, for example, that the average number of unauthorised absences for maintained primary school children in England was 10 half days in the 1997/8 school year, with secondary school pupils averaging 20 half days (Department of Health, 2000). Given the easy availability of means, nationally, by LEA and by school, due to the obligatory publication by schools of performance related data, this is an unfortunate omission. The largest survey undertaken in the UK using children already known to young carer services as its target population (n=2303) reported that 17 per cent of children in the 5–10 age group and 35 per cent of children in the 11–15 age group were 'missing' school (Dearden and Becker, 1998). However, this information was derived from agency respondents on the basis of a 'missing school'/'not missing school' answer, without any independent verification or any guidance as to how many absences were necessary for a 'missing school' designation to be recorded. Conversely, a two site study in England was unable to detect any significant impact on schooling of caring duties (Tucker and Liddiard, 1998), though again, this was based on self reports rather than records of school attendance. Even a study based on the extreme, by UK standards, experience of children in Zimbabwe, many of whom were caring for HIV infected parents, detected no elevation in school absences caused by caring duties (Robson and Ansell, 2000). This is a curious omission in our knowledge base given the importance placed on the right to education, especially as other childhood adversities have been explored in this way and have reached less than unanimous conclusions (for example, the effect of maternal and child asthma on children's school attendance (Parcel et al., 1979; McCowan et al., 1996; Cassino et al., 1997)). Despite claims to the contrary, we simply do not know to what extent, if at all, child caregiving results in higher levels of school absenteeism, after other confounding variables such as poverty and social class are taken into account.

Media Accounts

The media has a critical role to play in shaping and reinforcing our perceptions of social phenomena (Barthes, 1972). We are invited to perceive disabled parents and their children through a powerful cultural lens:

More than 100,000 children in Britain spend much or all of their childhood caring for parents made dependent by disability or illness.

(*The Independent*, 31.1.94.)

Children as young as three are forced to help care for disabled or terminally ill relatives, the British Association for the Advancement of Science was told yesterday.

(*The Independent*, 9.9.94.)

Headlines typically stress the assumption of caring roles:

Child carers hold the fort: survey says five year olds are tending sick relatives.

(*The Voice*, 9.1.96.)

Five year olds who care for AIDS parents.

(*The Daily Telegraph*, 24.2.97.)

Mother's little nurse: when childhood is shaped by responsibility.

(*The Daily Telegraph*, 1999.)

Many of the earlier headlines were generated by a Channel 4 documentary, *Looking after Mum*, shown in 1994, which generated a great deal of exposure in the trade and general press (Keith and Morris, 1995). In both the lay and professional world, the most important qualities for attracting attention were extreme youth, 'deserving' parents (alcohol or drug dependent parents, or parents affected by mental illnesses or learning disabilities were rarely mentioned), 'role reversal' and bravery (Deacon, 1999). However, the basic theme of disapproval and concern for children's role in caregiving can also be subverted. *The Daily Telegraph* (12.4.99), under a headline 'Gray's baby will care for brain-damaged sister', reported the case of a well-known TV personality, Muriel Gray, whose younger child suffered brain damage in an accident. Two years after the event, Ms Gray gave birth to another child, explaining that her decision to have another baby was prompted by the need to ensure that her elder son, after her death, would not be left to care for his younger sister alone.

Both disabled parents and their children have been affected by the emergence of a common discourse through which their circumstances are described and portrayed. Media exposure has often been less likely to draw attention to the extra help needed by many families, than to reinforce problematic constructions of both parenthood and childhood. A question mark is placed against the parenting potential of disabled people, and the act of caring by children subverts our notion of childhood as a chronological period free of domestic responsibilities. Both parties, it has been suggested, are not defined by what they are, but what they are not:

In its depiction of young carers, a very narrow range of ideologically distorted images of disabled people is employed by the various mass media, serving to reinforce an ideology of personal tragedy, and dependence.

(Stables and Smith, 1999.)

Young carer literature has acknowledged the need to provide whole family support as well as to help individual children, a tendency which has grown stronger in recent years (Bibby and Becker, 2000). The role of the media in promoting unhelpful stereotypes has also been noted (Becker et al., 1998). However, for many increasingly politicised disabled people, these objections have been insufficient in volume and frequency. The dissonance between these views is rooted in what has been described as the **social model of disability**.

Social Model of Disability

Recent decades have seen changes in the way the concept of disability is constructed, changes substantial enough to justify applying the rather over-used notion of a paradigm shift. Young carers exist because their parents become ill, are affected by disabilities, or experience other conditions that render them dependent to various degrees. If the needs generated by such dependencies are met from either formal sources, such as adequately funded community care support, or informal ones, such as friends, family or neighbours, then the *prima facie* conditions for child caregiving should be reduced. If such support structures are underpinned by a wider environmental and social architecture, physical, legislative and attitudinal, that diminishes the impact of impairments and promotes social inclusion, then the impact of such conditions may be largely eliminated. This, broadly, summarises the main dimensions of the social model of disability, or **social oppression theory** (Oliver, 1998).

Viewed from this perspective, the term **disability** becomes problematic. Terminology used to describe incapacities is inconsistent. Different descriptions are used by legislators, academics, and practitioners, members of the public, the press and disabled people themselves. Measurement errors are inevitable in epidemiological studies, and interventions cannot be standardised within populations and across international boundaries if there is a lack of consensus over the phenomena being investigated. The World Health Organisation thus developed a classification system, the International Classification of Impairments, Disabilities and Handicaps (ICIDH). The ICIDH means by *impairment* the loss of a physical or psychological function, by *disability* the inability to perform a commonplace activity as a result of an impairment, and by *handicap* the result of disabilities being of sufficient magnitude to exclude a disabled person from the performance of a normal social role. The social model of disability locates the genesis of disablement in the social environment and hence seeks solutions primarily grounded in social and political action. As a higher order concept the social model bases its rationale on human rights. The model implied by the ICIDH, often described (by its critics though not necessarily its proponents) as a 'medical' model, views disability as primarily a personal problem, arising from disease, trauma or ill health, which requires medical management and care by professionals. While the increasingly politicisation of the disability rights movement and the accompanying rhetoric has tended to excessively polarise these models (Bury, 2000), there is no doubt that the social model has been immensely influential, not least in driving the current revision of the ICIDH, re-named the

International Classification of Functioning, Disability and Health (ICF). The ICF model, adopted by the World Health Organisation as an international standard to describe health and disability (www.who.int/msa/mnh/ems/idich/ididh.htm) explicitly moves from indicators based on mortality and morbidity, to indicators based on 'life', that is, what actions need to be taken to promote and prolong healthy life years.

These models and the associated disputes are relevant to the subject at hand in that the most forceful challenge to the emerging concept of young carers has originated from disability rights activists, who have used the basic principle of the social model of disability, the proposition that people are disabled by socio-political rather than personal factors, to argue that the *primary* focus of intervention should be support for the parent, rather than support for the child. The genuine anger that has driven this discussion should not be underestimated. The dignity, rights, independence and self-esteem of disabled parents, it is alleged, are compromised by their portrayal as dependants, rather than citizens who are being failed by the state. The chairman of Aspire, the national spinal injuries charity, whose mother was affected by multiple sclerosis, writes of the publicity given to the plight of young carers, and his own childhood experience:

> *With the best will in the world, such official literature is once again contributing to the impression of disabled parents as short-changing their children. I felt enriched.*
>
> (Stanford, 2000.)

Disabled parents have not always received high marks for sensitivity in young carer research:

> *When asked a question about what they considered the main effects of caring on their children to be, the parents seemed unable to answer. This was an issue that few parents had either considered or articulated.*
>
> (Aldridge and Becker, 1994a.)

Insult is added to injury by the insidious suggestion that children have usurped the parenting role (Keith and Morris, 1995). Young carer services have thus come to operate in a heated ideological climate. Child caregiving, according to this analysis, arises from oppressive structures and would be unnecessary were such structures changed: investment should be directed towards adequate support for families not young carer projects (Morris, 1997). However, this objection carries some of the endemic weaknesses of the social model of disability itself, especially the proposition that impairment is only potentiated by oppressive social structures and has no (or limited) reality in isolation from these structures (Crow, 1996). To rectify an oppressive social structure by replacing steps with ramps, or through the provision of a home laundry service, is a somewhat simpler task than devising a support structure for a parent affected by a obsessive-compulsive or bi-polar disorder, or providing help for alcoholic parents who are unwilling to receive it.

This debate has important implications for the direction of social care services. If, as has been widely argued (Levin et al., 2000), parental disability – notably maternal mental illness – is a strong predictor of child protection registration, the pressure for an urgent response is likely to result in interventions based on a pathology model of mental illness. Conversely, if the impacts of parental disability, and again maternal mental illness is especially relevant, are exacerbated by structural inequalities and social oppression, then a disproportionate focus on child risk factors will further stigmatise and disable parents (Tanner, 2000). Both positions appear to have legitimate objections to the main propositions of the other. Disability is too heterogeneous for all its associated problems to be resolved through social action, however well resourced or planned. At the same time, families can undoubtedly care for their children better if adequately supported.

Nonetheless, this dispute starkly illustrates the collision between a model of child welfare services based on children's rights, and a model that sees parents as the main vehicle for the protection of children's health and wellbeing. Parents and children themselves seem rather better equipped to straddle this ideological divide and weigh up the respective advantages and disadvantages than professionals. Disabled parents report that,

alongside their concern that they may be unable to protect young children from some physical risks, their children become independent at an earlier age than the children of non-disabled parents, and are thus better equipped to deal with hazards (Wates, 1997). The author of this volume, herself disabled, cites one of her own children describing the gains and losses that result from parental disability:

> *There are some places we can't go without you, but when we go to a theme park we don't have to queue up for the rides. It's a pity you can't play running games but we like it when you can't catch us when we're naughty! It's horrible when you fall over but its fun playing with the scooter. Wherever we go you need help and so we're always meeting friendly people.*
>
> (Wates, 1997.)

When disabled parents themselves speak, they show a clear consciousness of dangers of making excessive demands on children, and no sign of abdicating, by acts of omission or commission, their status as parents:

> *It's really easy to get Melissa to work for me. She will do things I can't do. She'll go to get a tool, or I hold her up to get things I can't reach. But disabled parents have to be careful. We have to let our sons and daughters be children and do the things they want. They have their own little minds and their own priorities. We can't let them become robots for our sake.*
>
> (Brown, 1981, cited in Greer, 1985.)

Children's Rights and Adults' Wrongs

The social model of disability and the rights of children, despite being among the most important influences on social welfare services over the past few decades, have not always proved the most comfortable of bedfellows. The latter has been among the most powerful drivers of the young carer debate. Children's rights occupy a somewhat confused region within child welfare work, with the term being commonly applied to specific national or extra-national legislation, such as the United Nations Convention on the Rights of the Child

(UNCRC), but also to propositions that are non-judicial in nature.

The language of rights has assumed a powerful role within child welfare services. In addition to the judicial construction of children's rights, the medium is also used in a less precise manner, being rather more similar to suggested guidelines for good practice. A manifesto of rights for young carers has been proposed, and widely replicated, partially or in total, in the terms of reference and operational policies of a large number of dedicated young carer services (Aldridge and Becker, 1993a). This manifesto combined existing rights already met by UK legislation (education, health and social care, protection from harm, right to be treated separately from caregiver), rights proposed by the UNCRC (right to privacy), rights proposed but unfulfilled (right to befriending) and rights which are more accurately construed as perceived needs (right to be believed, right to stop caring, right to self-determination).

Whatever the mixed sources of this manifesto, and the occasionally slippery application of the language of rights, its influence has been undeniable. Possibly the most powerful impact of human rights discourse has been the changing weight of importance attached to the voice of the child. Both the UNCRC (article 12) and the 1989 Children Act make clear, from slightly different perspectives, that the views of a child in matters affecting their circumstances must be taken into account. In both cases, the crucial qualifying clause relates to the child's level of understanding. This is the key mediating factor in deciding the proportional weight that should be given to the child's views, a weight that, it has been strongly argued, is rarely given the emphasis that it deserves (Alderson, 1995).

Young carer literature has made a considerable contribution to the promotion of children's rights and facilitating the entry of children's voices into discourses on health and social welfare. However, the increasing relevance of children's rights to the way in which we respond to child welfare issues must be seen within the context of a broader debate about the nature of childhood. While

children's rights and their status as autonomous beings are promoted, children are affected by increasing restrictions on their liberty, characterised by curfews, electronic tagging, fear of unsupervised play, exclusion from informal work arrangements and heightened belief by adults in their vulnerability. While becoming more independent in some ways, they have become more dependent in others.

A perfect balance between rights and responsibilities, which has been the focus of much recent discussion (Selbourne, 1994; Etzioni, 1995) may be largely unobtainable, given that neither a categorical distinction between adults and children nor the elimination of such distinctions appears possible, or justified. Children appear well aware that they are denied rights that adults take for granted. However, older children express markedly different opinions about the optimum ages at which rights should be acquired than do children just a few years younger, illustrating that children are far from the homogenous constituency sometimes projected by children's rights activists (Newman, 1996). Equally, children appear to recognise that a more complex and relative approach to rights is needed which reflects differences in cognition, culture, gender and age (Morrow, 1999). Nonetheless, the dominance of the individual over the notion of obligations to others implied by human rights discourse has shallow roots. The United Nations Convention on the Rights of the Child grew largely from the manifesto of children's rights drawn up in 1923 by Eglantyne Jebb, the founder of the Save the Children charity, who proposed in the last of her seven rights of children:

> *The child must be brought up in the consciousness that its talents must be devoted to the service of its fellow man.*

Children of disabled parents dwell in a tangled web of reciprocal responsibilities, strong emotional ties and conflicting aspirations. In short, they live in families, social entities that are not easily deconstructed by the individualistic thrust of human rights discourse. While guaranteeing a child 'the right to stop caring' has a strong superficial appeal, the sentiment considerably underestimates the complex ties that bind families together. Rights, as the philosopher Benjamin Freedman has noted, are part of the justice of strangers, not of kinfolk (Freedman, 1999).

Child Caregiving and Culture

Like all other types of health and social welfare interventions, young carer services must consider the extent to which their activities, and the assumptions which underpin them, are applicable to all parts of our society. How are children in different minority ethnic cultures affected by parental disability?

A number of reviews of informal care in South Asian and African-Caribbean communities have concluded that levels of stress are proportionately higher than in white communities, due to a number of factors ranging from ethnocentric service attitudes to institutionalised racism (Atkin and Rollings, 1992; Hatton et al., 1998). However, only a very limited number of studies have specifically sought to examine the situation of young carers in non-white communities (for example, Hendessi, 1996; Shah and Hatton, 1999; Jones et al., 2002). Inequity in service is a common accusation (Dominelli, 1988). The core propositions cluster in two dimensions. First, it is suggested that disproportionately unsatisfactory services are provided to black and Asian caregivers due to Eurocentric assumptions or other forms of bias, not excluding racist attitudes. This includes inaccurate assumptions about family obligation structures, notably that intra-family or intra-communal support is both invariably present and that it is the preferred mode of social support. Second, qualitative differences are proposed in the construction of family obligations in migrant cultures, though inter-generational differences are a crucial variable, and inter-cultural differences within migrant cultures may be as wide as differences between migrant and non-migrant cultures. As one study of adult South Asian caregivers noted:

> The cultural norm of filial piety that influences the decision to provide care for elderly parents is more firmly rooted among first-generation immigrants.

(Gupta, 1999.)

This observation is supported by evidence that substantially higher proportions of South Asian adults, both male and female, and slightly higher numbers of black adults, care for elderly relatives than in the white population (People Science Intelligence Unit, 2000). We also know, from extensive survey evidence (for example, Policy Studies Institute, 1994) that family structures, and the views of members, of British citizens from African-Caribbean and South Asian communities may differ in some ways from white British families. While significant differences are typically found *within* South Asian communities, particularly between Bangladeshi or Pakistani and Indian families, differences have also been noted between all these groups as compared to white families. These include a stronger antipathy to divorce, less willingness for women to work outside the home, a preference for multi-generational households, a greater division of labour by gender, a more positive attitude towards marriage and a correspondingly negative attitude towards co-habitation prior to marriage (Beishon et al., 1998). An enhanced role for intra-family obligations has been noted in other communities where religious belief and practice may play a proportionately greater role (for example, within Jewish families, see Freedman, 1996, or within Chinese families, see Wong, 2000). While the importance of intra- and inter- family support in migrant communities has been emphasised (Ahmad, 1996), changes in cultural expectations have also been noted, as has the accumulation of greater cultural capital by children of migrants, and the corresponding effect this may have on normative values associated with family obligations (Modood et al., 1994). In addition, social class is known to be a powerful mediator of family obligations (Finch, 1989), a factor that has been noted as differentiating some dimensions of kinship support not just in white communities but also in working class and middle class black and Asian communities (Werbner, 1990). The stereotypes of both the endlessly supportive extended migrant family and, conversely, the oppressive restraint on young British Asians of traditional cultures unfortunately retain their power (Atkin and Rollings, 1996). Adding cultural expectations, particularly in the context of inter-generational change, to the intricate mix of gender and class further challenge our understanding of how obligations are fulfilled within families. In short, we might expect to find a more complex set of demands and negotiating positions within migrant families where a child finds itself in a caring role as a result of parental dependency.

Nonetheless, given the variations that exist in all populations, it is unclear to what extent these apparent differences will remain relevant when the experiences of children are examined. Furthermore, given the accumulation of inter-generational differences experienced by any migrant population, it is likely that the views and experiences of black, Asian and white *children* may not differ as significantly as that of their *parents*. While information on this dimension of child caregiving is limited, one of the largest studies conducted to date lent some support to this view. Statutory services came in for a certain amount of criticism from Asian young carers for having replaced a 'colour-blind' approach with excessive cultural sensitivity:

> *They seem very judgmental. They keep giving us an Asian social worker even though we've asked for non-Asian. They say 'Mum's Asian', we say, 'she can understand English'.*
> (Shah and Hatton, 1999.)

While Asian children perceived their burdens as being more onerous than white children (due to the greater difficulty of asking for help and the lesser likelihood of receiving it) they saw their experiences as being little different. A more recent study in Manchester of black families where children have caring responsibilities, while highlighting the more intense obstacles that black families faced, also stressed their common experiences (Jones et al., 2002). Absence of support to parents, the rejection by young black people of a 'young carer' label, the presumption of incompetence inherent in the assessment process where parental disability is present, and the confusion between 'having needs' and 'being in need' were features reported by

respondents, which echo observations increasingly being made by disabled parents in general (Wates, 2002).

Services to young carers are located within the complex and sensitive arena of reciprocal family obligations, expectations and duties. While the obligations of children to their parents feature powerfully in both Eastern and Western religious traditions, the ethical architecture of young carer work has emanated from secular sources, particularly, as noted above, human rights discourse, which is primarily concerned with the autonomy of the individual rather than the individual's perceived obligations to others. The diminution of obligation, and the corresponding emphasis on the primacy of the child's welfare might require us to consider, that in circumstances where the child's obligations to their parents, rather than the primacy of their needs dominate, a different kind of approach may be required.

Sources of bias

While some evidence exists for the long term negative consequences on children of parental disability, particularly parental mental illness, the long term impacts on children, specifically arising from the provision of care for parents or siblings, are unclear. In the absence of robust data, extrapolations from unrepresentative samples become recycled and become accepted as 'fact'. For example, self-reports of poor mental health, from a small convenience sample of adults with child caregiving careers described in a study for the Children's Society (Tatum and Tucker, 1998), are quoted uncritically in a leading mental health journal as indicating that up to three-quarters of young carers develop psychological problems as adults (Dearden and Becker, 1999). Absence of evidence is, of course, not equivalent to evidence of no effect. It is the not the fault of dedicated young carer researchers that no specific data on the issue are currently available from any large cohort study, or that prevalence is too low to be explored by any other than very large population surveys, nor that prevalence may be diminished by concealment. However, the almost total absence of studies that compare young carers with population controls, or which use validated instruments to test propositions about the mental, physical and emotional health of young carers has enabled the debate on the impact of child caregiving to take place in a vacuum of empirical evidence.

Many studies of young carers consist of surveys of known populations, and of non-replicable and methodologically unclear presentations of case studies. Negative findings predominate. Where more positive statements associated with caring duties are made, they are typically subject to stringent qualifications:

> Of course, it can be argued that such statements are little more than justificatory attempts to derive a sense of dignity and meaning from the caring work that has to be carried out.
>
> (Tatum and Tucker, 1998.)

The situation of the young carer, and that of their family, is presented as a distortion of the social arrangements that it is believed should pertain in 'normal' families (Aldridge and Becker, 1994a; Blyth and Milner, 1997). A few studies depart, however, from this approach. While denying neither the emotional and physical cost to children of some aspects of caring, nor that some children themselves recognised the debilitating effects of care, a study in Dorset emphasised the degree to which children regarded their situations as normal:

> The meaning that young carers attach to their caregiving experiences reveal that helping to care for parents is part and parcel of their experiences of family life: it is simply how things are, no matter how unfair.
>
> (Tozer, 1998.)

Positive benefits

A body of evidence also exists which provides some support for the proposition that the additional responsibilities involved in situations where children are having to deal with adversities may, in many circumstances, be a positive factor in a child's development. Self-reported positive dimensions of *adult* caregiving for ill relatives have been noted in a number of studies (Farren et al., 1991, Thompson, 1991, Hinrichsen et al., 1992, Beach, 1997). In relation

to parental disability and illness, it is suggested that more cohesive parent-child relationships may develop, and the accomplishment of tasks important to the household economy may result in enhanced self-esteem (Glass, 1985; Greer, 1985; Blackford, 1999). The Virginia longitudinal study of divorce and remarriage (Hetherington et al., 1982; Hetherington, 1989) found children of divorced parents exhibiting higher levels of maladaptive behaviour than children in the non-divorced controls. Many children in divorced families, however, coped extremely well, performing satisfactorily in school, being popular with peers and persistent in dealing with stressful situations, and exhibiting few behaviour problems. Some children in this group combined this competence with manipulative and opportunistic strategies. The most notable factor in the cluster of children in divorced families who exhibited highly competent behaviours and an absence of these strategies, was the responsibilities their family circumstances had steered them into undertaking, specifically the care of others, even at an early age:

> This usually involved the care and nurturance of younger siblings; in seven cases, however, it involved supporting a physically ill, lonely, alcoholic or depressed mother, and in three cases it involved helping to care for an aged or physically feeble grandparent. This early required helpfulness was the most powerful factor in predicting later membership in the caring-competent cluster.
>
> (Hetherington, 1989.)

We must clearly approach this issue with care. However, the above example illustrates that neither proposition, that child caregiving is inevitably damaging or inevitably positive, is necessarily true. What appears to make the difference is the range of factors, that when combined, result in a positive, or a negative, set of developmental opportunities.

While the image of children as passive and manipulated actors undertaking clandestine and damaging duties has clear appeal as a lobbying campaign, it has not been subject to the robust examination that such a major proposition should receive. To treat child caregiving as a previously concealed phenomenon that emerged in the late 1980s ignores both the lengthy history of domestic care by children, and over-simplifies the social roles children play within families. For example, while only being concerned with child caregiving in passing, Morrow (1996) found that, in a sample of 11–16 year olds (n=730), half the girls and a third of the boys reported regularly undertaking domestic work. Morrow categorised the work undertaken in two ways; help with housework and cleaning, and provision of care, mostly for younger siblings though, in a few cases, for adult relatives. The mother's employment pattern was the main factor affecting the nature and extent of the child's contribution. Children, however, presented themselves (the data consisted of self -penned essays) as active rather than passive agents in role negotiation, and not as victims.

Creating Identity

The allocation of a label to a social problem marks the entry of a phenomenon into a medical or welfare taxonomy. It enables a social problem to be officially recognised, enumerated and classified. Specialisms can subsequently emerge, organised professional groupings form, and diagnostic criteria can be developed. Those affected by the phenomenon, both personally and professionally, can build a shared language. Linguistically, varying competing descriptions will merge into one and the term will become capitalised, indicating its anointment as an official identity. Thus children become 'carers', then 'young carers' and finally 'Young Carers'. The identity may then be promoted among practitioners, parents, children and the public. The way in which all parties involved in the caring matrix perceive themselves and each other is a frequent preoccupation of carer research. For example, it is held to be desirable for adult carers to be treated, and to see themselves, as 'co-workers' (Moffat, 1997). Similarly, self-recognition is a common thread in young carer training material:

> *Getting children to recognise themselves as young carers is a fundamental issue facing professionals and (informal) supporters alike.*
>
> (Young Carers Research Group, Handout, 1a, 1994.)

While promoting the conscious awareness of the political context of suffering is hardly an illegitimate goal of child welfare services, the apparent inability of the parties most intimately

associated with a social problem to comprehend a situation without having it explained to them does deserve some critical attention. It is not altogether clear why children should benefit from such acts of recognition. Indeed, children themselves, as we have noted, appear wary of accepting a 'young carer' label.

Having discussed the main features of the young carer issue, the next step is to examine two important questions. Firstly, what are the known features of the young carer population, and secondly, what attempts have been made to measure the magnitude of the problem? The first question will be explored by summarising a survey of all young carers known to a large child care charity, the second by discussing and critically analysing attempts made to estimate the size of the population.

Barnardo's 'Young Carer' Survey

Barnardo's has been providing dedicated young carer services since 1990. In 1998, nine Barnardo's services provided data on 299 children and young people. Information was provided by agency workers involved with the children. Girls comprised 58 per cent of the population. The average of boys and girls was the same, being just over 12 years. Thirteen per cent of the sample was from ethnic categories. Almost half (47 per cent) of parents from ethnic minorities were lone parents, compared to 61 per cent from white families. Lone parenthood emerged as a notable characteristic of families involved with services, with 60 per cent living in one parent families. Mothers were, overwhelmingly, the main recipients of care, being the main care receiver in almost three-quarters of cases.

In 39 families (13 per cent of total), more than one person was being cared for. Thirty two per cent of the population of care receivers were single parents with mental illnesses (including schizophrenia, depression and phobic conditions). Ethnic minority parents were more likely to be reported as being affected by a psychological illness. Where the person cared for was the mother (single or not), the disabling condition was, in 60 per cent of cases, a mental illness. A picture thus begins to emerge of the most typical family structure and caregiving context encountered: a disproportionate skew towards family situations where mental disorders are affecting single mothers, a family context which we know is strongly associated with poverty.

Nineteen per cent of children were reported as 'missing school', though no independent verification of absences was available from school registers. As one would expect, a far higher proportion of older children (11–15 years) were reported as missing school. Many children were reported as carrying out more than one form of caring. Fourteen children (five per cent) were reported as carrying out intimate caring tasks for parents with a variety of physical disabilities (including spina bifida, multiple sclerosis, stroke and cerebral palsy). Almost as many (n=11) were carrying out intimate caring tasks for people with mental illnesses, a finding that raises a definitional issue regarding what is considered an intimate task. Girls, surprisingly, were no more likely to deliver intimate care than boys and, equally surprisingly, boys were just as likely to deliver intimate care to mothers as girls.

Profile of parental illness or disability

The distribution of illness and disability types is illustrated in Table 3.2. The diagnosis was written in by the service; no pre-set categories were given. Illness or disability types have been clustered into four categories; psychological, somatic, intellectual and sensory.

Twenty 'conditions' were generated by the Barnardo's data, and these conditions were subsequently compressed into the following composite classifications:

Psychological disorders   50% (including schizophrenia, depression, phobic conditions, drug or alcohol addiction).

Somatic disorders   38% (including chronic illness, ME, asthma,

Table 3.2: Young carers: condition affecting primary recipient of care	
Illness/disability type	
Mental illness*	34%
Learning disability***	11%
Depression*	10%
Chronic illness**	9%
Physical disability**	7%
Multiple sclerosis**	5%
Phobic disorder*	3%
Cancer**	3%
Stroke**	3%
Epilepsy**	2%
Alcohol dependence*	2%
Cerebral palsy**	2%
Myalgic encephalomyelitis (ME)**	2%
Arthritis**	2%
Mobility impaired**	1%
Spina bifida**	1%
Blind****	1%
Deaf****	1%
Asthma**	1%
Drug dependence*	1%
Total psychological disorders*	50%
Total somatic disorders**	38%
Total intellectual impairments***	11%
Total sensory impairments****	2%
Total other	–

Notes: 1) All those in the learning disability category are children, not adults.
2) Psychological disorders includes drug or alcohol abuse.

cancer, arthritis, epilepsy, MS, spina bifida, stroke, cerebral palsy).

Intellectual impairment   11% (learning disability).

Sensory impairment   2% (blind, deaf).

In the case of learning disability, all bar one of the care receivers was a sibling.

Sources of referral

Social service departments were the primary source of referral, followed by voluntary organisations and health services. Given the frequency with which poor school attendance is associated with child caring, it is surprising than less than 10 per cent of referrals were from educational sources.

Almost three-quarters of clients referred by *social workers* were lone parents, and 16 per cent of children in these families were reported as being involved in intimate care. Eleven per cent of children referred by social workers had received an assessment, 19 per cent were reported as missing school and 57 per cent of parents referred had mental disorders.

As one might expect, 63 per cent of those referred by the *education* sector were missing school, 74 per cent of whom were female. Almost 90 per cent were aged 13 and over. Only one child aged under 13 referred by the education sector was missing school. Parental mental illness accounted for 63 per cent of all education referrals, and 15 per cent of children were reported as being involved in intimate care.

Over half (56 per cent) of those referred by the *health* sector were 12 years and under; there were an equal number of one- and two-parent families. Seventeen per cent of children were missing school, a quarter of parents were depressed, and a further two thirds (61 per cent in all) were mentally ill.

While the above patterns inevitably reflect the particular responsibilities and concerns of the referring agencies – social services with disadvantage, health with younger children, education with school absenteeism – the phenomenon of parental psychological illness remains a common theme.

Where the parent was physically disabled, 14 per cent of referrals came from relatives. The largest number of 'relative' referrals was from families with a learning disabled child (38 per cent). Where referrals were from children *themselves*, in over half the cases (51 per cent), the parent had a somatic disorder.

Given the degree of adult impairment present, the levels of supportive services provided and assessments carried out, were extremely low. Only three per cent of children had been assessed under the 1989 Children Act, 2 per cent of families under the Carers (Recognition and Services) Act and less than one per cent under the NHS and Community Care Act. It was unclear whether this was due to a lack of response, inaccurate reporting, or whether the children or families were not perceived by statutory authorities as crossing the relevant needs threshold.

Parental psychological illness

The most important feature of this dataset is the distribution of disabling adult conditions, and in particular the high proportion of lone female parents who are affected by psychological illnesses. This is an extremely important issue. Physical impairments are strongly associated with the ageing process, whereas the population most at risk from psychological illnesses, especially depressive and affective illnesses and psycho-neurotic disorders, are women with young children, living in poverty, and lacking adequate social support, especially supportive partners (Brown and Harris, 1978). The Barnardo's dataset indicates that in only 38 per cent of cases is a second adult present in the home where the primary care receiver is affected by a psychological illness. In the case of a somatic illness, this rises to 66 per cent. A family where the main carer is affected by a psychological illness may impact on a child in a very different way, and require a range of support skills quite different from that where the main carer has a physical impairment. For example, while only 18 per cent of the primary dependants affected by a psychological illness received home help services, 28 per cent of those affected by a somatic illness did.

The question is also raised as to why so many families which contain two adults, where only one of which is reported as having an illness or disability, are also reported as containing children who have excessive caring roles. Perhaps more importantly, the extremely low levels of domiciliary support services reported indicate (assuming that levels of need within the families were not being misreported) a large scale failure by statutory services to provide adequate levels of help to disabled parents. If these data suggest a 'typical' family where a child with excessive caring responsibilities might be located, it is a family where a lone female parent is affected by a psychological illness. When the categories of mental illness, depression and phobias are combined, the relationship between lone parent status and mental illness in this data set is highly significant. If we isolate the care receiver condition of 'mental illness', which is the single largest category, accounting for a third of the total, the population consists of 71 per cent lone parents, almost three quarters of whom have more than one child.

What kinds of parental disability are most closely associated with a specific child outcome? The only hard data available are school absences. Conflating all care receiver conditions into psychological and somatic, we can see the highly significant impact of psychological illnesses.

It is clear from Table 3.3 that psychological illness is far more strongly associated with school absences than are somatic disorders (p<0.01). Non-psychological disorders of any kind, according to this dataset, have relatively minor impacts on school attendance, though it must be noted that in the case of both alcohol- and drug-dependent parents, reported school absenteeism was high, though these numbers were too small for

calculation. Many conditions noted were not accompanied by any associated school absences at all. Three quarters of all school absenteeism occurred in families where a psychological illness had been reported. The extent of the causal relationship between these two phenomena, without additional information on the socio-economic context of the families is, of course, speculative. School absences have a steep social class gradient and the substantially higher levels of poverty in lone parent households would be expected to depress school attendance regardless of the psychological health of the parent. However, these data do raise a question mark against the extent to which child caregiving can be regarded as an important independent variable in all cases of school absences.

The data also show the capacity of local circumstances to skew referral profiles. For example, 53 per cent of referrals associated with children caring for relatives with learning disabilities originated from a single source, a project that shared premises with a learning disability short term break service, illustrating the 'snowball' effect that can occur when families are in close contact with child welfare services. This, together with the above profiles of agency referral patterns, shows how the specific concerns of child care practitioners – whether arising from the purview of their agencies, their professional training or, in this case, simply the location of their service – may cause the profile of children's needs, the nature of the agency response, and the way in which children will become labelled to differ.

While there are numerous drawbacks to this survey (insufficient confidence in how representative

Table 3.3: Parental illness or disability type and school absences

Illness/disability type	Psychological*	Somatic**
Missing school	43	14
Not missing school	109	128

*Includes mental illness, drug and alcohol addiction, phobic conditions and depression.
**Includes learning disability, arthritis, physical disability, chronic illness, cancer, cerebral palsy, ME, stroke, impaired mobility, spina bifida, MS, epilepsy, blindness, deafness and asthma.

the sample is, lack of clarity on inclusion or exclusion criteria to many categories, and some doubts about the accuracy of the third party reporting) there is a consistent emphasis on maternal psychological disorders, especially when associated with lone parenthood. The importance of this issue has been highlighted in both a local (Seal, 1998) and a national (Edwards, 1997) context. In this important dimension, the Barnardo's data differs from that in the 1998 national young carers survey (the largest carried out to date) which concluded that 'the majority of young carers are caring for people with physical health problems, the most commonly occurring single condition being MS' (Dearden and Becker, 1998), and is more congruent with the variables most commonly associated with disadvantage.

Neither the Barnardo's survey nor the 1998 national survey were drawn from randomly selected samples, leaving an important question still unanswered: how typical of the actual population is the population encountered by services, and just how big is the problem anyway?

The Epidemiology of Children's Problems, or Why We Don't Like Counting

David was conscience stricken after he had counted the fighting men, and he said to the Lord, 'I have sinned greatly in what I have done'.
(Samuel II, 24:10.)

Defining both needs and numbers in child welfare services is often an inexact science, especially in cases where the distinguishing features of the target population overlap with those of the general population. How has the epidemiology of child caregiving measured up to these challenges?

Estimates of the prevalence of young carers in the UK have, with the exception of one study from the Office for National Statistics (ONS), been often less than robust. Early estimates of numbers varied considerably, with early studies in Liverpool suggesting a UK total of 10,000 and later figures of 212,000 being cited (Becker et al., 1998). The context in which prevalence of child caregiving is estimated can be illustrated with reference to a definition used by ONS for access to a survey

population, and one used by a young carers' service:

A young carer means a child or young person who is carrying out significant caring tasks and assuming a level of responsibility for another person which would usually be taken by an adult.
(Walker, 1996.)

A young person under 18 who cares for or about [my emphasis] *a relative with an illness or disability and who, because of their caring, has their own life significantly affected in some way.*
(Astil, 1998.)

The variation resulting from such differing definitions can be starkly illustrated by the resulting estimations of prevalence. The ONS survey identified 18 young carers in a survey population of 12,000 households which extrapolated, with a 95 per cent confidence level, to a national population of between 19–51,000. This finding was largely replicated by data from the 1996 General Household Survey, which used the same definition (personal communication, Office for National Statistics, 1998). A survey of schools in Bournemouth using the second definition resulted in one in eight children being identified as 'young carers' (Astil, 1998) which would result in a national estimate of some two million. Even the ONS estimate is typically quoted at its top end. For example, the Carers National Association asserted that 'official figures state that there are 51,000 young carers in the UK' (News release, National Carers Week, 6 May, 1998), a figure widely quoted in both professional journals and the national press, despite there being an equal chance of the actual number being 19,000 or 51,000 (or any number in between). The slippery approach to statistical calculation is further illustrated by a study of children affected by AIDS and HIV conducted in Wales (Thomas, 1997), which resulted in the following newspaper headline:

Care agencies let 400 children and teenagers look after infected parents, brothers and sisters.
(*Western Mail*, 1.2.97.)

In fact, no information had been collected in this study as to whether any affected children had caring duties at all. What the study had *actually* concluded was that, based on the undocumented recollections of staff in GUM clinics, 355 children had relatives, 46 per cent of whom were cousins, nephews, nieces and 'others', who were HIV-positive. The rationale given for regarding their being 'children in need' was as follows:

> It would be quite wrong to try and **predict** [author's emphasis] *which children will be affected. The nieces and nephews of gay men may be very much affected by their uncle's illness and death.*
>
> (Thomas, 1997.)

The reluctance, indeed the outright opposition, to propose that certain contexts, and certain relationships, are of greater or lesser magnitude than others – and hence potentially more or less distressing – has been present from the outset in young carer research. Scepticism as to the value of surveys appeared in some of the earliest studies:

> A survey might identify a teenager as the prime carer in practical terms but ignore young brothers or sisters on whom the psychological effects may be much greater.
>
> (Meredith, 1991a.)

The general point being made is unexceptionable; outliers may occur in any population and we would be wrong to discount the possibility that some children with apparently marginal contacts with adversity may not suffer harm. However, this stance suggests that proposing coherent causal relationships is not just subject to error, but that it is *impossible*, and immoral into the bargain. This view is not unique to young carer services. Advocacy research in social care has typically inflated prevalence where this might facilitate the acceptance of a desired view, stimulate welfare investment or increase the influence of a disadvantaged group, and similarly deflated it where the same aims require a perception of low prevalence. Child abuse is an example of the former, juvenile crime an example of the latter. Clearly, imprecise definitions enable such population estimations to be constructed with maximum flexibility, depending on the outcome required.

Estimating numbers

The difficulty of arriving at accurate estimations of imprecise or poorly monitored phenomena has major implications for a large number of child welfare problems and the resources we are prepared to allocate to discrete issues. For example, how many children live in families where the parent is affected by a significantly limiting illness? A major review in the US was only able to conclude that 'as many as 5–15 per cent of children and adolescents may have parents who suffer from a significant medical condition' (Worsham et al., 1997). Given that the child population in the USA is around 40 million, this is a variation of some four million children: not very useful for planning purposes. Similarly, epidemiological studies of children with emotional and behavioural disorders serious enough to warrant intervention give a range of prevalence figures from seven to 26 per cent in the UK (Stewart-Brown, 1998) and 15-22 per cent in the USA (Harrison et al., 1999). Some conditions are relatively uncontentious, though few are entirely without controversy. For example, if we accept a definition of poverty as having less than half average income, then we can estimate the number of children living in poverty in the UK as between a quarter and a third of the total child population. We know that around three to four children in 1000 have a severe learning disability and one in 1000 have a condition that will severely limit their life span. We also know that these conditions are not equally distributed in the child population. Socio-economic class, physical environment and ethnic group are among a range of factors that will skew the distribution. Conversely, many child welfare problems suffer from a lack of epidemiological rigor, due to the difficulty, or unwillingness, of practitioners to agree on a definition that may be operationalised. For example, rates of child sexual abuse within the population have been estimated by various studies as being between three per cent and 90 per cent (Pilkington and Kremer, 1995).

Prevalence and incidence

There is often confusion between estimates of **prevalence** and **incidence**. Figures for the prevalence, and cumulative incidence, of the same phenomenon may be very different. For example, the number of people suffering from influenza on Christmas Day 2001 (prevalence) will be much smaller than the number who had 'flu during the whole 2001 calendar year (cumulative incidence). The latter measurement is more meaningful if we are trying to estimate how many children grow up in situations of social disadvantage. Data from the National Child Development Study (Pilling, 1990) illustrate that while similar proportions of the cohort were socially deprived at age 11 and age 16, these were not the same children. 65 per cent of those disadvantaged at 11 were not so at 16, and 45 per cent of those disadvantaged at 16 were not so at 11. Estimating the number of young carers in a local or national population thus depends not just on a consensual agreement that enables a child to enter or be excluded from a definition with a large measure of reliability, but a decision whether to measure the number of children delivering episodes of care at a particular point in time or over a given period. Cross-sectional surveys which collect information about children from a representative sample of households at a single point in time will result in an estimate of prevalence. The estimate will be based on the numbers of children who might be carrying out defined caring duties on the day the survey was undertaken, or within a short time span (for example, over the previous month). A survey of an adult population, which seeks to establish how many adults undertook caring duties within their households as children would establish cumulative incidence, and the proportion would inevitably be higher than the prevalence, as a caregiving role may have been undertaken for short periods by large numbers of children due to episodic parental illnesses.

Are conditions also needs?

A further problem arises with estimating the volume of help required where the *presence* of a condition is equated with a *need* for an intervention, that is, assuming that the number of people affected by a particular illness in a population is a proxy for the number of people 'in need'. This is not necessarily a valid assumption. For example, 60 per cent of eligible men declined to participate in a randomised controlled trial of psychological therapy for patients with testicular cancer (Moynihan, et al., 1998). Apart from the study findings themselves (which were that no benefit was observed), the authors concluded that the refusal group differed in their psychological profiles from those who perceived a need for psychological support. A substantial part of a population with the same condition did thus not appear to 'need' the intervention. Given that some estimations of need used by child welfare services which derive from the 1989 Children Act equate a **condition**, such as being disabled, having an HIV positive parent, and being a 'young carer', with a **need**, we can conclude that, in many cases, *estimated* need may be in excess of *true* need.

The Walker Survey

To date, only one published survey using recognised sampling methods has sought to enumerate child caregiving, and this was conducted by the Office for National Statistics Social Survey Division (Walker, 1996). As we have seen, the prevalence of child caregiving has been a subject of some dispute, and the citing of figures, by welfare agencies, academics, practitioners and the press has often been undertaken in a somewhat cavalier fashion. It is thus worth highlighting the main points of the only robust epidemiological survey that we have to date.

The general population sample of 12,000 households yielded 29 households which appeared to contain a young carer, using the Department of Health criteria set out in the Chief Inspector's letter of April 1995. The survey consisted of interviews carried out in the household. In two thirds of cases, family group interviews were carried out, followed by individual interviews with the disabled family member and child, though in ten cases such privacy was not possible. In four cases, the child was not able to be interviewed.

On examining data from the interviews, it was concluded that 17 households contained 18 young people who met the Department of Health criteria. Most children lived in households where there was also an adult carer. While around half of the children had responsibility for the disabled adult at some time, the primary role of the child in the household was covering for the period where adult family members, or paid carer staff, were not present. Main tasks were giving physical help with mobility and generally keeping an eye on the disabled person. Only two children were involved in personal care. Half had caring duties for more than 20 hours a week. All bar four families received help from friends or relatives. Community care assistants provided help to three families. A UK-wide estimate of 19,000 to 51,000 young carers was suggested. The large range is a function of the comparative rarity of young carers within the total child population. To place this figure in perspective, this figure is similar to the number of children in the UK with severe learning disabilities (around 42,000) and some four times higher than the number of people with cystic fibrosis.

A common criticism of surveys of this type is that numbers have been underestimated due to concealment. 'Accurate figures', notes a widely consulted source for young carer data, 'are difficult to obtain due to the hidden nature of caring' (NCH – Action for Children, 1999). This proposition, despite having the status of a theory, is widely cited as fact. Counts of rare social groups tend to follow what statisticians describe as a **Poisson distribution**. Taking account of this, the ONS survey concluded that even with a frequency of occurrence in non-responding households 100 per cent higher than in responding households 'the grossed up population figure will still be of a similar order to that estimated from the responding sample' (Walker, 1996).

General Household Survey

While the 1996 ONS survey remains the most authoritative, the General Household Survey (GHS) for that year included questions on young carers.

Using the Chief Inspector's definition, a range of questions were asked of the head of household regarding any caring duties, undertaken by children, for sick or disabled relatives. The schedule investigated the range of help received from sources both within and outside the household, the number of hours spent on caring by children, the nature of the care receiver's impairment and the kind of help provided. The latter covered help with personal care, lifting and carrying, mobility, paperwork, keeping the disabled relative company, giving medicines, practical help and general watchfulness. However, the number of children caring for relatives identified in this sample was insufficient to warrant a statistical analysis, with only some 50 children being located in 10,000 households. These data have not been placed in the public realm and there were, at the time of writing, no plans to do so (personal communication, Office for National Statistics, 1997; 1999).

Secondary analysis

One attempt has been made to estimate the number of young carers using a secondary analysis of a large, cross-sectional data set (Parker, 1994). Analysis of data from the 1985 General Household Survey (GHS) suggested that 17 per cent of those aged 16–35 had caring responsibilities before their sixteenth birthday, a third of these being involved in assisting parents. The GHS identified 1.2 million adult carers. Using these figures, some 212,000 adults had been providing care before their sixteenth birthday, 68,000 of these for a parent. However, these data provide no information on what these caring duties were, and we are hence unable to know to what extent they would meet the definition provided by the Chief Inspector's letter, and hence how many of these 212,000 would be included in the formal definition of a young carer. This figure, however, is one of cumulative incidence and cannot be treated as an indication of prevalence, in 1985, or now. As noted above, the confusion between these two methods of calculation is one source of the large variation in young carer estimates.

The ONS and GHS studies were preceded, and have been followed, by a number of other attempts to reach a national estimate. While no other study has been based on a random selection of the population, a large number of local surveys have been carried out, in addition to the national survey of child carer projects in the UK to which the above Barnardo's dataset was compared.

Local surveys

The issue of child carers was first highlighted through a number of local surveys conducted in Liverpool a decade ago (Mahon and Higgins, 1995). The most frequently cited figure for the number of young carers in the UK during the emergence of the issue was 10,000 (White, 1989). Difficulties with both identification and definition, which were to prove recurring problems, emerged from the early surveys. A survey of 16,000 pupils in Sandwell secondary schools identified 95 young carers, with almost as many again 'suspected' (Page, 1988). However, a third were caring for siblings or grandparents, and while no data is given, the assumption must be that other adults were present within the house. The report suggested that higher numbers of children with caring tasks were found in schools with poorer catchments areas. However, as the definitional parameters have widened, estimates have increased:

> Local research has shown that in an average secondary school of 800 children, approximately 60 pupils will have significant caring responsibilities for a family member.
>
> (Hill, 1999.)

This figure would extrapolate to some 400,000 children nationally (11–18 years only); no methodology is cited and this article is not a serious scientific study. However, as it appeared in the only dedicated young carer journal in the UK, it is undoubtedly widely read and, presumably believed. We might also wish to note the gap between the 95 children identified from a population of 16,000 (1988) and the 60 from 800 cited a decade later; an apparent increase of 1200 per cent. The jury is thus still very much out on just how large the young carer population is:

however, more accurate estimates are not likely to be forthcoming without a closer attention to basic epidemiological principles by both researchers and practitioners working in the young carer field.

Definitions: counting what you want to count

> If you can't prove what you want to prove, demonstrate something else and pretend that they are the same thing. In the daze that follows the collision of statistics with the human mind, hardly anyone will notice the difference.
>
> (Huff, 1981.)

Inability, or unwillingness, to engage with the definitional challenges inherent in epidemiological studies has resulted in a rejection by many young carer services of attempts to estimate numbers of young carers based on a taxonomy of caring duties, and a preference for an approach based on the *impact* of caring on the child. It is argued that whether or not children meet the SSI definition of young carers should be irrelevant (Blyth and Milner, 1997). Noting that local authorities are most likely to refer to the definition provided by the guidance to the Carers (Recognition and Services) Act 1995, a definition based on the *nature* of the caring task, a more complete definition has been demanded, one which considers the *impacts* on children, and not just the content and frequency of their caring duties.

This course of action has several apparent advantages. A child who falls below a defined threshold of caring magnitude will still be served, if evidence of negative impact exists. The gatekeeping duties of agencies will be weakened and staff will not be placed in the invidious position of aggregating the weight of children's caring duties. It is furthermore suggested that:

> The terms 'substantial' and 'regular' care are ambiguous, and it is the responsibility of local authority social service departments to interpret them in relation to individual circumstances and needs.
>
> (Becker et al.,1998.)

The simultaneous complaints that a) definitions are too narrow and will exclude children in need and b) definitions are too broad and cannot be operationalised consistently, are familiar ones. However, it is not immediately apparent how shifting the definitional focus from acts to effects will result in any higher level of specificity. In fact, identifying impacts on children of caring (for example, depressive episodes, number of physical injuries, days of schooling lost, frequency of social contacts), may be a rather more arduous task than quantifying magnitude and frequency of care. The only avenue open that may avoid this dilemma is the very type of aggregation that the predictive model involves; an assumption that *all* types and frequency of caring have, or *could* have, damaging consequences for children. The shift from an external and objective mode of definition to an internal and subjective one is a significant change with considerable implications. The belief that the presence or absence of adversity can only be defined by the person affected has achieved widespread social penetration (Furedi, 1998). The post-modern approach to both needs and event definition is rooted in an attempt to remove the powers of categorisation from the powerful and place them in the hands of those who are actually oppressed. The locus of definition has thus shifted from observable, externally verifiable and measurable phenomena to the personal, subjective and non-quantifiable experience of the actors involved. In this context, estimating the number of children, or adults, affected by a phenomenon is largely a futile task. By methodologically fusing all varieties and intensities of a phenomenon, the number of people affected invariably increases.

These examples illustrate the kind of epidemiological inflation that can grip child welfare services and which affect attempts to estimate need. As illustrated above, there is a powerful belief in child welfare practice that seeking commonalties and finding patterns in human behaviour is inimical to the respect of individual differences. This is an ancient prejudice, as we can see from the Biblical quotation that opened this section, and one which has a long association with social work:

The certainty of value is not rooted in empirically verified results; it is rather derived from an unanalysable moral imperative.

(Halmos, 1965.)

Regardless of the origins of this bias, a reluctance to impose service parameters, whether by activity based or impact based definitions, has the inevitable consequence of creating a child welfare category proof against any type of quantification. A child will acquire a carer label if they or any other third party request it. Apart from the inevitable inflation in numbers that results from removing definitional barriers, it is unclear whether harm may be caused by the uncontrolled labelling of children and their subsequent admission to the domain of child welfare services.

Distortions may arise when basic epidemiological principles are ignored in the enthusiasm to convey a point, as the following example illustrates. A report produced for *Childline* details the circumstances of a sample of children who had called the helpline (n=792), and claimed that 30 per cent of children who discussed their distress at being affected by the illness of a relative also mentioned sexual or physical abuse. The *Childline* press release (10 June, 1998) publicising this report was headlined 'Children keep quiet about being sexually abused, for fear of upsetting a sick relative'. The author of the report commented, 'It often seemed that the illness of a parent had either opened the way for abuse, or made it impossible for a child to tell anyone about it' (*Community Care*, 11–17 June, 1998). However, in the absence of any statistical data, the reader is unable to establish the proportion of children in this situation, or the extent to which these figures can be extrapolated to the general child population.

Nonetheless, the association between parental illness and abuse is left strongly in the reader's mind. The dominance of lobbying or advocacy research in the young carer field illustrates another general principle of social investigation; as a rule, the more robust the enquiry, the lower the level of prevalence, and the less extreme the impact of a social problem. A study of young carers and bullying (Crabtree and Warner, 1999) suggested that 45 per cent of young carers were bullied on 'most days'. The largest survey ever conducted in the UK on bullying (Smith and Sharp, 1994) suggested that four per cent of a general population of children were bullied at least once a week. While there is compelling evidence that the vulnerability of children, including home circumstances and atypical family structures, increase the incidence of bullying (Salmon et al., 1998), the highly alarming figures often produced by young carer lobbying groups have the effect of blurring the distinction between research and advertising.

Conclusion

That *prima facie* reasons exist for a high contemporary level of child caregiving is undeniable. Increases in self reported levels of illness and disability, both child and adult, family re-construction, the increased prevalence of lone parenthood, and increased sensitivity to children's rights are all relevant factors.

However, many worrying factors remain; the large numbers of 'young carers' seemingly found in households where one parent has no limiting illness or disability, the dubious emphasis on sibling incapacity as a precipitating factor, the continuously 'hidden' nature of the phenomenon and the question as to whether children 'not in need' as well as children 'in need', are being drawn into services, with unknown consequences for their welfare.

Fear of harm and a re-assessment of the thresholds of risk has been a key feature in the evolution of child welfare services over the past generation. Furedi (1998) has described the emergence of a culture of fear, fuelled by the volume of demand for safety outstripping its

supply, a kind of Malthusian equation applied to risk. It has been proposed that these ecological niches periodically occur, where new social, cultural or medical phenomena may flourish, before eventually fading from view as the environmental ecology which sustains them diminishes (Hacking, 1995; 1999). The ecological niche is a chronological period where a number of over-lapping factors conspire to generate a phenomenon which rapidly assumes a level of magnitude and importance that can only be sustained by the architecture of the niche itself. The emergence of the 'young carer' issue during the last decade of the 20th century may be partly explained by the confluence of a range of social, cultural and demographic factors, which together have many of the features of an ecological niche. Jenks (1994), in exploring the perceived explosion in recent decades of concern over child abuse, suggests that our increased sensitivity to the welfare of children is based in our inability to find security in a supportive mosaic of trade unions, family and church. Similarly, Beck (1992) suggests that our preoccupation with the welfare of children derives from our perception that the parent-child dyad is the last remaining permanent primary relationship. A century ago, the plight of the orphan played an important role in late Victorian consciousness. Child rescue charities such as Barnardo's became indelibly associated with their care, despite the large majority of children cared for having one or both parents still alive. Similarly, 'young carers' have gripped the contemporary public imagination. Time will tell whether they are to become a permanent feature of our child welfare landscape, or simply a transient phenomenon specific to time and place.

4 Parental Disability: The Effect on Children

So much of the literature...has dealt with families as pathogenic agents that it may be difficult to reconceptualize family members in a nurturing role.

(Lefley, 1996.)

Key Points

- The over reliance on studies of clinical populations results in a consistent bias. Where studies examine general populations, the impact of parental disability and illness on children is less evident.

- The dominant motive for investigating the impact of parental illness and disability on children is a search for toxic effects: positive impacts are rarely reported.

- Evidence of negative impact on children of parental illness and disability is largely located in social, financial and contextual factors associated, but not correlated with, parental incapacity. Poverty, marital discord, lone parenthood, absence of extended family and low levels of social support appear to be of more relevance, in most cases, than any particular diagnosis or condition. Severe parental psychopathologies, especially affective and bi-polar disorders, are the most likely predictor of concern for children's wellbeing.

- The impact on children of ill or disabled siblings is unlikely to be more than moderate, in the absence of the above factors. Providing elements of care for dependent siblings may have positive developmental value for well children. It may also be of considerable benefit to their siblings.

- A range of information is necessary to fully explore children's encounters with serious family incapacities, including narratives of children themselves. However, these accounts should be subject to as much critical scrutiny as any other data source.

Despite controversy over the nature and extent of its distribution, there appears no doubt that disability and chronic illness in families has increased markedly in the past generation. The mixed evidence about children's 'caring' roles should not obscure the fact that many children live in families where serious disabilities or illnesses are present. Such children may be affected in a variety of ways, including situations that increase the likelihood of significant caregiving roles. What evidence is there that parental illness and disability is a threat to children's wellbeing? If it is, what is the magnitude of the effect and how do the effects manifest themselves? Under what conditions are the effects intensified or moderated?

The literature on parental disability and its impact on children is extensive, if preoccupied with a limited number of impairment types. For example, 'child of impaired parents' has been a MeSH (Medical Subject Heading) in the MEDLINE database since 1991 and a search by this heading yields around 1500 abstracts. The large majority of these papers deal with parental alcoholism, drug dependency, HIV/AIDS and psychological disorders, and their consequences for children. Other databases – notably PSYCHLIT and CAREDATA – provide rather larger numbers of studies, the majority concerned with young carers. The wider issue which this chapter addresses is the impact of parental disability on children, whether or not any element of caregiving by children is reported as being present.

Type of Disability

Reports and studies of adult carers often consider the type of disability affecting the cared-for person to be a factor which will affect both the process and impact of caring. For example, the provision of care for people with Parkinson's or Alzheimer's disease has been compared, as it was believed that cognitively impairing and non-impairing illnesses would have different caregiver impacts (Monahan and Hooker, 1997). In a study of children aged 6-13 in 72 two-parent households affected by a range of parental illnesses, including arthritis, multiple sclerosis and Guillan-Barre syndrome, it was *limitation* of parental functioning rather than the diagnosis that was related to any distress caused (Lange, 1996). While adult children of mentally ill, drug abusing and alcoholic parents tend to register lower self-esteem and higher levels of anxiety than controls, levels of self-esteem were found to be *highest* in the adult children of mentally ill parents, though good adult social support networks moderated the effects in all cases (Williams and Corrigan, 1992). While accounts of young caregivers in families affected by a specific illness are available, for example Huntingdon's disease (Power, 1977), Parkinson's disease (Grimshaw, 1991), HIV/AIDS (Alexander, 1995; Thomas, 1997; Wagner, 2001), parental alcohol abuse (Childline, 1997; Brisby et al., 1997) and as exemplars in wider discussions, for example, multiple sclerosis (Blackford, 1999; Segal and Simkins, 1996), drug abuse (Mounteney, 1998), mental illness (Marsh and Dickens, 1997) and alcoholism (Laybourn et al., 1996), nevertheless most studies discuss parental disability in more generic terms.

While this approach may be justifiable when dealing with some factors, others may need to be more sharply differentiated when considering impacts on children. Children may be affected in different ways by a parent's alcohol dependency, a degenerative illness such as multiple sclerosis, an illness that may stigmatise by association such as AIDS, an adventitious disability caused by accidental trauma, an 'invisible' illness such as chronic fatigue syndrome, a chronic mental disorder or inter-generational family dysfunction not characterised by any specific disability at all. The roles of children, the processes of interaction within the household, and the emotional, physical and contextual impacts (such as educational career and social networks) may differ according to the nature of parental disability. There is clearly no justification for not considering the nature of the parental impairment as a relevant independent variable, but as noted previously, the literature is dominated by a search for pathological child responses to parental impairment. However, in the case of some well explored parental illness types, such as cancer, a number of studies have noted *positive* family outcomes, such as enhanced interaction, involvement and intimacy between family members (Cooper, 1984; Lewis et al., 1985). A rare study of children affected by parental cancer who also had caring roles found a mixture of benefits and detriment arising from caring; the former being typically associated with responsibilities and enhanced skills, the latter typically with undertaking unpleasant tasks or witnessing adult distress. 'Hard but gratifying' was the dominant description of the caregiving role (Gates and Lackey, 1998). Whatever the respective balance of debits and credits, the impact on children of family disability is clearly not homogenous.

Differences do appear to exist between impacts on children of parental physical and psychological illnesses. Parental depression has been consistently associated with elevated levels of child malfunctioning, with child depression being accompanied by affective, conduct and eating disorders where other factors are present, especially parental alcoholism and marital disruption (Orvaschel et al., 1980; Kashani et al., 1985b; Welner and Rice, 1988; Beardslee et al., 1993). Conversely, a review of studies exploring parental physical illness and child functioning (Armistead et al., 1995) reached two relevant conclusions, firstly that the reviewed literature allowed no clear relationship to be proposed between specific kinds of parental physical illness and different types of child functioning, and secondly that we cannot conclude with any confidence whether any relationship exists between parental physical illness and child functioning at all.

Onset of parental disability may be as relevant as impairment type. While parental psychological disorder presents a number of potential threats to children's development, it varies in terms of risk depending on the child's developmental stage. Different factors may impact on children, depending on whether the parental illness or disability is adventitious or congenital. The former makes it more likely that the child's experience will be sensitive to family process, the latter that parental illness may be a predisposing factor in any behavioural or emotional child impacts (Coates, et al, 1985).

The two parental conditions deserve a separate note, though neither can be addressed to the extent they deserve, the first because of the brevity and typicality of the available literature, the second for quite the opposite reasons.

HIV/AIDS

The AIDS epidemic in the UK has primarily affected specific social groups; homosexual males, intravenous drug users, recent migrants from sub-Saharan countries and, in the early years of the epidemic, haemophiliacs.

The context of children with HIV positive parents infected through intravenous drug use may be seen as an outlier, at least in the UK, in terms of parental illness. Unlike most (though not all) parental illnesses, the condition is widely stigmatised, illness course is uncertain, lifestyle of parents may be chaotic, child welfare involvement not associated with HIV status more common, family support often poor or unavailable and single-parent status high. Children may also themselves be HIV positive. The educational status of the *non*-infected children (infected children are atypical as HIV affects cognitive abilities and outcomes are poorer, see Tardieu et al., 1995) appears similar to that of similar non-affected populations, with 20 per cent being classified as having special educational needs (Mok and Cooper, 1997). Children in this population have been the subject of a number of studies

(Alexander, 1995; Thomas, 1995) and convincing grounds for concern over their welfare expressed. However, the atypicality of the illness aetiology, both in its medical and social aspects, limits the generalisability of any conclusions we are able to apply to other groups with one possible exception; like other children affected by parental disability, it is neither possible nor desirable to consider the needs of affected children in isolation from their families (Imrie and Coombs, 1995).

Parental alcoholism

While this book does not address parental alcoholism, its close association with the subject matter renders it worthy of a short note. Parental alcoholism and its impact on children, from *in utero* to adulthood, is probably the most extensively explored dimension of parental incapacity; studies stretch back to the beginning of the 20th century. Despite the vast volume of literature, there is continuing disagreement concerning the magnitude of long term effects on children, as well as the perennial problem of distinguishing environmental and behavioural factors from genetic influences. While many reviews conclude that children of alcoholics (COAs) have raised vulnerability to emotional and psychological morbidity (for example, Zeitlin, 1994; Steinhausen, 1995), we again encounter the phenomenon of diminished impact where studies feature robust controls. In a longitudinal study following up COAs and matched controls after 12 years (n=474) few differences were found between the two groups on volumes of alcohol consumed or many major life problems (Schuckit, 1991). While stressing the long term impact of the home environment on COAs, it has been pointed out that the self-esteem of many adult COAs remains high (Robinson and Rhoden, 1998). While similar research overviews of children of substance abusers reach comparable conclusions on children's raised vulnerability to maladaptive behaviour (for example, Johnson and Leff, 1999), the much smaller volume of controlled studies, and the paucity of longitudinal research, raises similar questions regarding the magnitude and inevitability of long-term effect.

One dimension of parental alcoholism is of particular relevance. While children of alcoholics (COAs) have been a concern of health and social welfare services for some time, a more recent development is the concept of adult children of alcoholics (ACOAs). Particularly in the USA, ACOAs have organised themselves into a powerful social movement, sponsoring workshops, conferences and treatment programmes, and have achieved considerable influence over the direction of clinical practice (Brown, 1991; Johnson and Tiegel, 1991). The provision of a social identity, featuring a commonality of experience, a narrative of trauma, recovery and redemption and a growing ability to influence health and welfare responses, has many parallels with the current direction of young carer work. As the cohort of young people identified as young carers in the early- to mid-1990s ages, similar developments may occur in the UK.

Parental illness

Parental illness, particularly parental mental illness, is an issue of concern to child welfare services, both in the UK and indeed, throughout Europe, as international policy developments have made it increasingly likely that children will continue to live with, rather than be separated from, their parents (Butler and Kirwan, 1999). In terms of the risk posed to the child, parental mental illness and parental drug or alcohol abuse are considered, along with poverty and domestic violence, as being the primary reasons why the health and development of a child may be impaired (Department of Health, 1998a). Because of this association, the spectre of abuse is invariably a dimension that arises when children of disabled parents and their needs are discussed. The widespread association in therapeutic settings between parentified behaviour and earlier abusive experiences compounds the sense of unease felt by health and social care practitioners, especially where caregiving roles are encountered. However, polarised views on the dangers to children, particularly posed by parental mental illness, have helped perpetuate misunderstandings and stigma (Falkov, 1998). Parental impairment, in terms of

its potential impacts on children, can be considered along a number of dimensions (Rolland, 1987). Illness or disability may be congenital, or already be established either before the child's birth or in the very early years. If the incapacity is adventitious, onset may be sudden or gradual. While the parental disability will usually be unanticipated by the child, in the case of certain genetic disorders, prior warning may be a factor. Onset may also vary, occurring in four broad types. Incapacity may be episodic, with symptomatic periods alternating with periods of normalcy, such as in the case of epilepsy. It may be stable and predictable, as in the case of spinal cord injuries. It may be degenerative, as in the case of Parkinson's disease or multiple sclerosis, though this degeneration may be marked by periods of remission or episodic improvements. Finally, parental illness may be of relatively short duration, with a severe period of incapacity followed by an eventual recovery to normality or near normality, such as a period of convalescence from a coronary illness. This typology may also be applied to psychiatric disorders

Impact on education

Retrospective accounts by children whose mother or father had experienced cancer (Nelson et al., 1994) found adolescent boys experiencing the greatest difficulties. However, most children reported that family life had returned to normal after the episode. The majority of children (15 out of 27) reported taking on a range of domestic responsibilities, including care of younger siblings during the illness episode. This was remembered as causing problems for only five of the children, all boys. In relation to schoolwork, children's remembered experiences were, similarly, of only moderate negative effect although, again, boys appeared to suffer worse than girls, as illustrated in Table 4.1.

There is limited evidence associating parental illness with levels of school attendance, though it has been suggested that older children are more at risk from educational disruption and impeded

Table 4.1: Children's remembered problems with schoolwork and attendance during parent's illness (from Nelson et al., 1994)

Problems	School attendance (n)		Schoolwork (n)	
	Sons	Daughters	Sons	Daughters
No problem remembered	13	8	10	7
Problem(s) remembered	3	–	6	1

vocational careers (Garmezy and Devine, 1984). A small case controlled study (n=24, children >13 years)) examining the impact of maternal asthma on children's school attendance concluded that 27 per cent of children of mothers with asthma missed school at least one day per month, compared to five per cent of children of controls (Cassino et al., 1997). However, no independent verification of these figures from school registers was provided. Studies exploring school absenteeism of ill children, rather than ill parents, illustrate the importance of considering variables other than the illness itself. While childhood asthma has been found to increase absenteeism (Parcel et al., 1979, n=95), some studies have suggested other causal possibilities. A much larger UK study (n=773) found only minor differences between the absences of children with and without asthma, of around one day a term, which the authors speculated was likely to be largely explained by clinic appointments (McCowan et al., 1996). The latter study is instructive in terms of its attention to confounding variables. While absences due to asthma were unproven, wide disparities were found in mean attendance when a deprivation index was applied to the sample of children. Poverty had a much more powerful effect on attendance than illness. This factor is clearly also of importance when considering the reasons for any observed elevation in school absenteeism of children with ill or disabled parents. Patterns of school absenteeism are strongly associated with socio-economic class. Since the mean income of disabled people is below the average for the whole population, we would expect most child samples drawn from this population to have poorer rates of school attendance than population means.

Psychosocial adjustment

A number of reviews have identified associations between parental chronic illness and children's psychosocial adjustment, mostly focused on internalising problems (Armistead et al., 1995; Worsham et al., 1998). However, associations found have been modest and show considerable variation depending on the circumstances of the child and the nature of the illness. Severity of illness appears less important to the child's adjustment than the subjective response of the parent, as does extra-familial support compared to the child's *perception* of parental support; the latter, when strong, was the most important source of protection for the child (Kotchick et al., 1997). In other words, how ill a parent is appears of less importance to the child than the way in which the parent is able, or is enabled, to cope with their illness and provide emotional support and reassurance to the child. As a study of children affected by a parent's multiple sclerosis pointed out, the problems of children arose from inadequate levels of social support, not the condition of the parent *per se*. Even in situations of adversity, where children were undertaking a wide variety of helping tasks, they saw themselves as powerful and important social actors not dependants, the author noting that they 'appeared to take pleasure in the skills they possess' (Blackford, 1999).

Parental mental disorders

Between five and seven million adults in the UK are affected by a mental illness, of whom approximately 30 per cent will have dependent children (Falkov, 1998). This number, however, is based on a broad definition of mental illness. In the USA, exclusive of the institutionalised population, it has been estimated that the proportion of adults with a serious mental illness is between 2.1 per cent and 2.6 per cent of all adults, some 18 per thousand population (Lefley, 1996). These conditions primarily comprise the schizophrenias, major depressive, obsessive-compulsive and bi-polar disorders, and psychotic states. A number of post war studies described interventions aimed at moderating the impact on very young children of maternal psychiatric illness where hospitalisation was indicated, primarily by joint admittance of mother and child and subsequently the entire close family. Later, during the 1960s, outreach services were to develop with multiple interventions aimed at both mother and child (Goodman, 1984). However, the earliest comprehensive monograph on general parental illness (Rutter, 1966) raised many of the issues which have been addressed, in greater and lesser depth, over the subsequent three decades. Relying primarily on studies carried out on clinical populations in hospital settings and while recognising that the effect appeared most striking in cases where a parent was affected by a mental disorder rather than a physical illness, Rutter cautiously concluded:

> *Evidence suggests that chronic illness, physical or mental, may be associated with the development of psychiatric disorder in the children.*
>
> (Rutter, 1966.)

However, this conclusion was limited by the relatively few studies reviewed which explored non-psychiatric illnesses. Furthermore, the causal connection between parental illness and child disorder was, Rutter recognised, complicated by the unmeasured effect of genetic inheritance and mediated by a range of environmental circumstances. Specifically, risk factors were increased by the presence of a recurring or chronic illness, the involvement of the child in parental symptomatology (such as the parent's delusional states), parental separation, and severe disruptive events, such as financial catastrophe or parental

death, especially where death leads to a degradation of the family circumstances. Severity of parental illness was less important than the context in which the illness impacted on the child. The importance of using 'normal' controls was highlighted, a concern which has continued to be noted some decades later (for example, Hammen et al., 1990; Dodge, 1990). The capacity of clinicians to locate abnormalities in any group scrutinised is illustrated by Rutter (1966), who cites a pre-war study of 1933 which found only 13 per cent of children in a *normal* control group to be without psychiatric abnormalities. High levels of psychopathology have often been reported in adversely affected groups where no normal control is used, as, for example in a study which diagnosed clinical depression in *all* the children of parents in dialysis (Tsaltas, 1976). Assessment instruments of dubious reliability may inflate estimates of psychopathology, as, for example, occurred in a widely cited study which found (using Rorschach tests) a range of serious dysfunctional behaviours in children of parents with multiple sclerosis (MS) (Arnaud, 1959). Conversely, in a study where a normal control *was* used (Werner and Smith, 1982), no differences in body image of children whose parents had MS were reported compared to the control group.

A later study (Rutter and Quinton, 1984) confirmed the association of parental psychiatric disorder with child conduct disorder, especially where parents suffered from a personality disorder. However, a major feature of the families, who were studied over a four year period (n=137) was the high rate of marital discord. Noting that such discord occurs in many families where mental illness is present in neither partner, Rutter and Quinton concluded:

> *It seems that family discord and hostility constitute the chief mediating variable in the association between parental mental disorder and psychiatric disturbance in the children.*
>
> (1984.)

Alongside the difficulty in isolating causative factors of child disturbance, the study also noted that a third of children in the study showed no emotional problems during the whole study period and a further third only minor transient problems, which, Rutter and Quinton note, are common in any event in the general child population.

Reviews

Several reviews of studies on the impact of parental affective disorders on children were undertaken in the 1980s (Beardslee et al., 1983; La Roche, 1989). Beardslee et al., in reviewing 11 cross sectional and 13 longitudinal studies (retrospective accounts were dismissed as being insufficiently robust), concluded that children of affectively ill parents were at increased risk of developing psychopathology. However, there were again a number of complicating and limiting factors:

- Only two of the 24 studies used normal controls, again pointing to the need, especially for clinicians who primarily work with dysfunctional populations, to compare symptomatology in specific and general populations.

- The absence of any homogenous impacts on the child supported the proposition that effects need to be differentiated by illness type.

- The review supported the high recovery (or non-impact) rate, with only 40 per cent of children (in the three studies that involved a diagnostic procedure) found to have a diagnosable illness.

However, problems are clearly present, and should not be under-estimated. Re-visiting the material a decade later, Beardslee et al., (1998) concluded that higher levels of dysfunction are likely to occur in children of affectively ill parents compared to children with well parents, with a 40 per cent chance of children with affectively ill parents experiencing an episode of major depression by age 20. A meta-analysis of 17 studies on the prevalence of mental illness among children of parents with bi-polar disorder reported that these children were almost three times more likely to develop an illness than children with no such parental history (La Palme et al., 1997). Reviewing studies on child and adolescent psychological adjustment to parental

mental illness, Worsham et al., (1997) report only seven studies meeting adequate empirical criteria (i.e. the presence of chronic or acute parental illness, child aged 0–18 in family at time of illness, use of standardised measurements of psychological adjustment). While drawing attention to the methodological shortcomings of the studies examined, especially small sample size, and again warning of the wide variation in outcomes mediated by the above dimensions, the review concluded that 'parental illness is associated with moderate levels of psychological distress and maladjustment in children' (1997). However, it remains difficult to differentiate the impact of parental illness and disability on children from other stressors that may occur in any family. While La Roche (1989), in summarising developments over the following half decade, found evidence in some studies of increased morbidity in the children of parents with depressive and bi-polar disorders, several more found significant associations between disordered children and a range of family factors, including marital conflict, stress, parental dysfunction and poor family communication. La Roche concluded:

> *Measures of marital discord, family communication styles, expression of affect and levels of chronic stress are important variables that need further study.*
>
> (La Roche, 1989.)

Psychological disorders and parenting

That highly undesirable impacts on children may occur as a result of serious parental, especially maternal illness, is incontestable. Individual case studies which describe the effects on children of such combined adversities as parental schizophrenia, lone parenthood, poverty and criminality (for example, Mander et al., 1987) graphically describe life at the extreme margins. However, with some 10 per cent of the adult population experiencing mental illnesses at any one time, psychiatric disorder is clearly a common human experience. It is also characterised by a distribution of intensity from extreme to moderate, both in terms of the impact on the person themselves, and the impact on relatives, including children. Whole family perspectives are thus essential when considering how to respond effectively (Garley et al., 1997). Child care services have been accused of disproportionately focusing on the psychological deficiencies of parents, especially mothers, and interpreting illnesses as deficiencies likely to place their children at risk. The question 'will this illness endanger the children?' rather than 'what support does this mother need to help her parent better?' has been, it has been argued, the primary concern (Hugman and Phillips, 1993; White, 1996). The importance of helping the ill parent by supporting 'well' members of the family has also been emphasised (Hindle, 1998). This argument has strong similarities with those of Keith and Morris (1995), who argue that services are disproportionately concerned with the alleged effect on the child rather than the kind of help needed by the parent, especially the mother. Where adequate levels of social support are available, the differences in outcomes between children who have parents with mental health problems and those who do not become more marginal. In contrast to many other studies, little difference was found, over the period of their school years, between the progress of children born to mothers with perinatal mental disorders and a control group (Ruppert and Bagedahl-Strindlund, 2001). The reason for this anomaly appears to be the Swedish state welfare system, which is able to provide a wide range of both specialist and generic help to mothers, indicating that the extent to which disabled parents are judged adequate may be more strongly associated with the extent to which the state helps them to *be* adequate, than the characteristics of their particular impairment.

Gender, Age and Social Class

Parental disability appears to affect children differently depending on age and gender. Adolescents and particularly teenage girls seem to be the child sub-set most at risk, for reasons associated with affect, cognitive understanding and

the greater likelihood of being elected into a family caring role (Lewandowski, 1992; Grant and Compas, 1994). The large majority of studies on parental depression are in fact studies of *maternal* depression.

Adolescence, with its typical demands for greater autonomy and self identity is a particular period of vulnerability and along with early childhood, is a life stage where the child may be particularly at risk. The latter coincides with a phase of heightened risk of depression for mothers, with some 10 per cent of mothers suffering from periods of illness in the post-natal period (Cooper et al., 1988), and such periods of depression being associated with impeded cognitive abilities in the early school years (Richman et al., 1982; Wolkind, 1985; Murray, 1992). It is suggested that boys and girls are typically exposed to different risk profiles; boys being more vulnerable to parental criticism, resulting in conduct disorders, and girls to demands for emotional support, which increases the likelihood of depression (Radke-Yarrow et al., 1989). Open communication with children, however popular a concept it has become, may have contra-indicative outcomes in situations where coping through avoidance is the most effective strategy to combat adversities, as has been illustrated by several studies into children's methods of coping with cancer. Not knowing, or not wishing to know about the details of illness progression, appears, in these cases, to be better for children than being involved in all aspects of their illness management (Phipps and Srivastava, 1997). Younger children, who are typically told less about their condition, may not experience as much distress as older ones, who are may be told more (Claflin and Barbarin, 1991). Furthermore, children's responses to parental illness may differ according to age with, typically, children under 10 reporting feelings of sadness and fear, pre-teens being primarily occupied with their own lives and older teenagers, on the cusp between a desire for autonomy and parental attachment, experiencing the most problems (Lewis et al., 1985).

Up to half of adults who suffer from mental illness are mothers or fathers living with their children, a statistic with a steep social class gradient. Depressive illnesses affect twice as many women as men with prevalence rates heightened by the presence of young children at home, low socio-economic status and environmental stressors associated with poverty and social isolation. Brown and Harris (1978) found 15 per cent of women in an inner city area had suffered from an affective disorder in the previous three months, with half having a chronic condition lasting a year or more. Nineteen per cent of children referred to child and adolescent mental health services over a four week period (n=31, 032) were living with a mentally ill parent (Audit Commission, 1999), though this figure would not be replicated in a random population sample. This survey suggested that certain groups of children were at greater risk of developing mental health problems, with the largest risk factor (living with only one birth parent), being noted over twice as frequently as parental mental illness (39 per cent v 19 per cent). Working class women suffering a negative life event were four times as likely to develop a depressive illness as middle class women affected by a similar event. Especially at risk were women with no work outside the home, who had three or more children and no close supportive relationship. Cox et al., (1987) reached similar conclusions, also highlighting the risk factors of poor housing and unsupportive or non-existent relationships with the parent's own mother. While mothers struggling with physical, emotional and economic adversities are capable of nurturing their children even in the most desperate of circumstances, and may view their children as the one source of hope in a cruel world (Radke-Yarrow et al., 1993), the potential consequences for children remains one of heightened risk. In such circumstances, it is suggested:

The child could be experienced as a persecutor or as a saviour, be blamed for the mother's depression or praised for relieving it, but in either case likely to lose out on cognitive stimulation and support for his or her emotional development.

(Pound, 1996.)

As we have noted, the link between poverty and mental disorder, especially depressive illnesses, is well attested. Children of depressed parents appear at increased risk of psychological disorders, both currently or in adulthood (Richman et al., 1982). Rutter and Quinton (1984) found that two thirds of the children of parents referred for psychiatric disorder over four years exhibited transient or persistent disorders themselves. A control group had similar rates of transient disturbance but half the rate of more serious disorders. Marital discord was reported by 39 per cent of the patients compared to eight per cent of the control group. Outcomes associated with the children of depressed parents, particularly depressed mothers, include poor interpersonal skills, lack of social networks, conduct disorders, low self-esteem and clinical depression (Pound, 1996). Parental affective illness has been consistently associated with higher rates of disturbance in children (Cytryn et al., 1984; Kashani et al., 1985a), particularly where the mother is concerned (Keller et al., 1986), though the impact of maternal affective disorder on children is moderated when chronic stress is controlled (Hammen et al., 1987). However, social class remains a key mediating factor. In a white middle class sample (n=96), maternal uni-polar depression alone, when a supportive and well husband was present, was not found to be associated with any impact on children's social and emotional competence (Goodman et al., 1993). As Roy observed:

Middle class families with a stable marriage and good income without concerns about medical costs minimise the negative consequences of parental disability.

(Roy, 1991.)

Parental Learning Disability

In many ways, parents with learning disabilities have been exposed to the most damaging mis-attributions of any group of disabled parents. The capacity of any social group to resist damaging stereotypes is weakened by the absence of their voices in public debate, the greater likelihood of scrutiny by professionals, lack of social capital, and a history of oppression and discrimination. People with learning disabilities have been affected by these factors, arguably more than any other section of the population. Parents with learning disabilities, in addition to any intellectual impairment, are far more likely than other parents to encounter factors that make parenting harder, such as extreme poverty, bad housing, poor educational careers, weak social networks and lack of extended family support. People with learning disabilities are also affected more than non-learning disabled people by co-morbid conditions, such as a greater tendency to certain mental health problems and physical illnesses. While partners are often a source of strength and support, in some cases lone mothers with learning disabilities may become vulnerable to predacious men whose actions, rather than those of the mother, may become the primary source of concern for child protection services. Adult accounts of childhood abuse by the children of learning disabled parents tend to ascribe any abusive acts to fathers or step-parents not themselves learning-disabled, rather than learning-disabled mothers (Booth and Booth, 1997). Even where young people have supportive and caring family networks, it is often hard for parents devoted to their learning-disabled children to accept their transition from a dependant to a person who is capable of caring for another (Young et al., 1997).

While the numbers of parents with learning disabilities in the UK is unknown, it has been estimated that some 250,000 may be known to health and social care services (McGaw, 1997). Defining 'learning disability' for purposes of planning a social care intervention is invariably an unsatisfactory endeavour. Some 70 per cent of the population fall between a 15 point range either side of the mean IQ of 100. Borderline learning disability would normally be thought to fall between 70–80. However, the correlation between parenting competence and IQ is no more than moderate unless measured IQ falls below 60; other factors, especially environmental assets (or lack of

them), are equally powerful (McGaw, 2000). The real problems that people with learning disabilities have, even where sensitive and high quality professional support is available, can be considerable. Nonetheless, while not underestimating the real challenges that confront parents with learning disabilities and those who seek to help them, the parent's intellectual deficit, rather than the environmental circumstances they encounter, has invariably been the main service focus (Feldman, 1986; Booth and Booth, 1994). Assessment procedures are often driven by a fear of the potential risks rather than an exploration of potential strengths (Goodinge, 2000). Similarly, research has been primarily concerned with parental incompetence (Tymchuk, 1992). Unlike many other kinds of impairment, learning disability is likely to demand of parents the rapid acquisition of skills from an often low baseline; a basic understanding of early child development, the physical care of a baby, meeting a child's emotional needs. Unfortunately, the fear that a child's welfare will be imperilled leads to assessment and intervention strategies that are too often competency-inhibiting, rather than competency-enhancing (Booth and Booth, 1993). A general principle of learning theory is that skills are most effectively learnt in the situation where they are to be used. People with learning disabilities often have greater challenges transferring knowledge from one setting to another. Difficulties in knowledge transfer may require consistent and long term support services to be provided, often into early adolescence. While skilled support services record considerable success in family preservation services (Ray et al., 1994), generic family support services have not proved willing to accommodate parents with learning disabilities (Llewellyn, 1994) and where they have, staff often lack both the confidence and skills to meet their needs (McGaw, 2000).

The main concerns for children of parents with learning disabilities have centred around any genetic transmission of learning disability, and the environmental factors that may affect children as they grow from infancy to adolescence, notably developmental delay, abuse and neglect. There is no doubt that IQ has a strong genetic component (Rende and Plomin, 1993). However, the majority of children of learning disabled parents will have a higher IQ than their parents, with less than half having low-average IQ when both parents have learning disabilities, and less than a fifth when only one parent is learning disabled. Even so, these children account for only a small proportion of the total population of children with learning disabilities, with well over 80 per cent of learning disabilities being attributable to other factors (McGaw, 2000).

A number of problems have been identified as disproportionately affecting the children of parents with learning disabilities where families have been inadequately supported. These include problems with language and cognitive development (McGaw and Sturmey, 1994), psychiatric disorder, notably depression (McGaw, 2000) and behavioural problems (Feldman and Walton-Allen, 1998). Some difficulties have been noted in families where children are of manifestly greater intellectual ability than their parents, especially with regard to the maintenance of parenting capacity during the children's adolescence (O'Neill, 1985). Purposeful abuse by parents with learning disabilities appears rare; where abuse occurs, as noted above, non-disabled partners are often the main perpetrators (Tymchuk and Andron, 1990). Of more concern in unsupported families is neglect, often occasioned by lack of parental education (Seagull and Scheurer, 1986). The tendency for children of learning-disabled parents to be affected by a greater incidence of physical illnesses and disorders may also place greater demands on their parents to ensure that a high level of health care is provided and maintained.

Some half of all children born to parents with learning disabilities in countries with developed child protection infrastructures are, at least temporarily, removed from their parents. Both child protection and court procedures, it has been argued, have been so loaded against parents with learning disabilities, largely due to an ingrained presumption of incompetence, that an accusation of institutional prejudice is warranted. While we still lack data from representative populations on the adult careers of children of learning-disabled parents, adults who have been asked to reflect on their childhoods, do not report the disadvantages that are popularly believed to result from being raised by a parent with a learning disability (Booth and Booth, 1997). 'Good enough' parenting by parents with learning disabilities seems to result when the factors that make parenting successful for the rest of the population are in place – support from professionals, friends, neighbours and family, a decent income, adequate housing and respect for parental status.

Quality of parenting

The nature of parental illness and disability appears less important than the degree to which the quality of parenting is affected. The high levels of criticism and low levels of emotional warmth associated with families where children are at risk from a range of abusive circumstances (Department of Health, 1995) appear more damaging to children who have a mentally ill parent than contextual factors of environment and parental relationships (Richman et al., 1982). Children of depressed parents are significantly more likely to be exposed to parental disharmony and separation (Billings and Moos, 1985) and such exposure is associated with increased levels of disturbance and conduct disorder. However, the risk of such disorders is also strongly associated with marital discord in children of *non*-depressed parents (Fendrich et al., 1990). Conduct disorders thus appear to be most strongly associated with parental discord itself, particularly hostile behaviour towards children, rather than the parental illness *per se*, or any associated symptom (Beardslee et al., 1983; Cytryn et al., 1984). A study reviewing causal factors associated with high rates of disturbance in the children of psychiatric patients concluded that 'the major contributors are hostility, aggression, marital discord and disruption' (Hall, 1996). Children of parents with bi-polar illness appear to face particular difficulties, though the genetic component of the illness makes it difficult to attribute future outcomes to specific developmental factors (Thyer and Wodarski, 1998). Where adequate social support is given, the majority of children continue to function normally despite being exposed to disturbed parental behaviour, a finding that applies to both teenage children and pre-teens (Goodman, 1984).

A number of studies have concluded that, except in the minority of cases where severe parental psychopathology is combined with exposure to major life changes, children in families where parental disorders are present will not suffer significantly poorer outcomes except where marital discord or other severe domestic disturbance is a factor (Emery et al., 1982). In failing to detect any higher levels of negative symptomatology in adolescent children of depressed parents compared to children of normal controls, Hirsch et al. concluded:

> *When there is no marital discord present in families with an affectively disturbed parent, the risk for problematic school behaviour is similar to that found among children of normal parents. In the absence of other risk factors, parental depression may not be associated with heightened levels of child dysfunction.*
>
> (Hirsch et al., 1985.)

The relatively strong associations between parental illness and child psychopathology which feature in earlier studies have given way to more complex and ambiguous analyses. The confident determinism of Freud and Bowlby which proposed links of some certitude between childhood experiences and adult functioning, has been replaced by a growing interest in what we may learn from children who avoid apparently pre-ordained destinations. Far from there being a simple causal relationship between parental incapacity and child dysfunction, more recent studies highlight the many mediating factors which influence the impacts on children, including type, duration and onset of illness, familial, social support, and wider environmental structures. Inheritability also plays an important role in the development of many disorders, independent of environmental factors (Scarr and

McCartney, 1983; Wilson, 1985), though the influence of genetic predisposition is clearer for some illness types than others, notably schizophrenia (Farmer et al., 1998), affective disorders (Eaves et al., 1997) and, it is increasingly argued, attention deficit hyperactivity disorder (Silberg et al., 1996). The importance of genetic factors in explaining some aspects of causation has been traditionally neither accepted (Sheldon, 1984), nor considered relevant (Iredale and Cleverly, 1998) by social work staff. Such hostility is understandable; both parents with learning disabilities and mental health problems have learnt to their cost what happens when health and social care services become gripped by the fear of inherited impairments (Sayce, 1999).

'Role Reversal'

While the literature on the effect of parental disability and illness on children is extensive, the impact on children of assuming a specifically *caring* role is sparser, less robust and more ambiguous. Being a son or daughter is no less complex, in terms of role conflict, than being a parent. Not the least complex of these issues, in terms of both process and outcome, is the alleged exchange of roles between parent and child which has frequently been associated with parental illness or disability, and can, it is suggested, be accelerated by premature caring. The degree to which the notion of 'role-reversal', the psychological and functional exchange of roles between parent and child, grips the imagination of both lay and professional constituencies deserves some specific attention. In particular, role reversal and its analogues play a significant part in many important dimensions of the psychoanalytical tradition (Schmideberg, 1948; Freud, 1965).

There is a widespread belief that an early assumption of premature domestic responsibilities increases the likelihood of an adult career in the therapeutic professions. Often associated with the concept of the 'wounded healer' (Jung, 1933), it is suggested that the predisposition to help develops at an early age and is biologically determined (Stein et al.,1999). Parents whom, for whatever reasons, wish to exploit the child's growing feelings of empathy may prematurely encourage these strivings, resulting in a child excessively attuned to the parents' unconscious needs (Winnicott, 1965). However, it is held that inappropriate distortions of boundaries between adults and children will result in the inability of children (and adults) to resolve developmental tasks, risking the replication of family dysfunction in future generations (Goglia et al., 1992). The problem has been summed up as follows:

> When parents, because of loss, illness, emotional stress, or substance misuse, cannot function in their assigned roles, children will often fill the vacuum involuntarily or by necessity. If these children are required to over-function in an adult role, their individual development can be sacrificed.
>
> (Bekir et al., 1993.)

Role reversal, within the psychoanalytical tradition, has been described as 'parentification' (Boszormenyi-Nagy, 1965; Boszormenyi-Nagy and Spark, 1973) or 'spousification' (Sroufe and Ward, 1980). The earliest concern expressed by clinicians for children living in homes with highly dependent parents was the specific psychological effects of 'role-reversal' in the context of family psychopathology, associated with the development of attachment theory (Bowlby, 1971). Role reversal and its analogues, the 'parental child' (Minuchin, 1974) or the 'child-as-parent' (Walsh, 1979), refer to phenomena in the psycho-analytical tradition which are characterised by children prematurely assuming adult responsibilities as a result of family dysfunction. 'Compulsive' caregiving is seen as a pattern of adult attachment behaviour in which the individual is preoccupied with giving rather than receiving care. A number of studies have speculated that emotional role reversal, where the child takes on a disproportionate responsibility for ministering to an adult's emotional needs, is associated with insecurity, depression and relationship problems in later life, accompanied by an inability to express need or ask for care (Pound, 1982; Cox, 1988; West and Keller, 1991). Excessive 'parenting' behaviour in children arises, it is

suggested, from weak, infantile parents and is often a conscious or unconscious binding mechanism designed to keep the child tied to his or her family of origin (Bacciagaluppi, 1985). Role-reversal is thus held to result in, or be associated with, insecure parent-child attachment, and is therefore a legitimate item on the therapeutic agenda.

The dangers of parentification for the child's developmental progress, particularly in situations of marital breakdown, have been a major concern within the family therapy tradition (Goldman and Coane, 1977; Boszormenyi-Nagy and Krasner, 1986). Parentification is, according to this theory, a way of 'balancing the books' through the child's being coerced into fulfilling the adult's own missed opportunities (Jones and Wells, 1996). Damage is believed to occur when the process of 'giving' by the child becomes internalised to such an extent, that meeting the demands of others becomes an intrinsic part of the child's personality and is carried forward into adult life.

> These may include the loss of needed personal experiences, caring and nurturing involvement by parents...there is also the loss of purpose and identity, that might be experienced in more 'healthy' or boundary appropriate family environments. One of the more significant outgrowths...may be the inability to acquire true self-worth or entitlement.
>
> (Olson and Gariti, 1993.)

More darkly, role reversal or parentification and the corresponding insecure parenting attachment is proposed as a common feature of families where child sexual abuse is present (Alexander, 1992). Children in abusive situations may, it has been suggested, develop a precocious maturity, resulting in behavioural role reversals, and may prize the duties that result for which they may receive praise and encouragement (Mrazek and Mrazek, 1987). Psycho-analysts have expressed a particular interest in role reversal, partly because of its relevance to some factors fundamental to the practice of psycho-analysis in the Freudian tradition, notably the phenomena of transference and counter-transference (Ellman, 1996). The child may relish the praise arising from adult responsibilities at first, but will, it is theorised, eventually respond with neurasthenic symptomatology, as the following case study suggests:

> *In her disillusionment and depression, Mrs R. had unwittingly delegated Ellen to take over her role as mother and wife. Ellen, in her self-doubt and insecurity, had revelled initially in the sense of importance. Gradually, however, she had become aware of the consequences of accepting the invitation and become psychosomatically ill in an effort to escape the danger of the situation.*
>
> (Johnson and Irvin, 1983.)

In the Freudian tradition, the period of latency (from around five years to adolescence) is seen as a period where the child prefers magical rather than rational thinking, a major impediment in comprehending parental disability. During this period, it is suggested, undertaking tasks that subvert the parental role and result in the child 'having to parent the parent' is damaging to children's psychological health (Romano, 1976). Role reversal has also featured in historical discussions of childhood, particularly when authors approach the subject from a psychoanalytical perspective. De Mause (1976) proposed that role reversal was common prior to the modern period, due to the projection of repressed feelings by parents onto their children, going so far as to suggest that 'one receives the impression that the perfect child would be one who literally [sic] breast-feeds the parent' (1976).

Nonetheless, some benign aspects of parentification are proposed in the therapeutic literature, notably the recognition that non-normative responsibilities in lone parent households may constitute positive adaptive behaviour, and that the premature maturity of parentified children causes them to be sought out for help by peers and for their advice to be valued. Indeed, it is suggested that they may be especially popular with teachers due to their capacity to act as a 'teacher's aide' (Jurkovic, 1997). However, a more common assertion, and perhaps the one which will be most familiar to the public at large, is that a reversal of social roles may take place,

where the child becomes the 'parent' and the parent the 'child' (Johnston et al., 1992). This, however, is a highly simplistic construction of adult-child relationships (and to many disabled and sick parents, deeply offensive, see Keith and Morris, 1995). Regardless of the degree of responsibility a child may take for the welfare of their parent, caring within families will almost invariably be bi-directional, except in highly unusual circumstances. While the role-reversal dimension re-occurs throughout young carer literature, a few studies have actively sought to challenge it:

> *The research uncovered no evidence to support the hypothesis that young carers 'parent their parents'. The care they provide does not undermine the foundations of the parent-child relationship: young carers look to their parents for support, encouragement and nurturance in the same way that children everywhere 'depend' upon their parents.*
>
> (Tozer, 1998.)

Where bi-directional caring does take place however, we need to take account of factors other than the performance of tasks, such as personal care, sibling care and shopping. The appropriate model of emotional support in parent-child relationships is normally thought to be uni-directional, i.e. parent to child. However, concern over the impact of excessive child-to-parent emotional support is a legitimate anxiety; the rise in divorce in the last three decades has led to many children needing to deliver emotional support to one or both parents to an unprecedented degree (Winn, 1983). It has also been argued that social roles, not just tasks carried out, can be a potential source of psychological damage, regardless of the family dynamics present. Being stuck in an unwanted role, losing a desired social role, or being conflicted between several roles, may result in chronic feelings of stress (Pearlin, 1983). These observations, despite emanating from different theoretical bases, do add a new dimension to the proposition that children of disabled parents may experience higher levels of morbidity than their peers. However, the very large variation in the circumstances of young people should make us cautious of applying these concepts loosely. In cases of extreme adversity, some evidence of role reversal and accompanying negative impact exists. More internalised emotional distress, conduct problems and higher levels of illicit drug use have all been associated with parental role taking, by early adolescents, in families affected by AIDS, and parental drug use predicted higher levels of caregiving by adolescents (Stein et al., 1999). Inappropriate expectations of child responsibilities have been reported in families where one or both parents are alcoholics (Gallant et al., 1998). Childhood physical abuse has been associated with role reversal in low income, single mothers with young children (Lutenbacher and Hall, 1998). Adult sons actively caring for parents with dementia experienced a common perception of changing roles with their disordered mother or father (Harris, 1998). However, while these examples are very different, they have a common characteristic, that of extremity, suggesting that for parent-child roles to become bi-directional, let alone reverse entirely, highly atypical stress must be placed on normative family roles. A major problem in drawing lessons from the psycho-analytical tradition is the implicit assumption that parental responsibility has been wilfully, albeit as a result of inter-generational trauma, relinquished, thus pathologising all members of the family (Bekir et al., 1993):

> *Unpredictable events (e.g. parental death, divorce, or unemployment) often require children to assume increased instrumental and expressive responsibilities. Although these events may occasion parentification, consideration should also be given to the possibility that they serve only to exacerbate an already existing parentified pattern.*
>
> (Jurkovic, 1997.)

While insights derived from psychotherapeutic literature may undoubtedly be useful, the location of the problem in personal pathology rather than social oppression is unlikely to have much appeal to increasingly politicised disabled parents.

Children's Voices

A review of literature relating to a number of conditions, including parental depression, physical disability, multiple sclerosis and Huntington's disease, concluded:

> *For the most part, information about the effects of parental illness on children was obtained from the parents themselves and only in exceptional circumstances from the children either by interviews or objective tests or some other independent source.*
>
> (Roy, 1991.)

The dependence on proxy views by the majority of research conducted on parental disorders and child impacts, particularly maternal ratings, is a frequently acknowledged deficit in clinical studies (Stoleru et al., 1997). One of the most important contributions that social work literature has made to the subject of parental illness and child disorder has been the willingness to listen to and promote the voices of children. Exhortations to listen to the voices of children have become a commonplace plea in a wide range of areas, including participation in democratic processes (Willow, 1997), mental health (Laws, 1998), disability (Ward, 1997) and social research (Alderson, 1995) among many others. The views and opinions of children have rightfully become an indispensable dimension of many social investigations. We can add to this a legal desiderata, in the shape of the United Nations Convention on the Rights of the Child (UNCRC), which mandates that children have the right to be involved in all decisions that concern them (Article 12). In addition to any legal requirements, participation, it is suggested, has a beneficial effect in terms of promoting children's general health and wellbeing (de Winter et al., 1999).

Apart from any intrinsic ethical factors for this welcome development, sound methodological reasons exist for wishing to explore children's views. For example, the exaggeration of children's sleep disorders by affectively ill mothers (Stoleru et al., 1997), the closer correlation of independently observed levels of distress with children's accounts than with the accounts of parents (Worsham et al., 1997), the over-reporting of child behaviour problems by depressed mothers and a similar over-rating of child symptomatology compared to the reports of children themselves (Boyle and Pickles, 1997; Renouf and Kovacs, 1994) all illustrate the potential fallibility of adult accounts. In many cases, children are more accurate informants than adults. However, neither adults nor children may be sufficiently reliable sources of information by themselves; their respective accounts may vary, and independent observers may reach conclusions that differ from both parties (Puura et al., 1998). Replacing a belief in the inviolable accuracy (and superiority) of adult reports with a similar belief in the veracity of children's accounts is hardly a step forward; treating data from children as an equal, different – but also potentially fallible – source surely is.

Children's experience of illness

The view that researching children in isolation from their family environment was a meaningless exercise, and that focusing on children as research subjects in their own right required prior justification, was commonplace into the 1970s (Graham and George, 1972). This was compounded by a further belief that child psychopathology was inevitably a symptom of family dysfunction; sick children were the result of sick parents. Childhood depression in particular has been the subject of considerable theoretical controversy (Durkin, 1995). While differences in adult and child symptomatology are recognised, childhood depression has more recently been accepted as having a similar profile to adult depression and the same diagnostic criteria are typically used. However the capacity of children, particularly those under 12 years, to describe depressive states with sufficient accuracy for clinical diagnosis continues to be questioned (Kovacs, 1985). There is some dispute whether children, if given the opportunity to contribute to a diagnosis, are likely to estimate fewer depressive symptoms than their parents (Kazdin and Petti, 1983) or more (Barrett et al., 1991).

While depressive symptoms are normally thought to be less common in children than in adults (Dulmus and Wodarski, 1997), the steep rise in adolescent suicide rates has taken place in tandem with substantial increases in rates of childhood depression (Mental Health Foundation, 1999).

Reliability of testimony

In considering the reliability of children's reports of their health status, it is important to note that wide variations have been found between the prevalence of depression as reported by parents and as reported by their adolescent children. One large cross-sectional community study reported that adolescents described themselves as depressed six times more often than their parents, though whether this discrepancy resulted from parental under-estimation or adolescent over-reporting (or both), was unclear (Fleming et al., 1989). In relation to reports on emotional and psychiatric health, increasing age, it is suggested, results in increased reliability of child testimony, especially in relation to abstract concepts (Schwab-Stone et al., 1994). With the exception of some dimensions, notably children's own thoughts and fears, parental accounts prove more reliable (Fallon and Schwab-Stone, 1994), though not necessarily more valid.

Personal narrative

While robust data on children's experiences of parental illness remains scarce, the importance of personal narratives has become widely accepted (Davie, et al., 1996; Murray, 1998). Both parents' and children's voices feature prominently in a recent volume on families affected by mental illness (Cowling, 1999), and in a book otherwise dominated by clinician's reports (Gopfert et al.,1996) accounts by adults of their encounters, as children, with a parent's mental illness are a key feature:

> *Looking back to my childhood, a turning point was reached when my brother and I watched my mother being dragged up the drive of our family*

home by two uniformed men...they forced her
into an ambulance and drove off. We were
having tea with the family friends who lived
opposite us. Not an unusual occurrence and we
realised we had been invited over in order to get
us out of the way.

(Marlowe, 1996.)

I recall being dressed in a baby doll night suit and
going into the lounge where Dr Brown was
seated...he never asked me anything. He sat in
the chair in silence with a pleasant enough smile
on his face. My mother was taken back to
hospital that night.

(Roberts, 1996.)

Attempts to reclaim the value and power of
personal narrative are not confined to social care;
concern has been expressed at the devaluation of
narrative in medical training (Kleinman, 1988),
and several recent clinical papers have sought to
rectify this bias (Marshall and O'Keefe, 1995;
Greenhalgh and Hurwitz, 1999). The ways in
which details of parental illnesses are
communicated to children, even those with
learning or behavioural problems, is recognised as
an important factor in mediating outcomes
(Barnes et al., 1998). Recent volumes, drawing on
both clinical and anecdotal sources, have
reviewed the situation of children struggling with
adversities and are a source of practical advice for
both parents and practitioners (for example,
Marsh and Dickens, 1997; Katz, 1998). In volumes
that specifically address the situation of the
children of disabled parents, testimonies directly
from children are commonplace. These
approaches however, suffer from methodological
weaknesses, particularly in focusing on non-
representative samples that stress a range of
difficulties, usually extreme ones, which may or
may not be typical of the population as a whole.
Children may also provide inaccurate accounts of
the parental situation, by either mistaking the
volume of care one partner may give for their
spouse, or the degree of responsibility they
themselves believe they are carrying for their
parent's illness (Segal and Simkins, 1996; Lackey
and Gates, 1997).

Remembrance

There is no canonical way to think of our own
past. In the endless quest for order and structure,
we grasp at whatever picture is floating by and
put our past into its frame.

(Hacking, 1998.)

Retrospective accounts by adults of child trauma,
and the cultural changes that have encouraged
their recall and dissemination, have been an
invaluable contribution to our understanding of
childhood. They may be written, or told, partly as an
exorcism of past demons, or part of a therapeutic
process, or as part of the process of building a
resilient personality. However, the sheer
emotionality that may be involved in this process
can disarm the critical faculties that are necessary
in evaluating any piece of evidence from adult or
child. Consider the following passages, both from
prize-winning autobiographical accounts, written
by adults, who as children survived the Holocaust.
Nobel laureate, Elie Wiesel, writes of his first night
in Auschwitz:

Never shall I forget that night, the first night in
the camp, which has turned my life into one long
night, seven times cursed and seven times
sealed. Never shall I forget that smoke. Never
shall I forget the little faces of the children,
whose bodies I saw turned into wreaths of
smoke beneath a silent blue sky. Never shall I
forget those flames that consumed my faith
forever.

(Wiesel, 1981.)

A second, more recently published account
evokes horrors, both as graphically and as lyrically
as Weisel, and concludes:

I wrote these fragments of memory to explore
both myself and my earliest childhood; it may
also have been an attempt to set myself free.
And I wrote them with the hope that perhaps
other people in the same situation would find
the necessary support and strength to cry out
their own traumatic childhood memories, so
they too could learn that there really are people
today who will take them seriously, and who
want to listen and understand.

(Wilkomirski, 1996.)

Both the above accounts, equally moving, poignant and well written, differ in only one important factor. The former is true; the latter has been shown, some years after its publication, to be a fabrication. The psychological mechanisms that lead adults to falsify or distort childhood histories are not the subject of this book. However it is important to recognise that many positive benefits, such as acceptance, affirmation, sympathy, identity, membership of a group and more prosaically, financial gain, may accrue from either having, inventing, or embellishing a history of childhood trauma. As Rutter (1985) has pointed out, the factors and the personal characteristics that promote positive adult mental health are not necessarily attractive or socially valued. There is also some evidence that trauma disclosure, whether fictional *or* real, has similar cathartic effects and functionality in terms of emotional regulation, particularly in the construction of resilient personalities (Greenberg et al., 1996). In other words, lying may help us feel just as good as telling the truth. (Indeed, as the group in the Greenberg et al. study, who were asked to write fictional accounts of their traumatic encounters, actually felt less depressed and equally happy at post-test than the group who wrote true accounts, we might reach the conclusion that lying about trauma may make us feel even *better* than telling the truth.) While it may be unpalatable to those who rightly wish to ensure that the voices of the oppressed are heard, the manipulation, or even the creation, of past memories to achieve better adaptation in the present is an effective psychological mechanism, and not necessarily any less effective when the memories are distorted or fabricated. In contexts where particular narratives of childhood trauma are widely known, adults may reconstruct their memories accordingly. For example, UK studies, where former child caregivers recall their experiences, tend to be largely negative, and attribute poor adult outcomes to childhood experiences. In North America, where 'young carer' discourse is far less developed, accounts of former child caregivers are far more positive,

with little evidence of poorer mental health reported (Lackey and Gates, 2001; Shifren, 2001).

The capacity of personal accounts to disarm legitimate scrutiny must be recognised if we are to apply the same critical principles to this source of evidence as any other. Individual accounts may bring illumination and insight into a particular aspect of a child's experience. However, like all narrative accounts they are weak on several dimensions. They may be unrepresentative in that they present an extreme dimension of a phenomenon as being typical, they may be chosen for their dramatic qualities, they may be utilised in pursuit of a political agenda and, in failing to consider alternative accounts or to use controls, reliance on personal accounts alone may lead us to make incorrect assumptions about cause and effect.

Historically, professional belief in the systematic inaccuracy of children's accounts (due to their emotional immaturity) has been succeeded by a belief in their unfailing accuracy (due to there being no differences in child and adult cognitive functioning). A rather more balanced view is suggested by Bruck et al., (1998), who locate the main variable affecting the accuracy of child testimonies outside the child; that is, the validity of a child's account is most strongly influenced by the quality of the interviewing techniques, rather than any inherent tendency of children to provide accurate or false testimony. In our response to both child and adult testimonies of trauma, we may need to acknowledge that psychological integrity, not truth, is the dominant driver for recovery. 'The brain' as the biologist E O Wilson asserts, 'is a machine assembled not to understand itself, but to survive' (1998).

Long Term Effects of Caring

Where retrospective accounts by adults who encountered serious adversities as children are analysed, the extent of distal impact appears related to a) whether the population has been randomly selected and b) whether a control has been used. Where both are absent, estimates of negative long term impacts are higher, where both are present, estimates are lower. This can be illustrated by using the example of four studies of varying degrees of robustness, each concerning children of disabled parents.

At the least robust end, 25 adults were located by advertising in local journals in Hampshire for former 'young carers'. The authors reported that half had received, or were receiving counselling, 70 per cent had suffered long term psychological effects, and 70 per cent had poor educational experiences (Frank et al., 1999). All these consequences were attributed to their experiences of caring. The authors concluded that 'caring as a young person can have profound social, psychological and emotional effects in later life' (Frank et al., 1999).

A more extensive study, but one reaching broadly similar conclusions, examined the experiences of 60 young people (aged 16-25) who were, or had been providing care for ill or disabled parents (Dearden and Becker, 2000). The data comprised of accounts acquired through semi-structured interviews. Respondents were identified through existing carer service networks. While noting some positive self-reported outcomes, particularly maturity, responsibility and close relationships with parents, the general conclusions were highly negative. Unemployment, poverty, poor educational experiences and, for some, reception into care were typically reported. The authors concluded that inappropriate caring responsibilities have long term, as well as proximal effects, in terms of degraded life chances. No validated instruments or controls were used in either study.

Laybourn et al., (1996) sought to locate, from a non-random sample, adults who had grown up in a family where one or both parents had a drinking problem. Nine young adults were interviewed, no standardised instruments were used, but the population interviewed, the source of referrals and the methodology used are clearly described and the sample's lack of representation is acknowledged. While highlighting the predominantly negative consequences on the lives of the respondents, such as educational failure,

social isolation and drug abuse, all of which were attributed to the behaviour of parents, a few positive outcomes were associated with childhood experiences:

> *A number of older children and young adults seemed to be leading positive, sociable lives. A few even identified beneficial side-effects arising from the experience of having a drunken parent, such as enhanced academic motivation, improved coping skills, concern for others in difficulty and greater family closeness.*
>
> (Laybourn et al., 1996.)

The most robust study of the four (Neff, 1994) investigated levels of distress in adult children of alcoholic or mentally ill parents, collecting data from a random community sample (n=1784). Comparisons were made between effects of parental alcoholism, parental mental illness, both alcoholism and mental illness, and no parental pathology. A battery of psychometric tests were administered, including the Center for Epidemiological Depression Scale (CED-S) the Zung scale (for anxiety) and other measures for self esteem and locus of control. There was no support for the assertion that parental alcohol use differentially affected respondents on any measurement. Where effects were detected, parental mental illness was the most significant factor, with raised levels of depression for both the parental mental illness and mental illness/alcoholism sample combined. However, in relation to the overall result, the study concluded:

> *The lack of differences between parental pathology groups in background dimension such as education, income, employment, and current marital status generally fails to demonstrate effects of parental alcoholism or mental illness upon adult socio-economic achievements or social functioning. In other words, adults from pathological parental environments do not appear to be 'victims' in our data.*
>
> (Neff, 1994.)

As we can see from these examples, while self-selected case studies are able to dramatically illustrate the reality of some young people's lives, they suffer, inevitably, from bias. Half of the cohort studied by Dearden and Becker were children from lone-parent families; the majority lived in rented accommodation; and where a second parent was present, only a third were employed, and of those who were, almost all were in low paid manual or clerical jobs. Without a control, or data from longitudinal studies with representative populations, it is impossible to estimate the effect size of parental disability, or child caregiving in isolation from the effects of the poverty, low income and poor educational experiences that this sample would encounter, regardless of the presence or absence of family illness. *Any* child living in a lone-parent family, for example, will be over three times as likely as a child in a two-parent family to grow up in poverty. This is not to suggest that caring or parental illness has no bearing on future life trajectory (this would be an equally erroneous conclusion), just that the confident attribution of adult outcomes to family illness and disability is weakened by the limitations of the methodology used.

The final example given above differs in its conclusions from studies which use primarily in-patient or clinical samples, where adult outcomes for children of alcoholics are often reported as being worse (for example, Rydelius, 1997; Ackerman and Gondolf, 1991). One does not have to be a statistician to understand that examining an extreme sample of a social phenomenon, and then assuming that all instances of this phenomenon in the population have the same characteristics, will result in some highly skewed data. The popularity and power of narrative accounts which provide *post hoc* attributions of long term effects to childhood adversities is a core element in the tension between methodological approaches which seek to enumerate and those which attempt to illustrate through personal accounts. A critical appraisal of the former typically involves examining the data analysis of the *researcher*. Critically appraising the latter is more likely to require examining the validity of the *respondent's* account. Leaving aside methodological issues, the critical analysis of

powerful testimonies, especially from respondents who have clearly suffered distressing experiences, is a far more emotionally difficult task. Querying whether a confidence interval has been correctly calculated requires less personal investment than questioning the validity of a narrative. A crucial source of error in methodologies that rely on personal testimony is interviewer bias, which has particular relevance within professions that are characterised by a commitment to social justice. Interviewer bias is more likely to occur in contexts where the data collectors have strong *a priori* beliefs in a particular causality or frequency of events:

> *One of the hallmarks of interviewer bias is the single-minded attempt to gather only confirmatory evidence and avoid all avenues that may produce negative or inconsistent evidence.*
>
> (Bruck et al., 1998.)

This observation in no way invalidates conclusions reached by methodologies concerned with personal narrative. It does, however, imply that scrutiny of such accounts is as legitimate and necessary a procedure as the scrutiny of statistical tables, and that personal accounts should be no more exempt from critical analysis than any other data source.

Physical risks for children

Some evidence exists that associates parental incapacity with increased physical risk to children. A nationally representative US sample (n=11,248) found a greater likelihood of injury, including poisoning, for children with a disabled parent, but only where more than one disabled person was present in the household: this was also the variable most strongly associated with poverty. Around 25 per cent of all homicide victims in the UK are children, the majority infants. Where the perpetrator is female, as in about 60 per cent of cases, a diagnosis of psychiatric disorder is present in a quarter of these cases. However, the large majority of child homicides committed by parents are associated with sudden outbursts of violent temper, most frequently in circumstances exacerbated by marital discord, violent relationships and poverty related pressures such as low income and poor housing (D'Orban 1979). Lower levels of social disadvantage among mentally ill mothers responsible for child homicide suggests the illness itself, rather than deprived circumstances, as a precipitating factor. However, the extreme rarity of the event, and the fact that the huge majority of mentally ill parents do no deliberate harm to their children, should make us wary of seeking to construct a specific causal link.

There is little doubt that parental mental illness constitutes an elevated risk factor for children, though even where risk is heightened, as in the case of maternal depression, additional associated responsibilities of children may often function as coping strategies (Bifulco and Moran, 1998). The issue is how elevated and under what circumstances. A comprehensive review by Falkov (1996a) concluded that children whose parents suffer from psychiatric disorder are at increased risk of maltreatment. This is understood by parents themselves; the predominant fear of parents suffering from mental illnesses is the removal of their children by child care authorities (Cowling, 1996). However, as the above examples indicate, the elevation of a risk for a population neither constitutes the certainty that any single member of the population will be affected, nor that the elevation will be great enough to warrant an intervention in all cases.

Are things as bad as they seem?

In reviewing how outcome measures may be generated in researching children of disabled parents, the disproportionate focus on risk has been observed:

> *Many discussions of this type tend to focus on the deleterious effects of such influences as divorce or disability. This is the result of obsessive concerns with describing the normative experience in the social sciences. It would be a relatively easy task to provide a long list of problem behaviours which occur as the result of*

> *a child having a disabled parent. It would be less common to see a research project focus on the positive outcomes of having a disabled parent.*
>
> (Coates et al., 1985.)

A number of studies have, in fact, identified positive, rather than negative outcomes, arising from children's encounter with parental disability (Glass, 1985; Greer, 1985; Blackford, 1999). Greer, a disabled academic, locates the roots of children's feelings of inferiority in their early encounters with more physically dominant and competent adults. He queries whether the children of disabled parents, who are relied on by their parent for their superior physical or motor skills, would be advantaged in developing more enhanced competencies and maturity than their peers. In a review of different types of parental illness on children (Roy, 1991), the studies cited fail to conform to any clear structure. While reiterating the findings of increased psychopathology in children whose parents are affected by bi-polar disorders or chronic depression, the effect of other illnesses was far more ambiguous. Few associations have been found between severity of parental physical disability and child adjustment where the child's family situation was not threatened by marital discord or poverty (Buck, 1983). Children's health suffered no long term damage when a parent suffered a severe heart attack (Dhooper, 1983). Children of parents affected by tuberculosis (which involved their hospitalisation) were far less distressed than a comparison group of children with mentally ill parents (Rice et al., 1971). While two thirds of the latter sample (n=44) showed evidence of distress, the main reason for their anxiety was the witnessing of their parents' gradual deterioration, the corresponding financial pressures and the knowledge of their genetic risk. Even in this situation of extreme stress, a third of the sample perceived their encounter with parental illness as an opportunity for personal growth. Studies of children affected by parental cancer (primarily mother's breast cancer) are particularly inconsistent, with some finding heightened levels of dysfunction (Lewis et al.,

1985), some no significant impact (Boyle, 1994) and some a positive impact on intimacy and shared family activities (Cooper, 1984). While secondary analysis of data from the US 1988 National Health Interview Survey (n=11,246; range 5–17 years) suggested inflated levels of behavioural problems in children of disabled parents (Le Clere and Kowalewski, 1994), genetics, poverty, proxy reporting (accounts of children's health were from adults) are typical compromising factors.

We can thus see that the impact on children of parental illness and disability are highly variable, and strongly mediated by the quality of relationships within the family and the family's socio-economic status. Where heightened concern is present, psychological disorders tend to be the most important factor. The potential impact of parental illness or disability may be compounded where a disabled child is also present in the household, and may result in a considerable increase in responsibilities for any non-disabled siblings. What, then, do we know of the impact of sibling incapacity on children?

Effect of Child Illness and Disability on Well Siblings

Parental illness and disability may, where there are several children in the family, have implications for siblings, especially in situations where child as well as adult disability is present. While the effects of sibling illness and disability have received a good deal of attention, it needs to be recognised at the outset that disabling child illness is a relatively rare phenomenon, substantially more so than parental incapacity. In the USA, as in the UK, almost three times as many children live with a disabled parent than a disabled sibling (Le Clere and Kowalski, 1994).

Child care by siblings has received a rather more positive press in anthropological studies than in North American and European child care practice. Weisner and Gallimore (1977), in reviewing cross cultural studies of sibling caretaking, found that in over half of 186 societies, older children were the principal caregivers. They propose that Western

cultures have much to learn from societies where child care by older siblings is routine:

There is certainly no evidence that children suffer when cared for in part by older children as opposed to their parents. Indeed, aid or support to a mother from children or adults is likely to increase reported contentment...child caretaking thus contributes to role flexibility for mothers and caretaker diversity and skills for children.

(Weisner and Gallimore, 1977.)

The function of elder siblings is not confined to the provision of physical care or the substitution of other parental duties. Elder siblings also play a distinctive role of their own, that of 'culture-brokers', introducing younger children in the family to social and community traditions, rites of passage and work practices (Ervin-Tripp, 1989). Infants who are cared for by elder siblings in the absence of their mother exhibit the familiar proximity seeking and secure-base behaviours predicted by adult-child attachment theory (Stewart, 1983). Despite the often ambivalent nature of sibling relationships, siblings provide developmental opportunities that are distinctive and difficult to replicate, both in terms of modelling (Bukatko and Daehler, 1995) and the experience of coping with conflicting demands for co-operation and autonomy (Dunn, 1991). Distinctive differences exist between sibling and parental care, notably the greater provision by parents, where they are the primary caregivers, of more support and a wider range of coping strategies than older children (Bryant, 1992). Sibling care, therefore, can be construed as socially normative and having clear benefits.

However, changing demographics have reduced, in developed countries, the numbers of children who both give and receive sibling care, with the average family size in West European countries being well under 2.0. Increasing unfamiliarity with larger families, particularly by those in higher socio-economic classes, has led to sibling care being associated with deprivation and disadvantage. The discourses of children reported in one of the few studies to explore parallels between young carers in the North and children in the developing world illustrate the limited universality of the 'young carer' concept (Robson and Ansell, 2000). Zimbabwean schoolchildren described tasks and responsibilities, often driven by the African AIDS pandemic, far more onerous than those demanded of most children in the North. However, the children largely regarded these tasks as culturally appropriate and not problematic in the way that such duties would be regarded in developed countries, despite their often distressing nature.

Sibling disability

The implicit bias in sibling studies of disability and illness (not dissimilar to the bias in much disability research in general) is the *a priori* assumption made that negative impacts will be found. This bias is illustrated by the primary investigative technique used, which is to construct studies that are mainly concerned with locating pathology, with benefits, if any are noted, being reported as side effects. The main focus of concern is thus the impact the sick, disabled or otherwise dysfunctional family member has on others and the primary aim of remedial interventions is to prevent this dysfunctionality affecting the healthy members of the family unit. This is best illustrated by a comparison between the number of studies which explore the impact of a disabled child on a well sibling and the number exploring the impact of a well child on a disabled sibling (very many of the former, very few of the latter; see, for example an early review of studies by Lobato, 1983). Conversely, in families where no disabled child is present, an absence of at least *some* level of sibling care is generally considered a stress-inducing rather then a stress-buffering factor. In non-pathologised families, the co-operative nature of family units typically results in a collective response to the distress of any one member:

> *Well-functioning families mitigate stress of family members in part because they define and address the stressful situations of their individuals as familial concerns rather than as individual concerns.*
>
> (Bryant, 1992.)

The way in which children interpret family responsibilities can mediate the relationship between the work undertaken and its impact on the child's psycho-social development (McHale et al., 1990). The meaning attached by children to their caregiving experiences is thus not just of theoretical interest. When caregiving children interpret their roles and the competencies that arise from them as valued, positive consequences may follow. Where they are offered highly negative meanings for their actions, the psychological consequences may differ. Children with identical experiences may retrospectively view their childhood as stressful but rewarding, or as a theft of their youth (Gath, 1992). The views of foster carers' birth children are instructive in this context. Being part of a quasi-professional caring unit, the foster family, birth children typically play an important, if under-recognised role in the care of foster children (Natural Children's Support Group, 1990). While not all views expressed by children were positive, a survey of over three-quarters of all families with foster children in a Scottish region (n=75) concluded that 80 per cent enjoyed the experience of having foster children in the family. Looking after younger children, helping, and companionship were the three most important positive factors reported, with greater maturity being a frequently cited outcome (Part, 1993). A more recent review of the impact of fostering on foster carers' own children stressed both the important roles of children, and the need to provide support, including the provision of training, to enable the children of foster parents to play a more effective role in the foster care unit (Watson and Jones, 2002).

Swings and roundabouts

As we have seen, parental illness and disability have been predominantly viewed as a factor pre-disposing children to risk. Reviewing studies on chronic paediatric illness published between 1970 and 1995, Williams (1997) noted that some 60 per cent reported increased risks, while 30 per cent reported no elevated risks. However, many conflicting findings are reported, especially where studies are more tightly controlled, and where there is greater differentiation between different kinds of illness and impairment. For example, comparing siblings of children with pervasive developmental disorder and diabetes with well controls, Ferrari (1984) found no evidence to support the view that siblings of ill children are at greater risk of psycho-social impairment. As with parental illness and disability, little attention has been given to both the absence of effects and the positive benefits to children that may accrue. While some earlier studies suggested a favourable response of siblings to the additional responsibilities that often result from there being a disabled child in their families (Power, 1977), a more frequent finding has been the suggestion that siblings of ill or disabled children suffer a higher incidence of behavioural problems than non-affected peers (Gath 1973; Lavigne and Ryan,1979; Trevino,1979; Breslau et al.,1981; Tritt and Esses, 1988). Later studies into the psychological adjustment of children with chronically ill siblings have, however, found the incidence of behavioural and emotional problems to be within the range for a normative sample (Gallo, et al., 1992; Stawski et al., 1997; Taylor et al., 2001). Similarly, some well controlled studies have failed to find any variation in care activities by mothers towards well siblings in all-well families, compared to families where one child is ill (for example, Davies, 1993, in a study of children with cystic fibrosis). Even reviews that recognise childhood chronic illness as a potentially serious stress factor on well siblings warn that the strength of the impact is mediated by interaction with other variables, and that psychological adjustment is selective by age, sex and type of illness (Drotar and Crawford, 1985). Where impacts are noted, overall sibling health is only moderately affected, a conclusion reached in a large seven-site study of siblings of children with cancer (n=254), which noted as a primary effect a lower level of health care utilisation by siblings of ill children, a phenomenon attributed to greater levels of parental distraction (Zeltzer et al., 1996). As discussed previously, studies without controls

of any group impacted by adversities will tend to propose a stronger association between any negative outcomes found and the adversity under investigation. Hence, discursive accounts of children with ill or disabled siblings will tend to identify close links between child illness and sibling maladjustment or other psychosocial problems (for example, Seligman, 1987). An *a priori* assumption about the impact of an adversity will inevitably inflate the propensity of an observer to attribute a particular response to the presence of the adversity itself.

While it is fairly well-attested that siblings of disabled children are more frequently involved in caregiving of a greater and qualitatively different nature than children with non-disabled siblings (Powell and Ogle, 1985), there is less agreement as to whether, and under what circumstances, caregiving may generate positive or negative impacts on the non-disabled child. While studies have commonly reached equivocal conclusions, where more robust study designs are adopted, the results give little cause for concern. When siblings (mean age 10.1 years) of children with asthma and cystic fibrosis were interviewed and assessed on separate self-esteem measures, similar negative and positive findings emerged (Derouin and Jessee, 1996). Worrying, being jealous of excessive attention given to the ill sibling, and restrictions on family events were balanced by strengthened family relationships, more personal independence and satisfaction at seeing the health of a brother or sister improve. Where studies have sought to disaggregate child illnesses and disabilities, different impacts are noted. A longitudinal study comparing siblings of well children, children with Down's Syndrome and children with pervasive developmental disorder (PDD) over three years (n=46, 45, 46 respectively) found significantly more problems of adjustment in the PDD group, but not in the siblings of children with Down's Syndrome, who were similar to the control group (Fisman et al., 1996). As with adult incapacities, the nature of the impairment or illness appears highly pertinent to the outcomes.

Burton and Parks, (1994) examined the self-esteem, locus of control and career aspirations of two groups of college students. One group had grown up with disabled siblings (D), the other, a matched control of classmates (N), had not. The D group were of lower socio-economic status with a larger mean family size, which might be expected to introduce a negative bias. While some negative findings emerged from the D group, no overall differences were found on aspirations or self-esteem measurements between the two groups; the only differences found were significantly higher loci of self control in the D group. Self-esteem in the D group was inversely related to magnitude and visibility of sibling disability; that is, the more disabled the sibling, the higher the self-esteem. If our threshold for intervention is defined as an environment that is significantly more likely to induce damaging effects, these findings do not support the thesis that siblings of disabled children are, *ipso facto*, children in need of a substantial welfare response. It has also proved difficult to separate the effects of sibling caregiving from poverty and material disadvantage (Gath, 1992). Comparing 62 children aged 8-14 years, all with younger siblings, half of whom had learning disabilities, McHale and Harris (1992) found some minor negative outcomes associated with the siblings of disabled children, primarily raised levels of anxiety and slightly lower measurements of self-esteem, especially among the girls in the sample. However, contrary to claims that sibling care results in excessive restrictions on children's leisure time and other social activities, the study found no evidence that the daily activities of children with disabled siblings were unduly restrained. Pointing out the danger of diagnosing the typical internalising symptomatology of the child on the brink of adolescence as a consequence of caregiving rather than of hormones, McHale and Harris suggest an inevitable exchange has occurred:

> *The slightly higher levels of anxiety and lower self-esteem exhibited by children with disabled siblings in our study may be the price of a more mature outlook on oneself and one's world.*
> (McHale and Harris, 1992.)

Sibling welfare: whose is the more important?

The tendency of sibling studies to focus on vulnerability rather than resilience, and to be concerned with unsuccessful rather than successful adaptation was noted a decade ago (Leonard, 1991). Many intervention studies begin from the premise that well children need protection from their disabled siblings, and thus focus on helping the former rather than the latter (for example, Williams et al., 1997). Conversely, a small number of studies have begun from the premise that well children are a potential source of valuable help for their ill or disabled siblings. Several studies have reported highly positive outcomes for children with both physical and mental impairments resulting from structured teaching delivered with the help of well siblings. In customised intervention programmes, well siblings were reported as providing the most reliable baseline data, were the most powerful source of motivation for their brothers and sisters, and were the most influential change agents (Weinrott, 1974; Lavigueur and Ryan, 1979). Well siblings may be a greater source of influence on their disabled brothers and sisters than parents, due to the different style of socialisation patterns, the competitive nature of sibling relationships, the greater spontaneity of their interaction and the absence of detailed preconceptions about the ill or disabled sibling's potential (DeMeyer, 1979; Baskett and Johnson, 1982). One of the rare studies that addresses the welfare of the disabled instead of the well sibling, and begins from the premise that disabled children could be helped by their non-disabled siblings rather than viewed as a source of 'infection', studied an intervention that deliberately utilised well siblings as change agents. Using a more robust approach than the studies cited above, siblings of children with cerebral palsy were taught a range of activities aimed at increasing the independence of their disabled siblings and were involved as key actors in the children's care plans. Following the intervention, increased competence in motor activities, personal hygiene, dressing and eating were noted in the disabled sibling, along with self-reported increases in family cohesion and increased self-confidence in the well siblings themselves (Craft et al., 1990).

Growing up with an ill or disabled sibling may result in an atypical, and sometimes stressful childhood for well siblings. However, it is often balanced by experiences and the acquisition of useful cognitive and emotional assets (Meyer, 1997; McHugh, 1999; Sibling Support Project, www.chmc.org/deparmt/sibsupp; The Family Village, www.familyvillage.wisc.edu). What is unfortunately present in much of the literature is an assumption that negative impacts on the well child are of a higher order of importance than positive benefits accruing to the ill or disabled one. The latter has proved of less interest to researchers and clinicians because, one must assume, of the different value ascribed to ill and disabled as opposed to well children. To conclude, while the atypical demands made on some well siblings by ill and disabled children may be considerable, the capacity of siblings to help each other and to benefit mutually appears a grossly under-researched and under-developed practice area. The default position of treating the disabled child as a threat rather than an opportunity to a well sibling does little to rectify this imbalance.

Conclusion

The range of factors that can mediate the impacts on children of family incapacity are located in the particular features of the parental impairment, family structure and relationships, and the broader environment affecting the family (see Table 4.2).

Despite this apparently neat tripartite structure, difficulties prevail in drawing any consistent conclusions, or making simple generalisations, about the impact of parental incapacity on children. Studies that have explored the impact on children of a broad spectrum of parental disabilities, indicate that no close correlation exists between parental incapacity and poor outcomes for children, either in the short or long term, though there is compelling evidence of an association with the *consequences* of family incapacity, particularly poverty, especially when mediated through the quality of parenting (Pound, 1996). It is clear that a child cannot be defined as being 'in need' *purely* on the basis of their having a parent who is affected by a physical, chronic or mental illness, whether congenital, acquired, or even drug and alcohol related. The main finding from reviewing the literature on parental illness and disability is the heterogeneity of impact, depending on the nature of the parental illness, the economic circumstances of the family, their support networks and the immediate social environment. Some kinds of parental disability may heighten the risk of poorer outcomes for children, notably some kinds of maternal psychological disorder and parental learning disability. However, the disproportionate focus of previous research on risk, rather than protective factors, and clinical, rather than general populations, has tended to exaggerate the negative impacts on children, especially their long-term effects. The

Table 4.2: Factors associated with the impacts of family incapacity on children

Aetiological factors	Family dynamics	Contextual factors
Nature of onset	Parental relationship	Social capital
Status	Extended family support	Environmental
Degree of incapacity	Health of other family members	Economic
Course of illness		
Duration of illness		

consequences of factors such as poverty and low social capital have tended to be attributed to parental illness and disability. Both practice and research have sought to locate toxic rather than benign effects. Indeed, positive impacts on children, such as those arising from greater maturity associated with enhanced responsibilities, have been under-reported for fear of legitimising socially unacceptable roles. As in many other fields of health and social care, the increasing involvement of disabled people as active participants in practice and research, rather than as passive recipients of services or as research subjects, is changing the way in which policy is shaped. Both research and practice orientations that primarily seek to identify the harmful effects of disability on family members, and to protect children accordingly, are becoming increasingly less viable, and increasingly less tolerated, by disabled people in general, and disabled parents in particular.

5 Disability, Illness and Child Health

There are instances where parental illness has caused acting-out behaviour, poor performance in school, social withdrawal, sexual promiscuity and the use of drugs or alcohol in older children.

(Johnston et al., 1992.)

Key Points

- Very large numbers of young children in areas of high deprivation report encounters with family illness and disability.
- While many children describe playing a major 'helping' role within the household, claims of substantial contributions decline with age. Accounts by younger children of delivering high volumes of 'care' should be treated with caution.
- Higher reported levels of domestic responsibilities by children in a general population sample are not associated with any detectable levels of poorer health and wellbeing. This, however, is unlikely to be valid in more extreme cases.
- Children of ill or disabled parents involved with child welfare agencies show no detectable differences in many measurements of health and wellbeing from children in other families. They do, however, report lower self-esteem, more emotional problems and additional problems in school.
- Reports by young people who are affected by parental illness and disability indicate many areas where additional support to either the child or the family as a whole is warranted. However, problems associated with poverty or low social capital should not be inappropriately attributed to parental impairment.
- Children's accounts should be subject to the same critical scrutiny as any other source of information.
- School attainment should be supported, not undermined, by agency involvement, especially where this involves the offering of out-of-school leisure activities which may conflict with educational demands.

The previous chapter has suggested, with certain qualifications, that family disability and illness, whether or not this involves a degree of caregiving, is not as strongly associated with damaging consequences for children as is frequently proposed. A general principle has been suggested, that greater impacts will be observed in 'case studies' or in clinical samples rather than in randomly selected populations, and this may cause us to draw unnecessarily pessimistic conclusions. It has also been argued that our growing preoccupation with the elimination of risk factors has caused us to worry excessively about the potential dangers children may encounter, and that this may have resulted in children becoming less, rather than more capable of resisting stress and adversity. Finally, it has been noted that disability in general, and parental disability in particular, is a normative part of the lives of large numbers of children, and that the circumstances of both children and parents will not be improved by treating parental infirmities as potentially 'toxic'.

Opinions, however, need substantiating by evidence. We can attempt to shed some light on these issues by examining two child populations; first, a large, randomly selected 'non-clinical' population of children, and second, a population currently in contact with child welfare services, who report being significantly affected by parental illness or disability.

The impact of parental disability on children's emotional development, physical health and general psychosocial development has largely been based on data from clinical samples, and studies have been characterised by the search for problems. We have some robust information on the long term impact on children of parental disability, especially psychological illnesses, from which it can be concluded that in the absence of serious family conflict the impacts are no more than moderate, with a proportion of future ill health being explained by bio-genetic factors rather than environmental variables. We know that valued social roles undertaken by children, if recognised and rewarded, have the capacity to function as a protective factor, though this process will be weakened or reversed if the roles are excessive, or undertaken beyond a child's developmental capacity. However, we know little about how the psycho-social health of children exposed to parental illness or disability compares to other children. We also have limited information on the extent to which parental illness and disability affects children in the general population, especially the extent to which it is problematised by children or the extent to which it is regarded as a normal part of childhood.

In an attempt to shed light on some of these issues, a number of surveys were carried out. The first was reported in Chapter 3. That survey suggested that the greatest detectable cause of concern might lie in one-parent families where the primary carer, almost always the mother, was affected by a psychological disorder. A second survey was undertaken in a Welsh local education authority, and sought to establish the proportion of children who reported encounters with parental disability or illness, undertaking domestic duties or caring for siblings, and to explore relationships between these factors. This survey consisted of a large sample of children aged 7-11, and a smaller sample of 14-16 year olds. In the third survey, a sample of children with disabled or ill parents

(n=83), and known to two voluntary child care charities in England, completed a validated child health questionnaire. Follow up discussions were conducted with 20 of these children, who had indicated a willingness to be interviewed.

Children's Encounters With Parental Illness and Disability: A Welsh Survey

As we have seen, the proportion of both child and adult populations reporting an illness or disability that impedes normative functioning has undergone a considerable increase in the past three decades. The strong association between socio-economic status, impairment and illness would lead us to predict that in any area where poverty indices are significantly above national means, we would expect to find a correspondingly higher prevalence of disabling or limiting conditions, and thus a larger number of children and young people affected.

Identifying the numbers of children affected by parental illness and disability in a given population has been a strategy adopted in a number of surveys, with mixed results. School-based surveys have been the most extensively used method, though poor sampling techniques and low rates of return have undermined their usefulness. Several studies have attempted to identify the number of 'young carers' by asking teachers to provide an estimate, using their personal knowledge of children (London Borough of Enfield, 1994/5; Olsen, 1997). In addition to the obvious weakness of relying on incomplete knowledge and proxy opinions, poor response rates are typical, with the latter study, which surveyed all LEA schools in Leicestershire, achieving only a 29 per cent response rate. Attempts to collect information from staff in social care agencies have been similarly unsatisfactory (Jones et al., 2002). Studies which have sought out children rather than adults as informants have been even less successful, with Hendassi (1996) receiving 140 replies from 1000 questionnaires, none of them from boys. Not withstanding, the rationale for seeking to explore this issue through data collection in schools is compelling. One of the main concerns of services which support children of disabled parents has been the impact of the family context on children's education, and hence schools have an important stake in devising a response. Schools have one other obvious but crucial attraction for researchers concerned with representation – they contain the overwhelming majority of the target population. The survey set out to:

● Identify a representative sample of a school population, aged 8-16.

● Focus on an area with high levels of socio-economic deprivation.

● Explore the extent to which parental disability and illness featured in the lives of children.

● Quantify the extent to which children undertook some tasks associated with child caregiving, including sibling care, domestic duties and helping sick or disabled adults.

● Examine any associations between parental illness or disability and child psychological health.

Two versions of the questionnaire were designed, one for junior school children (aged 8-11) and one for seniors (11-16). The same structure was used for both (see Appendix 1). However, the junior school children were offered shorter scales, a more limited number of questions and questions with a less demanding vocabulary. Language and structure was kept as simple as possible, both in recognition of the youth of the children, and also of the low levels of literacy in the population surveyed.

The site

The area chosen was a Welsh unitary authority, affected by particularly high levels of unemployment, illness, poor housing and dependence on state benefits. Wales has one of the highest proportions of adult carers in the UK, lower only than NW England (Department of Health, 1999a). In the area where the survey took place, some 18 per cent of those of working age report a limiting long term illness. In the LEA area itself, pupils recorded the lowest number of five A to C GCSE grades in Wales, the highest proportion of adults out of work for more than 12 months and

the highest poverty score, by some way, of any authority in Wales (Welsh Office, 1996). According to the 1998 Welsh Health Survey (National Assembly of Wales, 1999), the borough reported the lowest score in Wales on the mental health component of the SF-36 health questionnaire used by the survey. One adult in 13 (aged 18 and over) reported being a carer that is, experiencing restrictions due to provision of care for another. In short, the area, in both a UK and Welsh context, is one strongly affected by most common measurements of deprivation, and where parental illness and disability is frequently encountered by children.

The population

The number of children in years 3-6 of junior school (8-11 years old) was 4,684, and in the senior school sector (11-16 years) was 4,681. A 20 per cent sample was sought; this being sufficiently large to enable trends to emerge. For the junior schools, a single deprivation index, the proportion of free school meals (FSM) supplied in each school, was used. Free school meals are provided for children where the parents or guardians are in receipt of income support, the income based Jobseekers Allowance, or where pupils themselves receive such benefits. Schools were ordered by proportion of free school meals the children received, and five selected from the top, seventh, fifth, third and bottom deciles. An additional Welsh language medium school, from the third decile, was selected, making six schools in all. The mean number of free school meals in the final sample of six schools was 33 per cent (range 12-68 per cent) the same as the mean of the total junior school population. The number of children on the rolls of the selected junior schools was 1203. The final number of questionnaires returned was 642, some 53 per cent of the maximum possible.

The senior schools

The senior schools (n=5) had a FSM range of 19-41 per cent (mean 29 per cent). However, the senior schools were much larger in size than the junior, as was the variation in numbers of pupils (high 1269, low 408). The senior school sample was much smaller, as it proved more difficult to justify the exercise to head teachers who were understandably concerned with the demands of the national curriculum. A sample of 87 14- and 15-year-old children in a single school was eventually negotiated.

The junior schools

The replies were distributed fairly evenly across the age range of 8-11 years, boys comprising 51 per cent of the total (n=325) and girls 49 per cent (n=315). Mothers were present in over 97 per cent of households, fathers in just over three quarters (80 per cent). Only 17 per cent of children lived at home with neither a brother nor a sister. A grandparent lived in six per cent (n=40) of households. The latter was twice as likely to be the case in one-parent as compared to two-parent families (11 per cent v. five per cent).

Main Findings of the Welsh Survey

Three factors (excluding age, which will be discussed subsequently) are likely to mediate children's encounters with adult disability and illness; family income, family structure and gender. As we have information on family income (measured by eligibility for free meals), family status (whether family is one- or two-parent) and gender of the child, the influence of each of these variables can be examined in turn. First, however, some of the overall findings are discussed.

Domestic care

Children's reported contribution to domestic tasks can be summarised in Figure 5.1 below. In all cases the data consists of children aged 7-11 years (n=642).

As we can see, the most striking aspect of these data is the extremely high proportion of children who report providing help for a sick adult, and the lower, but still substantial number of children who report undertaking sibling care. This issue shall be returned to when discussing the responses of older children.

Caring and health

Questions were asked about children's emotional health and the extent to which parental illness affected this. Figure 5.2 summarises the latter variable, and three measurements of the former.

The most notable observation in Figure 5.2 is

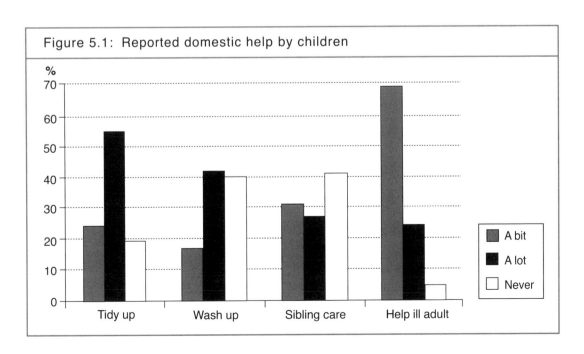

Figure 5.1: Reported domestic help by children

Figure 5.2: Concern about parental health and children's emotional status

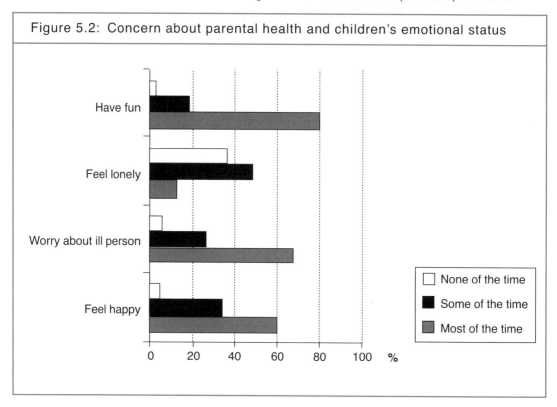

the apparently large number of children who worry most of the time about someone who is ill. While we cannot conclude from these data that this *necessarily* refers to a sick relative, it is clear that however children construct 'illness', and whatever part worrying about ill people plays in their day-to-day life, concern for sick people, or at least the public expression of it, is a normative, rather than an atypical expression within this population. Certainly, worrying about the sick does not prevent 61 per cent of the population feeling happy and 80 per cent having fun most of the time.

Poverty

There is compelling evidence that poverty strongly affects children's circumstances, including their health, their perspectives on life and the activities they undertake, or from which they are excluded. A number of comparisons were made using the proportion of free meals provided in schools (FSM) as a proxy measurement of poverty. Figure 5.3

compares the two schools at opposite ends of the range.

As we can see, there is a constant gradient in the direction of children who are receiving a higher proportion of free school meals. Children in the two schools differed on a number of measurements. Higher proportions of children from schools where the majority receive free meals (n=108) have more responsibilities for both siblings (p<0.05) and sick adults (p<0.05), worry more about ill people (p<0.05) and do more tidying (p<0.05) than children in the school with the lowest proportion of free school meals (n=129). These figures are consistent in illustrating the hypothesised effects of poverty in elevating the profile of illness in a child's environment, and increasingly the likelihood that domestic help by children may be more frequently needed.

Family structure

One hundred and thirty one children (20 per cent) were in families where no father lived in

Figure 5.3: Poverty: comparison of School A (68% free meals, n=108) and school F (12% free meals, n=129)

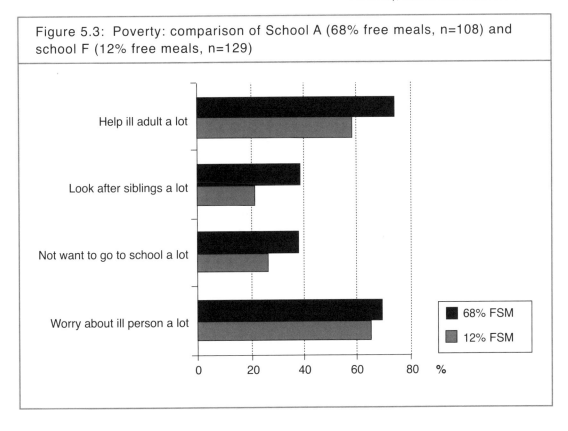

the household, 511 reported two parents at home. Given the strong association of lone parenthood, especially in low income families, with a range of adversities affecting children, the responses of children in lone-parent and two-parent families were compared. The mean age of these children was similar to that of the total population (9.3 v 9.2 years) and the gender split also similar (51 per cent male, 49 per cent female). On the majority of variables, no statistically significant differences were found. The differences that one might expect, should parental dependency and the consequent demands on children be greater in lone parent families, failed to emerge. Children in these families reported no greater frequency than their peers of tidying or washing up, looking after siblings or helping sick adults, though the reported prevalence of the latter, as noted above, is remarkably high in both. Poverty, in these data, appears to make a far bigger difference to children than family structure.

Gender

The profile of girls and boys in the sample was virtually identical, both genders having a mean age of 9.2 years, and having very similar family structures. As with comparisons of one-parent and two-parent families, there were no significant differences found between the majority of responses. In two areas of particular interest, sibling care and helping adults, no gender differences emerged; children of both sexes expressed very similar views on the frequency with which they performed these tasks. The differences that did emerge confirmed ancient gender stereotypes. Girls reported far more tidying and washing up than boys (p<0.01), were less likely to be able to do what they wanted (p<0.05) and yet were far more likely to want to go to school than boys (p<0.01). Gender differences can be clearly illustrated in Figure 5.4, which compares the responses of boys and girls in the 'a lot' or 'most of the time' categories on the questions that pertain to domestic chores and illness.

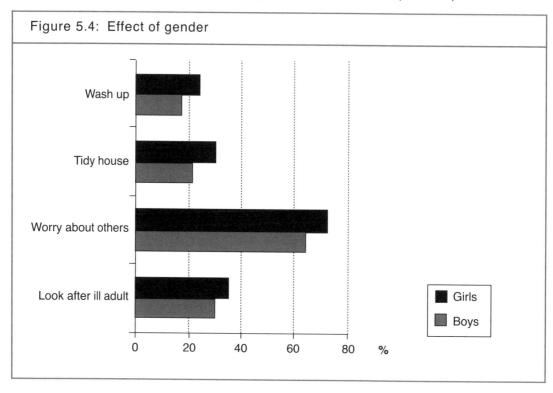

Figure 5.4: Effect of gender

Impact of caring

The distribution of responses in reply to the question on whether things were done for a sick adult made it impossible to compare children who 'did things' and those who did not, as over 70 per cent reported they did things 'a lot' and only five per cent never. However, we can attempt a comparison using the 'looking after sibling' question, where 32 per cent of the population (n=194) reported doing this 'a lot' and 41 per cent (n=248) 'never'. If excessive sibling care at an inappropriately early age is damaging to children, we should expect to find significant differences between the populations on variables related to psycho-social health. The data, however, did not support this belief. Children who reported looking after siblings were more likely to do other 'helping' tasks than children who reported no sibling care, in particular tidying up (p<0.01), helping ill grown ups (p<0.05) and doing the washing up (p<0.05), but there were no detectable differences in other dimensions of children's lives resulting from this increase in domestic

responsibilities. Figure 5.5 charts all the wellbeing questions (N12 – N25, see Appendix 1). Scores are presented for children who reported that they 'look after brothers and sisters' *and* they 'do things for a grown up who is ill' a lot (*high*), children who reported doing both a bit (*moderate*) and children who reported doing neither (*zero*). Negative health and wellbeing scores ascend on the *y* axis.

As can be seen, the 'high' line peaks at three points, indicating that children in this group, more than in the others, worried about people more (question N18), worried about people who were ill more (question N20) and reported tidying the house more than other children (question N24). However, none of the health-related scores were, compared to the moderate and zero groups, negatively elevated. In this population, no major differences in health and wellbeing scores appear associated with children's self-reports of involvement in domestic duties.

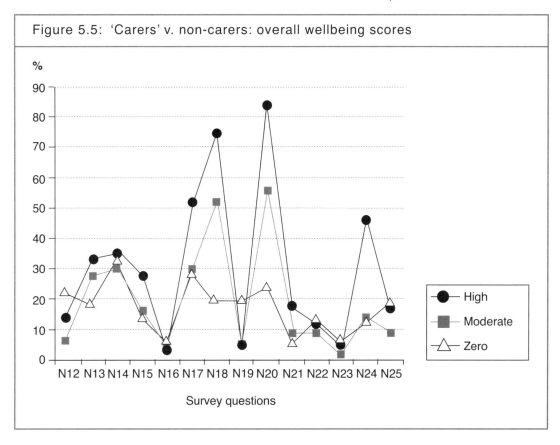

Figure 5.5: 'Carers' v. non-carers: overall wellbeing scores

Senior school children

In addition to the survey undertaken in the six junior schools, questionnaires were completed by a sample of year ten children in one comprehensive school. The sampling procedure adopted in the junior section was not possible in the senior schools, there being only five in the LEA. The school with the highest proportion of free meals was selected (41 per cent), due to the assumption of strong links between illness, domestic duties and poverty. The same questions were asked of year ten children as of the younger group, but additional questions were added of age appropriate complexity (see Appendix 1). Eighty seven questionnaires were returned from year ten children. Most of the children were aged 15 years (83 per cent), with smaller numbers aged 14 (two per cent) and 16 (15 per cent) years. The sample had a fairly even balance of males (47 per cent) and females (53 per cent). The proportion of children from one-parent families (22 per cent, n=19) was similar to the sample of younger children.

Encounters with illness and dependency

Responses to the key questions, concerning encounters with illness and contribution to domestic chores are given in Table 5.1, alongside the comparable figures for 7-11 year olds.

As we can see, where questions relate to non-abstract concepts, such as washing up or tidying the house, there are no statistical differences between the younger and older age groups. However, where questions require more abstract thinking, younger children are far more likely to conceive of themselves as worrying, looking after siblings or helping ill adults 'a lot', as illustrated in Figure 5.6.

Table 5.1: Comparison of children in year 10 with those in years 3–6

Question	Agree a lot 10	Agree a lot 3–6	Agree a bit 10	Agree a bit 3–6	Don't agree 10	Don't agree 3–6	p
How much do you agree...							
I worry a lot about other people	17	376	57	199	13	47	<0.01
How often do you...	A lot		A bit		Never		
Worry about someone who is ill?	20	425	45	171	22	25	<0.01
Tidy the house?	18	158	52	346	16	116	0.63
Do the washing up?	15	108	35	264	34	248	0.99
Look after brothers and sisters?	12	194	30	162	44	248	<0.01
Do things for grown-ups who are ill?	7	433	26	152	53	28	<0.01

Figure 5.6: Comparison of older (mean 14.9 years) and younger children (mean 9.2 years)

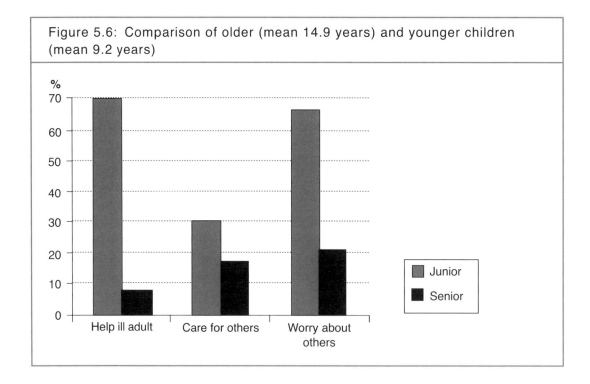

The enormous differences in the proportions of these responses indicate that we are dealing here with a conceptual issue, rather than a comparable measurement of activity, and go a long way towards explaining the extremely high proportion of younger children expressing encounters with, or involvement in, adult illness and its consequences.

This suggests that we must show extreme care when exploring both the impact of parental illness on children of different ages and the contribution they claim to the household economy. The responses of the older children are clearly far closer to the pattern of comprehension we might typically encounter in a population of adults. 'Caring', 'worrying' and 'helping', for younger children, these data warn us, cannot be necessarily understood within the same framework of comprehension we would apply to older children.

Family structure

Within-group comparisons using poverty as a variable were not possible for the group of older children. However, similar in-group comparisons were made using the factors of lone parenthood and gender. These data include a number of the more demanding questions asked only of the older group of children. On most comparisons, there was considerable similarity between children in one- and two-parent families. The mean age of children in one-parent families was 15.0 years, 53 per cent were boys and 47 per cent girls. There were only two children living with grandparents, and, as one might expect, these were both in lone-parent families. Few significant differences emerged on key questions pertaining to emotional health or autonomy. On measures pertaining to adult illness and its consequences, children in one-parent families appeared to do well. They were more likely to feel good about themselves, and although on a three point scale, no statistical differences emerge, proportionately more felt happy all the time. In relation to illness and the carrying out of domestic tasks, no differences emerged between children in one- and two-parent families. The sample is insufficiently large to give us confidence that these findings would hold for the total population, however, as few significant impacts on children directly attributable to family structure are detectable here.

Gender

Very substantial differences were noted between girls and boys in the 7-11 year old groups. We would expect similar differences to emerge between males and females in the older group. This expectation was, however, only partly confirmed. No significant differences emerged on any of the variables associated with emotional status or attitudes to school. The proportion of boys who

reported looking after siblings or helping a sick adult was similar. Where differences did emerge, they were, as with younger children, in the area of domestic help, where girls reported far more tidying and washing up. These findings confirm the normative assumptions about male and female profiles. As we know from reviewing the literature, boys and girls make similar contributions to sibling and adult care, and these data convey a similar picture. However, in terms of making contributions to the common domestic chores of washing up and tidying, girls conform to the ancient gender stereotype, being far more likely than boys to undertake both tasks (p<0.01), with over two thirds of boys appearing to have no contact with a washing up bowl at all.

Helping siblings and parents: impact on children

The key issue is whether parental illness or disability, especially where associated with caregiving roles and excessive domestic duties impact on children's wellbeing. We cannot know the extent to which tasks children reported undertaking in this survey fall beyond what might be considered normative activities. However, by isolating those children in the data set who reported looking after siblings and doing things for ill adults, the two most pertinent variables, and comparing them to children who reported that they never undertook these tasks, we can examine any differences that may emerge. Unlike with the junior section of the survey, the distribution of the data makes such a comparison feasible. We will do this by first comparing children who look after siblings with those who do not, second by making a similar comparison between children who do things for sick adults and those who do not, and finally by combining both variables, and comparing children who care for siblings and who do things for sick adults with children who do neither. Variables chosen for comparison are those related to aspects of functioning or emotional health that we would expect to be impacted should caring and domestic duties in general cause excessive levels of stress.

Sibling and adult care

First, let us compare those children who took no part in sibling care with those who undertook a bit or a lot. The groups have similar profiles; mean ages of 14.9 (n=44) and 14.8 (n=42) years respectively and the sibling carer group a slightly higher proportion of girls (57 per cent v. 48 per cent). Only one difference emerged between the groups; children who reported a high degree of sibling care also reported tidying the house a lot (p<0.01). No differences emerged on any of the health or wellbeing scores. It is not possible, given the evidence of these data, therefore, to support a thesis that sibling care has impacts on children that result in their expressing significantly different views on their quality of life across the dimensions explored here than children with no such duties. Second, let us compare children who reported undertaking no tasks for sick adults and those who did, either frequently or just sometimes. There were 33 children looking after sick adults (38 per cent) and 53 not doing so (62 per cent). Gender divides in both groups were similar, the first having 54 per cent female, the second 51 per cent female. Age difference was also minor, with the children reporting as looking after adults having a mean age of 14.7 years, the other group 15.0 years. Again, only one significant difference emerged; children who reported looking after sick adults 'a lot' reported, compared to children who reported no such activity, that they were less in charge of their own lives (p<0.05). Where children reported looking after adults, they appeared no more likely to perform routine domestic tasks than children who report no such tasks. Emotionally, looking after adults was also not associated with significant differences, with no more children in the former group worrying about people, or reporting having less fun or more frequent feelings of sadness than children in the latter group. While we have very limited information on these tasks, other than the extent to which children report performing them, and should thus interpret the results with some caution, these figures do not confirm the hypothesised effects on children of caring and domestic chores.

Finally, in order to explore any differences between groups that are at the most extreme ends of the continuum that our data can illuminate, children who reported caring for siblings and looking after adults were compared with children who reported doing neither. The two groups were very similar. Twenty children reported undertaking both tasks and 31 neither. Mean ages of both groups were similar, 14.7 and 15 years respectively. The gender split in the former group was exactly 50/50; in the latter there were 58 per cent boys. Only two significant differences occurred when the two groups were compared. Children with dual caring tasks reported having significantly less fun (p<0.05) and tidying the house a lot more (p<0.01); overall however, the profiles of the two groups are largely the same. Even when we attempt to compare the two extremes of our data set, in terms of those who report the maximum range of family caring tasks and those who report the minimum, we are unable to separate the two groups on the large number of measurements.

Figure 5.7 illustrates all the wellbeing scores, with negative impacts increasing on the y axis.

The moderate line represents those who reported *both* that 'looking after a grown up who is poorly' *and* 'looking after brothers or sisters' was 'a bit like me'. The zero line represents children who answered both questions, 'this is not like me'. No children chose the option 'this is a lot like me'. As can be seen, no overall pattern emerges favouring one group over another.

Perception and age

In this general population we find very large proportions of children who report encounters with, or consciousness of adult illness. Younger children's perceptions of illness and the contribution they report themselves as making differs to a great degree from that of older children. The difference was quite startling, with over 70 per cent of years 3-6 children reporting that they helped ill adults 'a lot' compared to only eight per cent of year 10 children. These findings, while apparently surprising, have been replicated in some dimensions at least, in similar questionnaire-

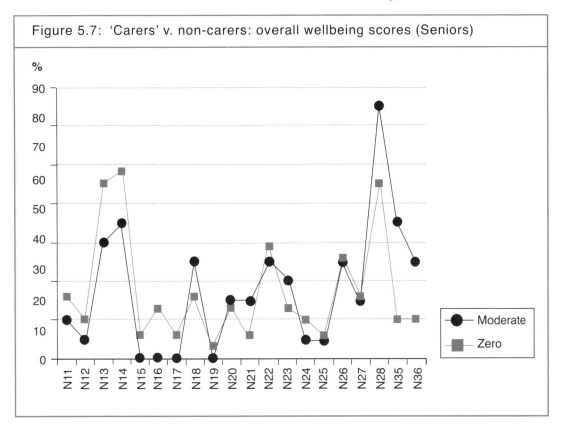

Figure 5.7: 'Carers' v. non-carers: overall wellbeing scores (Seniors)

based schools surveys. For example, some 40 per cent of refugee children, ages 11-14 years, in a study by Candappa and Egharevba (2000, n=325) and 20 per cent of a non-refugee control group reported taking responsibility for the care of siblings. Over a quarter in both groups undertook shopping for food, with similar numbers undertaking other household tasks. A widely accepted premise of child developmental psychology, is that up to the age of seven or eight, children will typically over-estimate their physical and mental capacity to perform tasks (Dweck and Elliot, 1983). This characteristic diminishes as the child approaches early adolescence and acquires a more realistic self-assessment of their strengths and limitations. The changing perceptions of children of the volume of help they deliver to adults can also be seen by examining, by age of child, responses to the question of how much help is given to adults.

As can be seen in Figure 5.8, there is a slow but steady decline in numbers of children perceiving

that they help a great deal as their age increases, fitting the theory suggested above.

Discussion

The population explored was a general one, deliberately skewed towards the most disadvantaged when measured by poverty indicators, in order to maximise the number of children affected by family illness and disability. This was, according to local estimates, not inconsiderable; the borough's Community Mental Health Team estimated that 40 per cent of all children of parents known to the team could be classified as 'young carers' (personal communication, 1999). The main issues that emerged from the survey can be summarised as follows:

● No consistent relationship between caring roles and self-reported wellbeing was evident in the younger group. Children who reported the most caring duties had less fun and did more tidying

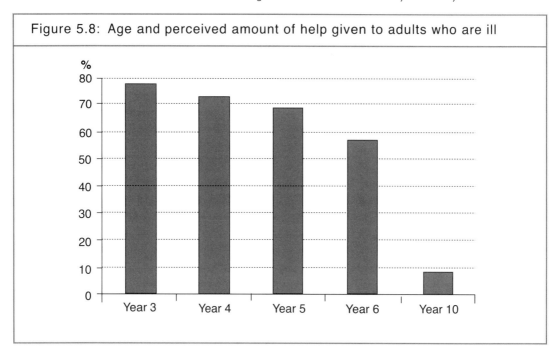

Figure 5.8: Age and perceived amount of help given to adults who are ill

up. However, they felt no more jealous of their friends, paid as much attention in school, felt unhappy no more frequently and could do what they wanted as often as children who never cared for siblings or looked after sick parents.

- In the older group, few differences were apparent when the children who reported both sibling and adult care were compared with those who reported neither.

- Younger children may have had inflated perceptions of the volume of domestic help they contributed. Perceptions of the volume of help provided declined with age.

- In the younger group, poverty and especially gender emerged as the main variables differentiating children's encounters with disability or illness and their consequences.

- In terms of contribution to domestic chores, gender was a predictably powerful variable for both older and younger children. Gender has proved a consistent source of variation in responses to questions in school based surveys. Girls worry considerably more about most issues, notably family, friends and the way they look, and they are far more likely to

seek help from friends than boys (Balding, 1999). There is also evidence that girls, even at a pre-school age, exhibit more caring behaviour towards ill parents and more intense levels of parental disorder are necessary to produce similarly elevated levels of caring behaviour in boys (Radke-Yarrow et al., 1994).

The drawbacks to this survey are clear; the instrument was not validated, it is not known whether children interpreted the questions relating to adult illness, sibling care and domestic help consistently, the year 10 sample was too small, and we cannot know for sure whether some children with disabled parents were in school the day the survey was completed. It is also impossible to differentiate between children with normative and non-normative domestic responsibilities. However, the substantial volume of data collected does provide a considerable insight into children's encounters with, and perceptions of, many of the issues pertinent to parental illness and disability.

Our conclusion from these data is thus: illness, personal, familial and general, is an important factor in children's lives, in terms of the frequency with which it is encountered. While we would expect, given the demographic profile of the community studied, that illness would play a disproportionately large part in the lives of its citizens, the belief of younger children in particular, that they were encountering and helping sick adults with such a high degree of frequency, comes as a surprise. This is not, however, unprecedented. Studying children in families where a parent had cancer, Lackey and Gates (1997) noted that children described giving a greater intensity of help to adults than was reported by adults themselves.

Furthermore, younger children typically described providing a more primary caring role than their elder siblings where independent observation concluded the opposite was the case. This finding is congruent with the data presented above. Adult illness, in fact, is presented in this section of the data as normative rather than atypical phenomena. While some small differences emerged between children who reported caring for both siblings and adults, it is not possible to conclude, without additional data (such as school attendance records), whether these differences translate into any circumstances that would, for example, lead such children to be classified as 'in need', or for these children, or their parents, to be eligible for assessments under the Carers Act, the Children Act or the NHS and Community Care Act. For more fine-grain comparisons, an additional approach is needed. Either the caring reported was not of a sufficient degree of magnitude to register differences on the variables used, or the instrument was not sufficiently sensitive to detect any differences, or the impacts of caring are less intrusive in the lives of children than claimed. In order to explore these options further, we will need to examine a specific rather than a general population: children of disabled or ill parents already receiving the support of child welfare agencies.

The Health and wellbeing of Children With Ill or Disabled Parents: An Agency Survey

The Welsh schools survey discussed above provided few examples of differences between children who report responsibilities for looking after siblings and

helping adults and those who do not, though we have no information from this survey on what these responsibilities were. These data, however, are reported from a general, not a 'clinical' population and are unlikely to contain many accounts from children who are severely affected by family impairment. While, according to these data, some minor differences exist, it is unclear whether these differences are a cause for concern, or whether, indeed, they affect the health of children in any detectable way. In order to explore further whether parental impairment is associated with poorer child health and wellbeing, we need to examine the health of children who have already been brought to the attention of agencies charged with helping children affected by family disability and illness.

Measuring health and wellbeing

The main requirement for such a survey was an instrument that could be completed by a child without assistance, was appropriate for a general population and which covered a wide range of child health and welfare outcomes. Child-completed instruments are less readily available than those designed for adults. The instrument most widely used in general UK health surveys, the SF-36 and its shorter analogue, the SF-12, is unsuitable for those under the age of 16. The instrument thus chosen was the self-report version of the Child Health Questionnaire (CHQ-CF87), which covers a wide range of child health outcomes and is intended for use with any child population (Landgraf et al., 1996). The self-completed version of this instrument is designed for children of at least 10 years of age. All the children in the agency sample exceeded this age. As with the general population survey, the instrument uses Likert-type scales. Options mostly range along a five point scale. Scores of 4.0 or greater indicate that the problem rarely occurs, scores of 2.0 and less indicates it is fairly or very common. The CHQ has been validated in child populations of several different countries, including the UK (Landgraf et al., 1998) and has been used in a number of different child illness settings, for example, cancer (Nixon et al., 1999) and diabetes (Wake et al., 2000), as well as general adolescent populations (Waters et al., 2001).

Administration

Access was negotiated through two voluntary agencies. Letters were written to each child explaining the purpose of the study, with corresponding letters to the parents of the children. Children were asked, in the covering letter, whether, in addition to completing the questionnaire, they were willing to be interviewed. Eighty-three questionnaires were returned. There was a gender imbalance in the returns, 33 (40 per cent) being from boys and 50 (60 per cent) from girls. The mean age of the respondents was 13.8 years (range 10-19 years). Many of the children had been involved with the agencies for some time, the shortest reported contact period being 14 months and the longest just over 6.5 years.

Questionnaire domains

The Child Health Questionnaire (CHQ) was designed to take account of an understanding of health as a broad, multi-dimensional construct, in the sense of its being 'a state of complete physical, mental and social wellbeing and not merely the absences of diseases or infirmity' (World Health Organisation, 1948). The 12 **domains** covered by the CHQ are designed to accommodate this holistic understanding of health and wellbeing. The domains, the corresponding numbers of items covered by each domain, and a brief description of their function, are shown in Table 5.2.

As illustrated, all the relevant areas of concern expressed in the literature concerning children of disabled parents are addressed across these domains; impacts on physical and emotional health, restrictions on friendship networks, and effects on

Table 5.2: Child health questionnaire domains

Domain	Number of items	Function
Physical functioning (PF)	9	The presence and extent of physical limitations
Role/social emotional (RE)	3	Limitations in school and friendship related activities
Role/social behavioural; (RB)	3	Limitations in school and friendship related activities
Role/social physical (RS)	3	Limitations in school and friendship related activities
Bodily pain (BP)	2	Intensity/frequency of pain
General behaviour (BE)	16	Frequency of behavioural problems
Mental health (MH)	16	Current mental state
Self-esteem (SE)	14	Degree of life satisfaction
General health perceptions (GH)	13	Subjective assessment of health
Change in health	1	Changes in the past year
Family activities (FA)	6	Limitation in activities
Family cohesion (FC)	1	How the family gets along
Total	87*	

*Though the number of questions totals 87, the CHQ users manual omits 2 questions (the 'Change in heath' category above and one question from the 'Family activities' category, questions 8.2 and 9.1e respectively, due to ongoing interpretation difficulties. In order to retain comparability, these questions are also omitted from the following discussion.

self-esteem, school career and family. Should exposure to parental impairment be associated with degradation in health and general wellbeing, we should expect to find scores across these domains lower than normal population means.

Main Findings of the Agency Survey

While the length of the scales in different domains varies, the general rule is that lower scores indicate worse health, higher scores better health. The questions address behaviour, emotions or activities over the preceding four weeks. The mean score for a general child population (GP), based on a middle school sample (n=263) provided in the CHQ manual (Landgraf et al., 1996) are given opposite each domain score as a point of comparison. Standard deviations for both the agency sample (AS) and general population (GP) sample are also given. As well as the general population sample comparison, mean scores on the CHQ of out-patient samples of children with cystic fibrosis (CF) and end-stage renal disease (ESRD) are provided, where appropriate, as a further point of comparison (source: Landgraf et al., 1996).

General health perceptions (GH)

When children surveyed were asked to estimate, on a five point scale, their overall health, their mean general health score was very close to the general population mean (3.76 v. 3.79), with a similar standard deviation. When combined with the other 11 global health-related items, the full domain score was slightly worse than the general population mean, 3.54 to 3.61 respectively, though the range of scores was narrower, and both were considerably larger than the CF comparison of 3.36. On overall health perceptions, relating to past, present and future health, the differences between the two groups are thus relatively minor.

Physical functioning (PF)

This domain explores the extent to which normal activities, such as walking, climbing stairs, doing

tasks around the house, getting around the neighbourhood and playing are restricted by physical health problems: there are suggestions that the physical health of children with disabled parents may be impaired by, for example, having to lift or carry ill parents. Mean scores for both groups were very similar on all items; small standard deviations within this domain indicate that little variation is present between the group members. The overall mean for this domain, in fact, slightly favoured the agency sample, 3.70 to 3.65 respectively.

Bodily pain (BP)

Associated with the PF domain are two items that query how frequently and to what extent pain has been suffered in the preceding four weeks. Slightly lower scores are recorded in the agency sample (4.52 v. 4.65), but both scores fall well within the mild to very mild part of the scale.

Effects on school work and friendships

This dimension is explored through three domains which address the question of whether school work or activities with friends are affected *emotionally* (RE), *behaviourally* (RB) or *physically* (RP). No differences between the groups were observed in the domains of physical health or behaviour, with scores in both groups being almost identical (RB 3.56 v. 3.57; RP 3.69 v. 3.63). However, the GP group was favoured in the domain that investigated emotional health. Children in the agency sample reported schoolwork and activities with friends being more affected by sadness and worry (3.34 v. 3.65). To put this score in context, the comparable score for ESRD children is 3.11 and that for children with CF, 3.70. We can infer from this figure therefore, that emotional interference with school work and friendships is a notable phenomenon reported by this sample of children.

General behaviour (BE)

This domain addresses behaviours or problems that children may exhibit, or encounter at home, with friends or at school. There was virtually no difference in the domain mean (agency sample 3.99, GP 4.03). The only score falling below the midpoint of 3.0 was common to both groups; everyone had argued rather a lot in the preceding four weeks.

Family activities (FA)

This domain investigates whether the behaviour or health of the young person had caused difficulties at home, for example causing tensions, limitations on activities, disagreement or conflict. The agency sample was favoured in comparison to the GP group within this domain (3.77 v. 3.48), suggesting that in relation to these issues at least, the young respondents had no particular problems in this area.

Family cohesion (FC)

A single question is posed in this domain, which explores the extent to which family members get along which each other (q.9.2). The mean scores for both groups were very similar (3.58 v. 3.62), again indicating that this is not a dimension in which children with disabled or ill parents are distinguishable from most other children.

In most of the domains discussed so far, little difference can be observed between the agency sample and the general population, with the exception of children's reported difficulties, with schoolwork and friendship, RE due to worry. The final two domains examine different aspects of children's emotional lives; their moods and feelings, and self-esteem.

Mental health (MH)

This domain asks a range of questions about the extent to which children are scared, nervous or worried; and conversely, the extent to which they feel cheerful or have fun. As with the earlier domains, the questions relate to emotional affect in the previous four weeks. While both the agency sample scores and the GP scores are closer to the 'feeling positive most of the time' or 'only feeling

negative a little of the time' points of the scale, the difference between the two mean domain scores is similar to that in the domain which addressed emotional difficulties with school and friendships, around 0.20 (3.65 v. 3.86). Notable differences emerged when children from the agency sample reported the extent to which they had difficulty sleeping (3.53 v. 3.98) and, especially, how much they liked themselves (3.23 v. 4.22). This figure also compares poorly to children with CF (4.13) and even the children with ESRD (3.79).

Self-esteem (SE)

Mental health is obviously related to the theme of the final domain, self-esteem. This domain reveals by far the greatest difference of any between the agency sample and the GP, with a mean domain difference of 0.49 (3.65 v. 4.25), and is the only dimension where a substantial difference can be observed between the two groups. The difference appears startling; putting the mean score of the agency children in context, the associated CF score is 4.17. The agency sample score is barely higher than children suffering from end stage renal disease (3.74). Particularly depressed, in relation to the GP group, are the scores relating to questions on school work, feelings about body and looks, and health in general.

The line graph in Figure 5.9 summarises this data, comparing the mean scores of both the agency sample (AS) group with the general population (GP) sample by summed means in the eleven domains.

As we can see, the lines shadow each other across many of the dimensions. However, we can also see the gaps emerging in the domains of self-esteem (SE), mental health (MH) and also the dimension that assesses emotional interference in school or friendship networks (RE).

Gender

Notable gender differences emerged in the school survey. In line with the expected direction, girls were more likely to project caring attitudes and behaviours than boys. The capacity of girls to be

Figure 5.9: Health of children affected by parental illness and disability: comparison with general population

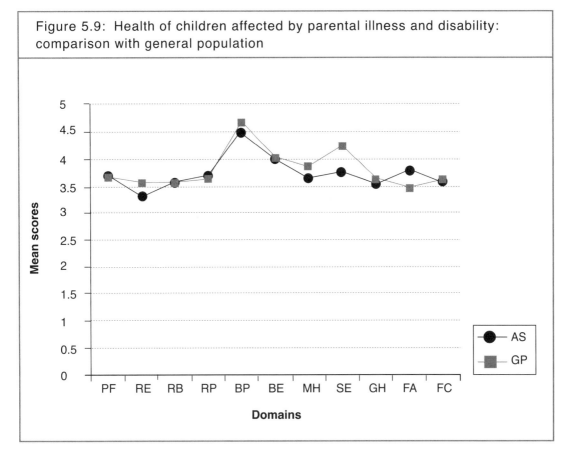

more emotionally expressive and more sensitive to the emotional states of others than boys is well attested by the literature, as is the tendency of girls to show more anxieties in adolescence than boys about health, family issues and other concerns (Bukatko and Daehler, 1995). We would expect therefore, in relation to comparative health, to find gender differences between the responses of boys and girls. The different profile of boys and girls are illustrated in the Figure 5.10 line graph. As noted above, the number of female respondents (n=50) exceeded that of the males (n=33).

The gender profile illustrated in Figure 5.10 largely supports the predicted gender differences. Boys, as one might expect, report more behaviour related problems at school (RB 3.39 v. 3.66) and girls have consistently lower scores than boys in the domains of mental health (MH 3.60 v. 3.73), self-esteem (SE 3.67 v. 3.91) and general health (GH 3.46 v. 3.66). In the domains related to family

life, girls are considerably less likely than boys to encounter difficulties associated with family activities (FA 4.01 v. 3.31) and are more likely than boys to be satisfied with family cohesiveness (FC 3.69 v. 3.39).

Age

Are younger children more likely to be affected by parental impairment than older children? There are two factors to consider here, the age of the child and, given the help provided by welfare agencies, the prophylactic effect of a social care service. On both counts, we might assume that younger children would be more affected by caregiving duties than their older peers, and that a longer exposure to a welfare service should result in improved health and wellbeing. The graph in Figure 5.11 compares the CHQ scores for children above and below the age of fourteen (ages ranges 9-13 and 15-19 respectively).

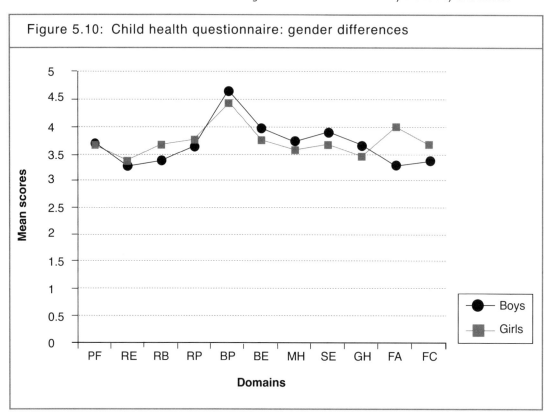

Figure 5.10: Child health questionnaire: gender differences

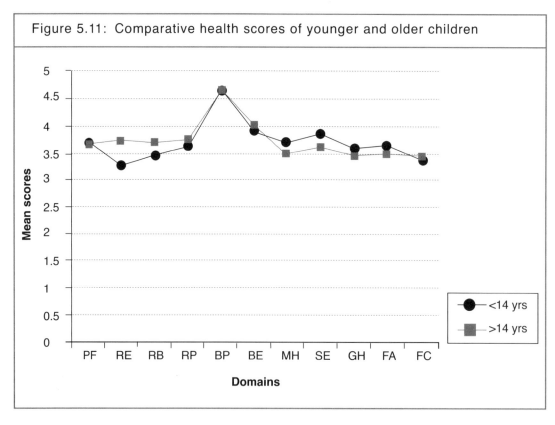

Figure 5.11: Comparative health scores of younger and older children

As can be seen, the expected direction is reversed in many domains. Across the three domains associated with restrictions on school work and friendships (RE/RB/RP), the younger children record lower scores, a finding consistent with the inverse relationship between perceived volume of 'helping' and age discussed earlier. However, in the domains which address mental health (MH), self-esteem (SE) and general health (GH), the younger children are consistently favoured. Older children, it appears, report greater emotional difficulties and feel less good about themselves than the younger group.

Discussion

What conclusions can we draw on the central issue addressed by the agency survey data? While we have little prior information about the health of children with ill and disabled parents known to child welfare services in the UK, it is suggested that in one well-explored and analogous group, children of alcoholics, typical health related problems we might expect to find include psychosomatic complaints (notably sleeplessness, fatigue, nausea and eating problems), compulsive disorders and work addiction (Robinson and Rhoden, 1998). While not all these factors can be explored by these data, the older informants (aged >14 years) reported considerably higher levels of sleeplessness than the population mean (3.03 v. 3.98), though this was not evident in the younger (<14 years) children (3.92 v. 3.98). The mean score of our sample on the question regarding frequency of headaches was almost identical to the population sample (3.34 v. 3.33). The expected differences between males and females were evident. Boys reported more behaviour related problems, girls more problems relating to self-esteem and emotional difficulties. This fits with what we know about gender differences in adolescence. Younger children appeared to be less affected in the domains relating to general and emotional health, and self-esteem. The findings relating to gender and age replicate those from one of the largest general population surveys carried out to date (n=2361) which has utilised the self-report version of the Child Health Questionnaire (Waters et al., 2001). While any conclusions about the impact on children's health through involvement with child welfare services is impossible without prior baseline measurements (would it have been worse without involvement, the same, or better?) the poorer scores of older children, particularly in the domain of self-esteem are clearly unsatisfactory.

In some health-related domains, no apparent differences emerged between the agency sample and children in the general population. Reported physical and general health was similar or superior, no raised frequency of behavioural problems was noted, and family activities and cohesion showed no heightened difficulties. Where a difference was clearly evident, particularly for older children, and especially girls, was in the domains associated with emotional health. Children reported more disruption in school and friendship related activities through emotional disturbance, more sadness, some heightened psychosomatic conditions, notably sleeplessness, worrying and associated co-morbidity at home and, in particular, depressed levels of self-esteem. The latter is particularly important, as mean scores in this domain were barely higher than a comparison group of very ill children with end stage renal disease. That lowered self-esteem should be encountered in this sample is not in itself surprising. Using again the example of alcoholism, children of alcoholic parents have consistently recorded lower levels of self-esteem than controls (Post and Robinson, 1998). Similarly, a Scottish study of children with disabled parents reported lower levels of self-esteem among children with caring responsibilities compared to those with none (Banks et al., 2001).

The overall health scores of the agency sample, especially in the realms of emotional health and self-esteem, will inevitably suffer by comparison to any random population sample because of the larger proportion of girls in the sample (60 per cent), as adolescent girls invariably score lower than boys on these measures of wellbeing. However, given the length of time that the older child informants had been receiving help (a mean of just over three years), it is clearly disappointing that such depressed measurements continue to persist, especially given that improving children's self-esteem is frequently cited as a core objective of child welfare services.

While quantitative explorations of children's health are essential in order to avoid mis-attributions of cause and effect, to reduce bias and to standardise responses, a full picture of children's complex encounters with parental impairment cannot be achieved solely by enumeration. To enrich the overall data profile, a series of interviews were carried out with a sample of young people who had completed the questionnaires.

Survey Four: Talking to Young People

The questionnaires completed by children in the agency survey included a covering note asking if they were willing to be interviewed. Thirty agreed, though only 20 were eventually interviewed due to school holidays. The children preferred to be interviewed in peer groups, with other children of similar age whom they already knew. CHQ scores for the children who were interviewed were calculated and compared to the whole group. Differences were minor; the interviewed group was representative of the larger population.

Nine clusters of issues became apparent. The children described the domestic circumstances that had resulted in their involvement with the child welfare agency. School and education in general was the source of many observations, as was the content, intensity and impact of their domestic circumstances. Children discussed the nature of the activities provided by the child welfare agency, any paid work that they did, the wider support they received from neighbours and relatives, and how effective they perceived this to be. Finally, they discussed their ambitions for the future. These issues are discussed, in turn, below. Quotations

given exclude or change any personal identifying details.

Domestic problems

The children present described many of the domestic situations which have been reported previously in literature concerning children of disabled parents. Mental health issues, autism, sensory impairments, learning disability, chronic illness, multiple sclerosis and non-specific disability were mentioned by children as incapacities present in their families. The illness or disability of mothers, as in most previous studies, was the main feature of their domestic situations, although the young people also mentioned the illness or disability of brothers, fathers and grandparents. Many of the children, though not all, were in lone-parent families. Mothers, as expected, were mentioned most frequently:

When I was 14 me Mum was diagnosed with having a mental health problem.

My Mum's got MS.

I've been coming here five [years] 'cos me Mum's got a disability, she can't get out so I come here.

Me Mum's going to have an operation and she won't be able to do anything for weeks and weeks.

In one case, both parents had impairments, and the father, rather than the mother was the recipient of care.

Me Mum and Dad can't go out very often without me being with them, 'cos they're blind.

I look after me Dad what have got a disability.

Siblings were frequently mentioned as care recipients.

I help my brother and sister. They're younger.

I got involved [with the service] about ten months ago 'cos I look after me little brother who's autistic.

While, as previously discussed, the complex texture of family relationships rarely emerges from children's accounts alone, with a single exception, discussed below, children's descriptions of family impairment implied no abdication from, or reversal of, the paramount role of an adult as the family member responsible for the child's welfare. Children helped impaired adults and siblings, by their own accounts sometimes considerably, but not in the context of the major psychological shift in function implied by the concept of role-reversal.

School

Educational issues, as we have seen in reviewing the literature, are one of the most widely reported problems that are alleged to be associated with parental impairment, especially where excessive domestic care by children is present. This factor, not unexpectedly, emerged in these interviews. Many, though by no means all of the children's comments with respect to school were negative. Lack of knowledge by teachers of the child's domestic situation, or a diminution of its importance, were highlighted. Not all children reported difficulties with attendance, but many children's observations were blunt:

> *I'm always early for school because the bus comes at five to eight and at twenty past eight I'm there. I get up at a quarter to seven.*

> *You haven't got time to study.*

> *You're too busy to do homework.*

Other comments were more detailed:

> *What gets me is I have to write me own notes for school* [child's mother is illiterate], *like when I have athlete's foot or something and the teacher doesn't believe me.*

> *Some teachers don't understand, they just ignore you, they say, well, just get on with your work...you explain to them but they just don't, like, understand. They should be better informed about the children with needs for extra help and extra time to do the stuff.*

In some cases, the absence of teachers' accounts renders us unable to judge whether the urgency of children's perceived duties at home are congruent with real domestic need.

> *...she* [headteacher] *said she'd tell other teachers* [about child's home situation] *but she never. She told two of me teachers I think and then I was in the French class and had a 15 minute whole class detention and me teacher wouldn't let me out of the lesson and I have to get out of school on time.*

Is completing homework, considered vital to future educational attainment, of greater benefit to children than a leisure weekend with a child welfare service? Both conclusions are possible. However, the following passage does raise the issue, though cannot answer it, of whether provision of leisure opportunities by child welfare services relieves children from stressful duties, or impedes educational progress.

> *I remember a while back asking me teacher, I had to have work in for Saturday but I went away with* [agency] *for a break and that, and I told her that I was going away and she said 'well, that's no excuse because your homework's more important than going away'. But you feel that you need a break and that from home.*

Similarly, both the conclusion that serious damage has occurred to a child's educational career, or that the correlation between caring and educational outcome is minor or spurious is possible from the following passage:

> *My attendance was quite poor. If I wasn't looking after me Mum I used to get loads of migraines so it was affected by that. Some teachers would understand and others were a bit funny over it even though I told each year head about the problems. Only last year when I was doing GCSEs I was doing all the work, the course work and everything, but at the time of the exams me Mum was ill so I only got into one part of each of the three exams so I didn't get any grades.*

Not all observations about the children's schools were negative, some children expressed appreciation of the level of understanding displayed by teachers:

> *...the school know about me Mum's problem and they help me 'cos I can talk to them if I can't get homework in at the right time. I can tell them why.*

Me Mum's getting better now so I have got more time to go out with me friends but the school know about me Mum's problem and they help me 'cos I can talk to them if I can't get homework in at the right time.

Some accounts of school absences were detailed and coherent:

I had to stay off a few times 'cos when me Mum was sick I had to pick up her money and all that from the Post Office. I have been off lately a few times because she had this illness, I don't know what it was, and she couldn't even get off the couch so I had to stay off for a week.

Others are less so, and suggest factors other than family incapacity may need to be considered:

I missed half a year because I had some trouble in school because some people were bullying me about me brother [who is autistic].

I missed a whole year in year 10 helping at home.

The difficulties in educational careers caused by chronic and unpredictable illness courses in lone-parent families were clear, as was the impact of a second adult in the home:

It wasn't too bad [in primary school] *because when I was seven she was taken into hospital every couple of months, so most of my juniors was fine. My rate of work got behind but I did catch up. The infants wasn't too bad because I didn't notice. Later on she was out of hospital for a good couple of years. When I went up to seniors she was ill again.*

It's happened to me a few times [problems at school] *but now me Mum's got a boyfriend, he helps a bit now so I've got a bit more time.*

The suggestion that children of disabled parents may suffer from excessive bullying has been discussed previously. Here, the observations were mixed:

School's all right...it's not really the teachers or anything, it's just the children. They bully you but I don't have a problem there. They don't push me about but just tease me but I'm not really bothered.

Some teachers can be really nice about it and others can really put you on the spot in front of the rest of the class as well, but your friends are good.

As with many other young person testimonies on educational issues, the above material raises as many questions as it answers.

Distractions over and above those normally affecting children will inevitably have educational consequences. But how large? The more moderate effects of caring on education, missed days, late arrivals and assignments, occasional longer periods of absence, are coherent and congruent with what we know of the impact of domestic responsibilities. Missing years, or extensive periods of time lost because of disabled siblings are less so, and demand additional or alternative explanations. Most importantly, the caring element of children's duties needs to be isolated from other factors, particularly those associated with poverty, disadvantage and low educational aspirations that may be part of the causal chain, rather than making the assumption that parental impairment alone is the source of the child's difficulties.

Helping

What did children actually do at home? As discussed previously, it is unreasonable to propose a simple relationship between tasks undertaken and child impact; this will inevitably result in disproportionately highlighting tasks that are more easily quantifiable, observable and, importantly for a child, describable. The wide variety of domestic tasks undertaken was illustrated by the children's dialogue. In a few cases, these responsibilities were clearly beyond what any child should encounter; the following description is from a child of a lone parent affected by mental illness:

I've been caring for me Mum since I was about seven. I used to do a lot of housework, cooking and cleaning and stuff. Me Mum was mentally ill so I'd have to talk to her, let her talk to me and be there for her emotionally as well. Check tablets and make sure she got to the day centre on the right days.

In some cases, the tasks seemed unexceptional, especially where sibling care was described:

Me Mum and me look after our [sister], *I had to pick her up from school so I have to get out about ten minutes earlier to pick our [sister] up and take her home and sometimes I do dinner for her.*

I've got a one year old and a two year old brother and sister and they're very friendly to me Mum and they'll cry when they can't get me Mum.

I look after me little brother who's autistic. It's a bit difficult to lift him upstairs and into the car and into his bed...He's nine and really really heavy.

Sometimes I have to stay with my Mum and tidy up.

Again, mothers were the main object of caregiving, which the presence of other adults did not always minimise:

I've got two brothers and one sister. Me and me Dad were doing most of the caring for me Mum. The other kids sort of got to go out with their mates and basically to do whatever they wanted whereas I had to stay and look after me Mum. Me Mum takes so many tablets she's, like, on another planet.

Me Mum broke her leg last September so I had to stay off school for a few weeks and help and a few days later when we got back from our holidays she fell out of her wheelchair and broke her right arm.

Obligations mixed with affection were typical of the parent-child relationships described:

Sometimes I've got to be protective about me Mum. I don't like her going up the stairs too much because she fell down the stairs and smashed her face on the wall, that's what caused her epilepsy to come on.

Some domestic tasks were enjoyed, rather than seen as a restriction:

I put the Hoover around before I came here. I do the Hoovering and I do bits of shopping. I did the patio with the hose pipe yesterday. I quite like working.

As can be seen, the caring relationships described vary from the extreme to the more mundane. As with the claims of the children in the junior school survey, it remains unclear from this testimony alone to what extent children's roles demand external intervention.

Impact of parental illness and disability on children

It has been extensively argued, not without some justification, that the *impacts* of parental impairment on children, especially where caregiving elements are present, must take into account *restrictions* on children, not just activities. Many of the impacts mentioned by children did, indeed, feature descriptions of restrictions:

When you're at home and your friends ring you, unless your Mum and Dad is safe, you can't go out with them.

You can't go to Alton Towers and all that, you have to stay in.

If I do go out I have to ring her all the time to make sure she's OK, or I don't go that far so I'm near if she needs me.

I have friends but I can't do as much with them as other people can.

The pain of feeling 'different' was vividly described by children:

Some people know that your Mum's got something wrong but the other kids, their Mums haven't got nothing wrong and sometimes you feel left out.

Like, some of me mates, going back to when I was in school and they were saying 'I hate me Mum' or 'I hate me Dad' because of some like stupid petty argument that's gone on, they'd tell me all about it and I'd think, 'my God, I'd love to just have normal parents', Or they'd go shopping with their Mum and say she bought me this, this and this. I was made to feel different.

In some cases, the general drabness of poverty and the confusion of children faced with events beyond their understanding were evident:

Me Mum can't read or write...she has these bad headaches...she goes to bed early and I come back down and watch a film before I go to bed.

I remember weird stuff when I was in primary school and it sort of snowballed from then when she got worse, but she weren't diagnosed until I was 14.

Apart from educational impacts, described above, restrictions on normal activities, rather than any health-related damage, were most frequently mentioned. Clearly, the importance of friendship networks for children, particularly teenagers, would make such restrictions particularly irksome. However, not all the accounts of children's domestic situations appeared likely to lead to the draconian restrictions often described. Certainly, children spoken to, and many more that were not, regularly attended events at the child welfare service offices without any special arrangements made for care of their parents or siblings, and weekends away were enjoyed by many. Again, while more independent accounts of the nature and extent of restrictions placed on children are needed, these anomalies are sufficient to place at least a question mark against the claims that excessively restrictive lives are normative for children with ill or disabled parents.

Activities

Apart from help of an emotional nature, described below, leisure activities were by far the dominant features of the children's conversations:

They take you out, so you can meet other people.

You can come down here and do the girls or boys groups in the evenings and plan what you do and that and just make your own rules. Through the summer holidays and Easter holidays you go on activities, like a playscheme.

We used to go for meals and go to the park, now it's like canoeing and swimming.

We go to [name] Friday to Saturday on adventure weekends. We go about twice a year in a mini-bus. There's a hotel we go to, that's a chill-out weekend.

Sometimes when we're on holidays they have little trips. One went to the [name] docks and on the ferry and places like that.

While undoubtedly providing considerable pleasure and clearly being very popular with children, it is unclear the extent to which leisure activities have anything other than a marginal effect on children's health and wellbeing. Taggart (1999), albeit in a very limited study, was unable to find any evidence of positive change in psychosocial health as a result of the involvement of children with disabled parents in a leisure programme. This is insufficient evidence on which to base a view on the utility of this kind of activity; in any event, enabling children under stress to enjoy themselves hardly needs justification by demanding evidence of a positive effect on child health. However, the question must be asked as to whether such a large investment in this particular approach is justified, given that it appears to have no immediate relevance to many of the problems reported by young people, in particular, their educational difficulties.

Work

One of the main complaints of children in the previously cited Office of National Statistics survey (Walker, 1996) was that the excessive domestic responsibilities associated with parental disability made it difficult to maintain a part-time job. This factor affected several of the children in this cohort; however, some of the children described current and past part-time work, both formal and informal:

There used to be this lady in our street, she was dead old and she used to have problems and we used to help her clean the house and that and she used to give me money and that.

I worked for an agency called [name]. It's a care agency for the elderly disabled. I just used to put people to bed and sit with them for an hour and talk and make them meals and stuff like that. And I work in an off-licence now.

I work in Macdonalds in the dining area. I earn good money.

I used to have a paper round but I found I was too tired to get up.

While several of the children indicated that part-time work was not possible due to their domestic circumstances, these descriptions again raise the issue of whether, however difficult some of the children's lives may be, they are not necessarily so constraining that working outside the home becomes an impossibility.

Support

Where do, or did, the young people receive support? Three sources were evident; the child welfare agencies with whom they were involved, other statutory services and relatives. The child welfare agencies were perceived as providing, in order of how frequently the issues were mentioned, a listening ear, breaks away from home and general leisure activities, a forum where they could meet others in their situation and mediation with other service-providing organisations.

Professional help was described at the greatest length; however relatives were an important factor. Some obviously played (or had played) a major role, and appear in most cases to be the primary caregivers in the households:

I live next door to my Nan so she can take care of her [child's mother].

I've got me auntie, she lives more or less down the road from me Mum's. When me Mum's bad she'll say well, you come to ours and stay the night and I'll go down and look after your Mum. Then she'll come back later and say everything's alright now, you can go back tomorrow after school. So I have been helped quite a lot by me family and other people.

When I was in the juniors my Nan looked after me and me Mum when she was ill, but when I got into the seniors, me Nan had angina so I started looking after me Nan as well. From time to time I used to go and stay with a friend of the family because sometimes they both had to go into hospital at the same time. If I was in school sometimes my Mum's friend would do the shopping so I didn't have to do it but it was just like mainly if they were both in hospital

'cos I was too young to stay in the house by meself.

My Dad cooks and does things. We have help with the ironing and a woman comes to do all the cleaning.

Sometimes I stay off if me Mum's bad and then me Nan comes up and I can go to school. She's got a car so she only takes five minutes to get there.

Not all relatives were perceived as helpful, or even present at all:

I've got a half-brother but he never comes near.

Me aunt comes round about every two months and decides to dust everywhere.

I haven't got any nans or aunties or uncles or anything.

As we can see, accounts of help from relatives are variable. The importance of family and community networks, stressed in the literature as the most powerful source of buffering to stressful situations, is clearly crucial in influencing the experiences of children affected by parental incapacity.

The large majority of comments concerning support described the help given by child welfare agency staff to children. The value of having a listening ear and have another take responsibility for logistical problems was highly stressed, as was, less frequently, helping with confidence:

Being able to talk to someone. When you come here if you're feeling down about it, you like to talk it over.

It [agency] *gives us help with our troubles and worries. They take you out. You can talk to friendly faces.*

...give advice which is important. They [agency workers] *also give you a lot of confidence in what you do when you get a problem.*

It's solving your problems. They just help your Mum and yourselves, like they take some of the problems away from you so you don't have to worry about them, they sort them out for you and help.

The receipt of advice and support was often associated with the opportunity to meet and make friends:

> We've been involved for about a year. It has helped me. When you call [the agency centre] in you're getting away from your problems at home and you make friends here, other people come here as well so it's like a place to get away from everything, relax or go out on activities.

> I've been coming here about six years, me and a couple of others since the start. You get away from your problems, make friends, people to talk to, get advice and stuff. If you've got a problem and you need to talk to a doctor, they listen and it gets done.

The particular insight of staff who had intimate knowledge of children affected by parental illness was valued by children; these personnel were compared favourably to other professionals:

> If you need to talk to an adult, a professional, when you're younger they don't listen to you very much. If they do listen they don't take it seriously. I know to you it's more serious than it is to them. If you tell someone at [agency], they will talk to them and tell them how serious it is and they listen to it more. Same with meeting people and making friends because I found that I didn't have time to make friends. I had friends to talk to at school but I didn't have time to go out after school and meet them. When I'd come here [agency offices], this would be my time and I could talk to people and make friends and every time you'd come here they would probably be here so it was easier to make friends that way.

> ...it's just being able to talk to someone and have an adult listen to what I have to say and help me sort it out because when I've talked to other professionals that was helping, they weren't listening.

Older children, in this case a late teenager, described the ongoing support of the child welfare agency through to early adulthood:

> As I got older, they've [agency staff] helped me out in different ways. At one point I was moving house, out of the family home, and they helped me get in touch with organisations that were to

do with that, 'cos I was only 16 then. They put me in touch with flats, Shelter, but I didn't end up moving. I live by myself but I live in the family home and me Mum's moved to a hostel so now if I have any problems with what to do about bills or benefits or whatever, I come in and they get in contact with the right people and find out the information for me and I know where I am then 'cos it's difficult when you are on your own.

A variety of other agency staff and resources were described as helping, including social workers, day centres, nurses and home helps. Again, there were varying opinions as to their usefulness:

> We used to have a community psychiatric nurse that used to come to our house and he'd take me Mum out in the car and help her get shopping.

> We used to have a home help to come in and give her [mother] her dinner and that was it really.

> We've got a carer that comes in once a month to stay in with me brother and we go out as a family for the day.

Identity

As has been discussed earlier, the belief that carers, both adult and child, need, often with the assistance of professionals, to be helped to see themselves as 'carers' is held to be a necessary pre-condition for accepting help, and more broadly, for healthy psychological adjustment. However, as has been noted previously in a minority of studies, this group of young people largely rejected an understanding of their caring role as abnormal:

> ...it's just like if your Mum's sick, it's just natural to help.

> It's families, you just help them out.

> It's natural, if they're ill.

> They do enough for you, it's like paying them back.

For some, 'normality' was attributed to an under-exposure to alternatives:

No, you just don't know any other way.

You think that it's just normal except when you get out and see the other kids.

For a majority of the children, a 'young carer' label was more a matter of professional convenience than a description of themselves they recognised:

...you just take it as it comes. You don't go round saying 'I'm a young carer'; you're not.

It seems what you normally do. If you think about it all the kids have got chores to do, it's just that I had a bit extra. The only difference I noticed was, as I said, I didn't get to be out as much as other kids, I just thought I did what every other kid does and then you come along with this nice little label 'young carer'.

The tension between the children's perception of their domestic activities and responsibilities and the social role offered to them by their involvement in child welfare services is apparent in these comments. The term 'young carer' had little utility to children themselves in their day-to-day life; it was potentiated when contact was required with welfare systems. As one child commented of the expression:

It's helpful with professionals but to everyone else it doesn't mean much. If you were talking in the street and someone asked you what you do and you say 'I'm a young carer', they'd go, 'what's one of them?'

For professionals, however, the application of a label subordinates a complex web of phenomena, conveniently, under a single heading, generating a common understanding of a situation and legitimising a response:

When me Mum first got diagnosed, and she got a social worker, and we got lawyers, and like it was all being categorised under the one label – what we'd been doing for years.

The application or withholding of welfare labels is, apart from its other functions, a political act. The main purpose of using the term 'young carer', whenever children affected by family incapacity are discussed, is to ensure that this particular dimension of young people's lives is rendered paramount to an observer, and to the children themselves, at every possible opportunity. In professional discourse, children or young people become 'young carers' or 'the Young Carers', with both the definite article and the upper case spelling having a linguistic function. This identity, from the perspective of professionals and public, may swell to encompass their whole being. To the children themselves, however, their role appears more changeable and less prescriptive.

The future

The future aspirations of the young people varied little from those of most other young people:

I want to go to law school.

I want to be a doctor.

I want be a lorry driver when I'm older.

I'd like to be a professional footballer.

A good job with loads of money but I don't know yet. I'm not really bothered as long as it's some work.

I want to be a hostess or something to do with languages.

...join the Royal Navy.

In addition to career ambitions, using the past in a positive way to build the future was implied in some children's comments:

Make sure my Mum does eventually get better and not to worry about her and leave it in the past, and if it does get mentioned, be proud of it [caring].

I think it's made me more prepared to be an adult really.

The belief that childhood adversities tend to increase the likelihood that a person will consider a future in a helping or therapeutic capacity is widely held. It was noticeable that, of the children who expressed a view, a quarter indicated that this option was under consideration:

I want to work with kids and families when I'm older, and help them out, having been in that situation.

I'd like to do that [work with children and families] *because I've been through it all and I know.*

I'd like to do the job that [name of agency worker] *does because it would help other people.*

I'm doing an NVQ level 2 in care with a year on placement. I want to be a social worker.

To what extent a close causal relationship exists between a premature caring career and these aspirations is difficult to evaluate from these data. Of rather more interest, though equally unanswerable, is the question, if such a relationship does exist, whether it is involvement with child welfare services, rather than children's domestic roles that renders such future aspirations more likely.

Conclusion

It is easy to fall into the trap of presuming causal relationships between past experiences, current dispositions, children's domestic roles and future life trajectories. Offering an explanation associated with a single variable – caring – may be both functional and attractive to all parties involved, and made more plausible by the probability that at least *some* of the causal links may, indeed, arise from caregiving. The occasional intrusion of professional jargon into the language of children indicated their degree of proximity to a social care culture:

[I've] *been given me childhood back again.*

You can just hang out, or you can do the one-to-one work.

However, the utility of this approach for child welfare services, which lies in the ability to convey a powerful, simple message and to maximise the impact on public and political support, may have unforeseen consequences for children. What effect will the acquisition of a 'young carer' identity have on children in later life? If unpaid caregiving as a child increases the likelihood of paid caregiving as an adult, does close involvement with a child welfare service accelerate this tendency? If so, is this a good thing?

It was suggested in Chapter 4 that the same kind of scrutiny should be applied to narrative accounts as to quantitative data. Problems with education, for example, featured prominently in the children's narratives. Children's difficulties at school are well documented in literature concerning children of disabled parents, though, as pointed out previously, no study has, to date, isolated 'caring' as an independent variable and estimated what contribution it makes to unauthorised absences, or diminished academic performance. Unauthorised absences from school have a steep social class gradient; children involved with child welfare services, who are disproportionately drawn from lower socio-economic classes, are likely to have attendance records lower than the mean for their area. That children with difficult domestic circumstances should be supported by schools and allowances made for atypical domestic demands is unlikely to be disputed by any party. However, the extent to which poorer attendance, and poorer academic performance may be tolerated *because* of a child's reported domestic circumstances, is an unexplored realm. This dilemma illustrates the potential for unintended consequences of social care interventions. Children with low educational aspirations compounded by domestic demands may have their commitment to education weakened by an excessive toleration of absences derived from reported caring duties. To attribute difficulties at school entirely to tasks at home, *solely* on the basis of children's accounts, is neither sound research nor sound practice. A balance clearly needs to be struck in this area, a balance which recognises the genuine difficulties of children and parents, and the importance of educational attainment, and does not under-estimate the potential for children of disabled parents – like any other children – to rationalise and justify non-compliance with academic requirements by virtue of their domestic circumstances.

To a certain extent, the questions that have been raised in this chapter are less associated with the young people's accounts than with the nature of much of the literature on this subject, which accepts, largely uncritically, children's accounts of restrictions and adversities and, typically, highlights the most extreme examples encountered. Avoiding this approach, as this chapter attempted, and asking reasonable questions not about the general context of children's roles, but about the claims of extremity, in terms of amount of work done, extent of restrictions, or depth of damage, illustrates how a less draconian view of children's lives may be constructed. This by no means implies that these children, or children in similar situations, are unaffected by the adversities they have encountered. In the case of some of the above accounts, this is clearly not the case. However, the inability of children to leave an ill or disabled adult unattended, a common feature of case study material and associated media publicity, appears the exception, rather than the rule, in these narratives. Distressing as some of the children's experiences clearly are, it is unclear how many may be equated with the restrictions placed on adult carers looking after, for example, a partner with Alzheimer's disease, especially as in most cases, another adult with primary caring responsibilities was present in the household. This factor, noted also in Walker's ONS survey (1996),

does require some explanation if the term 'young carer' is to be treated as the juvenile version of an adult carer. That children may be affected by parental illness and disability, in often unpleasant and undesirable ways, is clear from these accounts. Why all, as opposed to some, should be legitimately described as 'carers', in the sense that this term is commonly understood and defined, is less clear.

We do have clear evidence, however, of some dimensions of psychological morbidity greater than we should encounter in an adolescent population, particularly in relation to self-esteem, though this finding is skewed by the over-representation of adolescent girls. This, as noted, still pertains despite a mean of some three years of involvement with a child welfare service. Children, regardless that the tasks they undertake are highly valued socially, appear to value themselves *less* as a result of undertaking them. Is the status of a fragile victim, destined for a future marred by the long term effect of caregiving likely to strengthen a child's self-esteem and capacity to resist adversities? Or can we offer a more positive model of how to support children and families affected by parental disability and illness?

Supporting Children and Families

The key issue is whether the child's welfare or development might suffer if support is not provided to the child or family.

(Department of Health, 2000.)

Key Points

● Encounters with illness and disablement are a normative, rather than an atypical experience for many children, particularly children living in more disadvantaged communities.

● The impact on children of parental illness and disability is greatly intensified by the presence of aggravating factors, particularly poverty and a lack of social support networks.

● While no systematic relationship between types of parental illness or disability and a specific child response can be proposed with confidence, maternal psychological disorders are a greater potential cause of concern than physical illnesses or disabilities, especially where lone parenthood is a factor.

● The most powerful mediating factor in children's welfare is the quality of parenting. Supportive interventions which promote a parent's ability to care for their children are likely to be the most effective single mode of assistance.

● The potential of well brothers and sisters to help their ill or disabled siblings is greatly under-exploited, and greatly under-reported in the literature.

● The capacity of children to resist adversities has been under-estimated, as has their capacity for recovery.

● The promotion of resilience in children is a key factor in boosting levels of self-esteem, and improving emotional health and wellbeing.

● Whole family support is the preferred option, in terms of its being able to deliver better outcomes for both parent and child.

● An intervention framework, based on an ecological application of the concept of resilience, enjoys the most robust support as an effective method of ensuring resources are applied to families where children are affected by parental or sibling incapacity.

The mixed evidence of the impact of parental illness and disability on children, the tensions between the constructs of the competent and the vulnerable child, and the inflation of concern over the alleged dangers facing children have been discussed in previous chapters. However, none of the foregoing negates the proposition that, for some children, and for many families, parental illness and disability, especially where associated with an excessive caregiving role requires an efficient and competent welfare response. In discussing what this response might be, we are faced with the difficulty that very little empirical evidence exists as to the effectiveness of strategies used by social welfare services to help children of disabled parents and their families. This chapter summarises the information we have, the kinds of knowledge which we need to acquire, and discusses, from the limited information we have available, which approaches enjoy the strongest support.

The evidence discussed so far can be briefly summarised as follows. While parental disability, most notably psychological illnesses, is associated with some long term effects on children's psycho-social wellbeing, these effects are mediated by factors other than the nature of the parental illness of disability; notably socio-economic circumstances, parenting style and social capital. On a broader canvas, the way in which 'disability' is perceived socially – as a personal tragedy, an object of charitable concern, or as just an unremarkable feature of human diversity – will have an equally, and many would argue more important impact on affected children and adults. There is less convincing evidence for any degradation in health associated with sibling disorders. These observations must be set against the finding that encounters with illness and disablement are normative experiences for many, if not most, children, especially in more disadvantaged communities. Where we have specific information about family-based caregiving activities, some dimensions of children's wellbeing appear affected, specifically emotional health, with evidence that this may affect school performance, and self-esteem. Successful child welfare interventions will achieve positive change in these dimensions. How should child welfare services address this issue?

Evidence-based Practice

As in other professions, it is important that professionally qualified social workers base their practice on the best evidence of what works for clients and are responsive to new ideas from research.

(Department of Health, 1998b.)

It is suggested that investment in the fields of both health and social welfare should be based on evidence that an intervention is capable of positively altering the natural history of a problem (Cochrane, 1972). Evidence-based practice seeks to reduce variation in theory and practice where there are compelling reasons to choose one approach over another. Activities which add value to the welfare of children should be promoted and replicated, those which appear to do no good, or which cause harm, should be avoided. This approach requires judgements to be made about the validity of particular theories and forms of

practice. Meaning well does not inevitably translate into doing well (MacDonald, 1997) and the consequences for children of ineffective interventions may be damaging (McCord, 1978). Evidence-based practice tends to demand higher levels of verification from professionals that their activities are, indeed, resulting in better outcomes for their users. Claims of large effects tend to be associated with weaker methodologies. In addition, studies which suggest that interventions have poor or no results are published less frequently and there is a tendency to inflate the importance of studies that confirm *a priori* beliefs. An evidence-based approach also emphasises the need to encourage expressions of uncertainty, on the grounds that it is the function of scientific enquiry to continually challenge authoritarian views in order to improve our basis for planning and acting (Chalmers, 1983).

This approach depends on both an ability and a willingness to diminish intuitive approaches to problem solving and to appraise evidence critically (Gambrill, 1990). Critical thinking in the context of an evidence-based approach requires our making fair demands for verification from those promoting a particular course of action (Gibbs and Gambrill, 1996).

Users' Views

There is little dispute that the views of users are crucial to the delivery of effective child welfare services (Alderson, 1995). Continual dissonance between research evidence and the views of users may raise serious questions about the relevance of the intervention being tested. A variety of methods have been suggested to overcome this, including the use of focus groups (Bradburn et al., 1995) and the participation of children in research design (Boyden and Ennew, 1997). In many cases, interventions may be justified on the basis of positive user accounts alone, especially where no harmful effects are likely, the views of all users involved in the programme (including drop-outs) are solicited and no obvious alternative is present. Equally however, regarding users' views on the effectiveness of an intervention as the sole criterion ignores a substantial body of evidence (MacDonald et al., 1992) on the poor correlation between the strength of user approval and the impact of the intervention when measured by third parties.

Evidence-based practice is not widely discussed in relation to the children of disabled parents, though one recent text on the subject acknowledges that positive advances 'will only be possible if both policy and practice become more evidence-based than they are at present' (Becker et al., 1998). This is not unusual. The majority of research published in dedicated social work journals is devoted to descriptive and theoretical issues. Few studies address the relationship between interventions and outcomes and fewer still are described in detail sufficient to permit replication (Rosen et al., 1999). For example, only five outcome studies, from 356 articles, none featuring controlled trials, appeared in the UK's premier social work journal, the British Journal of Social Work, in the decade 1990-9 (Sheldon and MacDonald, 1999). Findings from evaluative studies are subject to a number of typical sources of bias, among these being the strong tendency for internal, self-evaluated work to claim a greater problem-solving efficacy than studies carried out externally by independent researchers (Gorey, 1996).

Methodological disputes among researchers notwithstanding, it is clear that substantial investment by government in specific areas of social welfare is only likely to occur in domains that have been subject to robust investigation and where clear implications for practice have emerged. Recent examples of this are in the fields of youth justice and pre-school services, where the establishment of Youth Offending Teams and the Sure Start programmes respectively have been able to draw on substantial evidence from experimental research that contain encouraging findings on the effectiveness of specific strategies (for example, Furniss, 1998; MacDonald and Roberts, 1995, respectively). It seems unlikely, in a climate where both health and social welfare investment is increasingly contingent on prior evidence of effectiveness, that any population served by child welfare services can attract substantial, long term support, without more robust evidence that the children served actually accrue significant benefits.

Taking account of this brief outline of what an evidence-based practice approach might require, how can this help us answer the question 'what works best for children of disabled parents'? One of the consequences of constructing powerful social identities, indeed one of the strategies for accomplishing this construction, is the minimisation of within-group differences and a corresponding stress on between-group differences. As a result, both the members of the social group, and those observing it, will develop a tendency to make attributions of cause and effect to the key characteristics associated with the group, with less consideration of other explanations.

Jumping to Conclusions

A major concern of services that support children of disabled parents is to draw the attention of teachers and others working within the field of education to their situation. This is not an unreasonable strategy; teachers encounter children with a far greater degree of frequency than most childcare workers. The relationship between school absences and educational attainment is, however, not as obvious as it first appears. A number of cohort studies (for example, Douglas and Ross, 1965; Fogelman and Richardson, 1974) have found no simple relationship between absences and attainment, with the association holding for children in lower socio-economic groups, but being absent for children with fathers in professional and managerial classes. Bullying is also a problem faced by many children and disproportionately affects vulnerable children with visible impairments or other non-valued attributes, who are already likely to be suffering from low self-esteem, high anxiety and depressive conditions. The proposition that characteristics associated with an atypical family, especially where family crisis is present, may inflate a child's vulnerability to bullying, is well supported by the literature (Salmon et al., 1998). A meta-analysis of peer victimisation studies leaves little doubt as to the negative impact of bullying on children's psychosocial adjustment with a heightened vulnerability to depression being the worrying factor (Hawker and Bolton, 2000). Not surprisingly, bullying is widely reported as an adversity affecting young carers. However, studies to date, while highlighting this issue, have typically conflated different variables – child caregiving, parental illness or disability, poverty, individual characteristics of the child – and attributed any increased exposure to bullying to 'young carer' status (Crabtree and Warner, 1999). In order to avoid a false perception of causal processes, some consideration of how and why we may jump to conclusions is necessary.

Attributional bias

Attribution theory suggests that people's behaviour is influenced by the kinds of inferences individuals make about the motives of others; what has caused someone to act in a particular way, why they possess certain characteristics, why they have succeeded or failed (Bukatko and Daehler, 1995). The functioning of an attributional framework is critical to the growing child's psychological development, notably to the growth of self-esteem and self-efficacy, in that the child infers causality regarding personal success or failure from the feedback they receive, and this in turn influences patterns of thinking and subsequent behaviour (Weiner et al., 1971).

This has particular pertinence to the main health-related issue that emerged from the survey described in Chapter 5, the apparently degraded levels in self-esteem of children of disabled parents. The relevance of attribution theory to these young people is the tendency of adults to infer causality from the perceived characteristics of actors in specific social roles (Dix and Grusec, 1985; Harris et al., 1992). If, for example, we assume that parental disability or illness is associated with child depression, inflated school absences and poor educational attainment, then, when we encounter a child who has a disabled parent, is depressed, is missing school, and has poor exam results, we will be more likely to assume this causal relationship and less likely to seek alternative explanations. Studying older children of disabled parents, Wates (1997) noted that a high proportion of them were receiving child guidance. Was this, she queried,

because children of disabled parents have more emotional problems, or because children whose parents are in regular contact with health and welfare services are more likely to come to the attention of staff?

Attribution theory and self-esteem

This model is important to the ways in which children develop a belief that they can affect (or not affect) their circumstances, and thus to the emergence of the factor highlighted in Chapter 5 as the main deficit in the health profile of children of disabled parents, low self-esteem. A consistent pattern of negative attribution, 'I could do nothing about it'; 'even when I succeed, it's just luck', as opposed to positive attribution, 'I can do it next time if I try harder'; 'I'm much better than people think I am', is likely to result in a belief that what happens is independent of volition, a phenomenon described as 'learned helplessness' (Seligman, 1975). Where the natural instincts of children towards the mastery of competencies are thwarted by continual failure or insufficient reward for success, the result is typically lack of motivation accompanied by depressive disorders. Optimism in young children appears to be an instinctive response; at age five a child will typically over-estimate its ability to accomplish tasks and will exaggerate their achievements, a tendency that diminishes from around the age of seven (Dweck and Elliot, 1983). This phenomenon was well illustrated by the steep decline in child perceptions of the volume of help delivered to parents from age seven to 11 and then again at 15 years, in the Welsh school survey data described in Chapter 5.

We can thus infer that the mastery of tasks and the reinforcement of adaptive behaviour through recognition and praise are key protective factors in resisting negative attributions by children. Learned optimism mediates the growth of self-esteem and we could expect from this model that children who were given the opportunity to occupy socially valued roles, were enabled to succeed in them, and were rewarded accordingly, would have correspondingly higher levels of self-esteem than children not given such opportunities. Encouragingly, there is compelling evidence that such attributional patterns are not immutable and that social processes, rather than cognition, is the key mediating factor (Durkin, 1995). Given the opportunity, sufficient support and adequate rewards, children can unlearn destructive thinking and learn to make attributions that will enhance rather than degrade their self-esteem.

Effective Interventions

> *As in other areas of pediatric psychology, empirical studies of interventions that ameliorate the effects of parental health risks on children and families lag behind descriptive studies.*
>
> (Drotar, 1994.)

The disproportionate generation of explanatory rather than applied knowledge is not confined to sociological disciplines. The impact of serious illness on children has been extensively explored in clinical literature, yet reviews of the effects on children of disease have found relatively few studies with immediate practice implications (La Greca and Varni, 1993). Interventions aimed at children are often similar despite addressing the differing problems of parental, sibling or child illnesses (Wallender and Varni 1998).

Social and emotional support

A number of robust studies have illustrated that social and emotional support can offer protection against premature mortality, prevent illness and diminish levels of emotional stress (Berkman and Syme, 1979; House et al., 1988). Communication within families about the nature of parental illness is a protector against distress for children (Barnes et al., 1998), and even young children are able to reach a detailed understanding of disease (Eiser, 1994). Despite the impact on children of maternal depression, and the known efficacy of social support in helping mothers through periods of illness (Johnson et al., 1993; Oakley, 1993), childcare social workers have not provided interventions with depressed mothers which differ in any respect from interventions in families where maternal depression is not present (Sheppard, 1997). Intensive, highly trained social support does not appear to differ

markedly in its impact from less intensive approaches; no significant changes were found in child or maternal functioning in the Threshold Mothers Project in Chicago compared to a less expensive and less intensive home care programme (Stott et al., 1984). In one of the few randomised controlled trials carried out in this area, clinic-based interventions rather than lecture group discussions proved more effective in promoting the resistance of children with affectively ill mothers to depressive disorders (Beardslee et al., 1997a; 1997b). Some protective actions do not rely on any particular clinical skills; for example the maintenance of familiar family rituals, such as communal meals, have been associated with positive long term consequences for children living with alcoholic parents (Bennett et al., 1987).

However, the most consistent body of evidence suggests strongly that parental functioning is the most heavily weighted factor on which children's adjustment depends and thus the main focus of intervention should be on parental support (Sandler et al., 1997). Some studies aimed at reducing emotional disturbance in children have concluded that only interventions involving the mother's participation had any appreciable positive effect on children (Lucas et al., 1984). The end product, however, is not parental adjustment but the child's enhanced capacity to cope with stress. We have consistent evidence that parental and extra familial support to children affected by parental illness is the most important source of stress-buffering (Kotchick et al., 1997). Social support to parents, by relieving parental stress, will make it less likely that the child will witness parents confronted by uncontrollable events and hence reduce the child's exposure to situations where their main sources of support appear impotent. Where social support to the child, whether from parents, the wider family or external sources, is directed at increasing the child's ability to exert more control over events, we can expect the child's experience of stress to decrease as self control increases. The mechanism driving this cognitive restructuring is the increase in the child's ability to attribute failure or unwanted consequences to internal rather than external factors. Social support thus has the capacity to help them make realistic assessments of their capacity to influence a situation and help them make positive attributions – 'my own effort is the main factor in this situation' – rather than negative ones – 'it doesn't matter what I do, it's going to happen anyway' (Sandler et al., 1989).

Serving the whole family

> *Services providing support should not undermine the parent's ability to parent or make the child feel that he or she has failed.*
>
> (Department of Health, 2000.)

That psycho-social support has the capacity to meet the needs of adult carers enjoys some qualified support, though the impacts appear greater on the affected person rather than the carer. For example, increased compliance with medication regimes and fewer relapses was noted by a systematic review into family interventions for schizophrenia (Mari and Streiner, 1996) and replicated by a more recent randomised controlled trial (Barrowclough et al., 1999), the latter finding corresponding decreases in carer needs compared to a control group. Neither research nor services which treat carer and cared-for as entirely separate entities can be entirely satisfactory, a factor recognised by the call in the Carers Act practice guidelines (Department of Health, 1996) for 'an integrated family-based approach which does not see either the service user or carer in isolation' (p1).

While some support services to families with disabled parents take account of whole family issues, their main focus remains the child, rather than the family. A recent review by the Social Services Inspectorate of services supporting disabled parents emphasised this point:

> *The focus of staff appeared to be either on the children in the family or on the impact of the adults' disability on their personal needs. Workers rarely looked beyond this and seldom focused on the whole family and how to support and help the parents in the discharge of their parental duties in their social setting.*
>
> (Goodinge, 2000.)

It is a common belief in the voluntary sector (Aldridge and Becker, 1998) that non-statutory family support is more easily accepted by parents. However, questions were raised in this review as to the extent to which dedicated young carer services might reinforce parental anxiety that local authorities would be unreasonably judgmental about their parenting abilities. Despite this fear being raised by some parents and children during the course of this review, the majority of families who were in direct contact with local authority social service departments were satisfied with the service received, reporting 'that services had helped them to stay together' (ibid.). From this perspective, we might query to what degree the emphasis on the *rights* of children impedes the development of approaches which address the whole family situation when the biggest single factor contributing to the health and wellbeing of children is the capacity of their parents to provide effective care. Focusing on the support needs of families is thus indicated by both research evidence and policy guidance, especially where an excessive concern with protecting the child from any 'toxic' effects of disablement or illness may lead to the undermining of parenting capacity.

Learned optimism

Children are not passive templates on which outcomes are etched, but have the capacity to actively play a part in shaping their own responses to family stress. The changing of children's patterns of thinking from negative to positive through the medium of cognitive behavioural therapy (Seligman, 1998) has been implemented with some success in the Penn Prevention Programme (delivered to a general not a clinical population), which found a 50 per cent drop in levels of depression in the intervention group and no change in the control, where both groups had identical baseline profiles. Strategies involved the use of comic strip characters ('Hopeful Howard', 'Gloomy Greg', 'Pessimistic Penny', and 'Say-it-Straight Samantha'), role playing, games, discussions and videos, in a 12 week programme. This type of intervention is highly relevant to the promotion of effective coping. Coping styles, as described in the influential work of Lazarus and colleagues (Folkman and Lazarus, 1980; Lazarus and Folkman, 1984) may be of two kinds:

- **Problem-solving coping:** developing skills, suppressing irrelevant activities, seeking information and planning is thought to be more effective in that it involves the affected person taking active control of the situation.

- **Emotion-focused coping** reduces emotional stress and has a supportive function, but is less adaptive in that it fails to address long term issues, though it may be inevitable in situations where the individual has no control over their circumstances.

While for children affected by parental illness information and support-based interventions based on groupwork may be effective (see, for example, Greening, 1992; Walsh-Burke, 1992, on children affected by parental cancer), the promotion of emotion-focused coping needs, in order for a child to actively manage their situation, needs to be complemented by programmes that enhance problem-solving also. Support services to children of disabled parents tend to be stronger on the former, but weaker on the latter, driven, perhaps, by a belief that children should not have to cope with and solve problems. The extent to which children are able to affect the course or texture of the adversities they encounter should influence the nature of the intervention. A focus on children's own capacity to cope in some situations will be justified; in others, interventions are likely to be more effective if they also seek to manipulate factors in the external environment (Roosa et al., 1997).

Resilience and Self-esteem

Perhaps the best, albeit the most depressing, example of how the indiscriminate application of welfare can teach pessimism and weaken the innate resilience of populations is the catastrophic social impact of aid programmes following the Chernobyl nuclear accident in 1986. An authoritative report prepared for the United Nations concluded that the negative impact on morbidity and mortality of strategies intended to help the affected population was greater than the accident itself:

> ...the Chernobyl accident led to a wide range of psychological problems including a sense of being a victim; a sense of social exclusion; lack of initiative; a low level of adaptation to the new environment and an expectation of external support. Significantly, the state of mind of the victims was not connected to their objective living conditions. This situation has produced a culture in which ill health is the expectation for many people, including doctors, nurses and teachers; a phenomenon particularly prevalent where children are concerned.

(United Nations Development Programme/UNICEF 2002.)

The populations that suffered most were those that allowed themselves to be resettled away from the affected areas, to become dependent on welfare payments and to internalise their status as victims. Families who refused to leave fared better; best of all in terms of health outcomes were those who were evacuated and then chose to return and resume their former occupations and way of life.

Resilience has been closely associated with gains in self-esteem (Newman 2002). While the study of coping and resilience has been increasingly well developed in psychology, it is less familiar in social work practice and where it is discussed, clinical skills are eschewed in preference to the undoubtedly important but basically procedural tasks of networking, collaboration, team-building and advocacy (Smith and Carlson, 1997). Despite this, resilience has been recently discussed in social work and allied journals in relation to sexual abuse (Spaccarelli and Kim, 1995), child maltreatment (Heller et al., 1999), the children of alcoholics (Palmer, 1997), child placement and children in need generally (Gilligan, 1997, 2000), children with emotional and behavioural difficulties (Lewis, 1999), looked after children (Jackson and Martin, 1998), family therapy (Rutter, 1999), personal development in schools (Raphael, 1993) and, more generally, as a conceptual framework for social work practice (Saleebey, 1996). As we have noted, the development of positive thinking in children is an important factor in protecting children against depressive disorders. There is considerable evidence that children's latent resilience can be stimulated by interventions aimed at promoting learned optimism through the medium of cognitive restructuring

(Seligman, 1998). This is particularly important in the case of young people such as young carers, whose circumstances may render then vulnerable to pessimistic cognitive styles of thinking, resulting in, as we have seen, lowered levels of self-esteem.

Balancing factors associated with caregiving

As we have discussed, much of the concern about children of disabled parents is based on the proposition that their circumstances may have both immediate and long term effects on their health and development. While we must be cautious in drawing parallels between adult and child experiences, the general issue of the impact of caring on emotional and psychological health is of clear importance. Caregiving cannot, it appears, be measured by a single construct: both positive and negative outcomes are reported, frequently by the same respondents. While caregivers experience stress, physical ailments and psychological problems (Baumgarten et al., 1992), positive outcomes such as satisfaction, increased wellbeing and emotional strength are also reported (Brody et al., 1995). It appears therefore, that in some situations – and we must recognise that all adult, let alone child, caregiving situations are not the same – enhancing the *positive* effect experienced by the caregiver will reduce the impact of any caregiving-induced stress, despite the level of care remaining the same.

The actual process of caring has been ascribed a negative role in terms of child development. Adult responsibilities, particularly when they are a source of status and rewards, can compromise, it has been suggested, a child's essential developmental opportunities (Johnston et al., 1992). However, these impacts tend to be diminished (by no means to the point of extinction) when methods of investigation are more robust. A key learning point highlighted by a comprehensive training resource for staff working with mentally ill parents and their children supported by the Department of Health (Falkov, 1998) made clear the need to both provide adequate levels of support, but also to enable the young person to retain the status as a skilled helper they may have earned:

Recognise the delicate balance between **provision of adequate support** *for children and young people who look after a parent who is mentally ill, whilst not removing* **the competency-enhancing responsibilities** *the young person has taken on [author's emphasis].*

(Falkov, 1998.)

Mixed messages

There are very few examples of child welfare interventions in this field that utilise experimental methodologies, though a few exceptions to this are beginning to appear in the literature. Taggart (1999), sought to measure the impact on children of disabled parents of two different services, with the addition of a non-intervention control, using a pre- post-measurement model and four validated instruments, the Adolescent Coping Scale, Self-Efficacy Scale, General wellbeing Index and the Significant Other Scale. Though small in scope (n=38), and conducted over a relatively short time period (four months), the study was able to identify some modest improvements in the psychological wellbeing of children involved in the education group, but none in the recreation group or control group, though no effect was noted on perceptions of social support, coping strategies or self-efficacy. The poor quality of much research is beginning to be recognised, as is the need to conduct studies that differentiate between types of caring roles and parental dependencies (Becker, 1999). Groupwork, for example is a common approach used in the majority of support services and has much promise, especially where group members have a common stress experience (Sandler et al. 1997). However, in this context, it remains almost entirely unevaluated, despite the relative ease with which pre- post-measurement designs may be utilised (for example, in relation to a cancer support group, see Magen and Glajchen, 1999). 'Befriending' features as a service offered by a large number of dedicated services (Aldridge and Becker, 1998). Some narrative accounts report positive feedback by children on its value (Traynor, 1999). However, the effectiveness of this activity also remains largely unevaluated, despite some cautionary evidence from other fields, where the creation of artificial friendships has been found to be both transient (Hughes, 1999) and in some cases, to jeopardise existing friendship networks (Bayley, 1997). The range of services provided by dedicated services to children of disabled parents are widely reproduced nationally, but is unclear to what extent these approaches are selected with specific child outcomes in mind, or to what extent they simply reflect the available skills, resources and intuitive beliefs current in the services themselves. Where the possibility of unintended consequences is present, such as undermining parental competencies or reducing the likelihood that social support might be provided, a more explicit relationship between activities and outcomes is clearly warranted.

The Theft of Childhood

A powerful theme runs throughout narratives, both factual and fictional, where children encounter stressful family situations: adversities tend to make children grow up faster. The titles of many associated studies are sufficient in themselves to illustrate this tendency: *Stolen Youth* (Lyall, 1989); *You Grow up Fast as Well* (Bilsborrow, 1992); *My Child, My Carer* (Aldridge and Becker, 1994a); *On Small Shoulders* (Frank et al., 1999); *Too Much to Take On* (Crabtree and Warner, 1999). This is not in dispute; what is in contention is the extent to which this should be a cause for public concern, and which dimensions of premature maturity we should strive to inhibit. As we have noted, there is substantial evidence that, within limits, both adversities and helping others may have positive long term consequences for children. Where tasks fall within the developmental capacity of children and are valued and rewarded, required helpfulness (Rachman, 1978) may result in increased personal strengths. The specific tasks of caring for siblings, helping sick parents and undertaking part-time work have been identified as protective factors in a range of influential studies (Elder, 1974; Bleuler, 1978; Garmezy, 1985; Werner and Smith, 1992). Conversely, unsupported, excessive and undervalued activities, especially when compounded by multiple and continuous adversities, are unlikely to result in positive outcomes. Our conclusion must thus be a cautious one. Both ignoring the consequences of excessive premature responsibility *and* exaggerating its impacts are likely to result in adverse consequences for children. However, the largest volume of commentary on this issue has, by far, erred on the side of exaggeration. We have limited evidence, due to the absence of data from cohort studies, as to the long term effect of premature responsibilities, though evidence from the psycho-therapeutic literature suggests that where these are linked with severe family pathology, negative outcomes may occur. Conversely, there is some evidence of the effects of excessive *dependency*. The Berkeley Guidance Study, a cohort study initiated in 1928-9, suggested that men with a history of childhood dependency were more likely to follow stable occupational, educational and marital patterns but be less ambitious for success:

> *It may be that childhood dependency fosters the internalization of societal norms about reliability and competence in the workplace, but it does not provide an extra push towards achievement.*
>
> (Caspi et al., 1990.)

Trade-offs occur in terms of dependency and independence, risk and protection. Accelerated emotional or functional competencies in one area may be balanced by compromised development in others. However, there is compelling evidence that the paramount protective factor for children is the relationship they have with their primary carer. Children's psychological health largely depends, not on professional support, but on the quality of their relationships with friends and family. Similarly, the most common reasons for psychological disorders stem from conflicts and loss associated with a child's family or peer relationships (Mental Health Foundation, 1999). Interventions that enhance these relationships will promote the child's welfare. Conversely, child welfare activities that weaken, undermine or threaten the parental bond will have the opposite effect.

Getting the Balance Right

No supportive service is likely to fundamentally change the ambiguous relationship within families between minors and dependent adults. Children who provide elements of care, emotional or physical, for adults may see their role as both gratifying and burdensome, their school as both oppressive and supportive, and may simultaneously feel a need to fulfil obligations and for personal gratification (Lackey and Gates, 1997). However, social work, like medicine, is largely preoccupied with unhappiness, pain and loss. Both disciplines seek to identify effective interventions, yet also need to be concerned with the potentially harmful effects of intervention. Child welfare interventions are justified when children are exposed to harm or the risk of harm. The obligations of social services departments are clear; if a child's health or development is likely to suffer without the provision of support, there is an obligation to provide help. The National Carers Strategy (Department of Health, 1999a) requires local authorities to identify children with extra family burdens which result in these risks being present.

A very high proportion of support services for children of disabled parents depend on short term funding. The longevity of funding sources in a competitive welfare market will inevitably have consequences for the way in which services are structured and, in particular, for the client group served. Security of funding is typically related to the extent to which children are perceived as likely to suffer if an intervention is unavailable. A welfare trajectory which stresses potential harm and diminishes potential benefit will be more likely to drive the issue from its current position as an essentially supportive service to children in need (and to varying degrees, their parents), towards the other end of the child care continuum as a service for children at risk. As illustrated in earlier chapters, the boundary between children of disabled parents as children 'in need' and children 'at risk' is permeable. The concerns of ill and disabled parents that asking for help may result in their being judged and found wanting are not, from this perspective, unreasonable. On which part of the

continuum any family is placed, will depend whether children are judged to be in 'essentially exploitative caring relationships resistant to change' (Aldridge and Becker, 1999). However, a loose epidemiological definition will lead to increased claims of prevalence, accompanied, inevitably, by increased numbers of children judged to be at the 'at risk' end of the spectrum.

Volume of demand being a key element in whether sustained financial support may be forthcoming, the adoption of broader definitions of who may be 'in need' clearly has the effect of inflating potential demand and hence the urgency of the support requested. Preceding chapters have noted how, despite decreases in physical illnesses, the health of the nation, as measured by the perceptions of its citizens, has steadily declined over the last generation. As self-defined parental illness increases in prevalence, and the threshold of what is considered a legitimate childhood helping task weakens, then clearly the proportion of children in the UK who may attract an 'in need' label will increase proportionately. Indeed, some four million children in England, over one in three of the child population, are now regarded by the Department of Health as 'vulnerable' (Department of Health, 2000). Whereas the potentially damaging impact of interventive social work services may be recognised, for example in the fields of child protection or youth justice, the proposition that supportive services may have unwanted consequences is not one that is typically considered. If we proceed on the basis that a bigger child 'in need' population is better for the health and welfare of children than a smaller one, we are conceding that more welfare is better than less. A broad definition of, for example, an emotional or behavioural problem will, according to this approach, result in more children being served and more overall health gain. However, the distribution curve of any population will include a proportion at the more serious or challenging end. The bigger the total population, the bigger this more demanding group. As we have seen in the USA, and more recently in the UK, the substantial increase in the numbers of children being prescribed stimulant medication has followed the larger numbers of children who are now classified as having emotional and behavioural disorders serious enough to warrant intervention. The activities of social work services at tier one in terms of problem definition are thus intimately connected to clinical interventions at tiers two and three. Bluntly, while the relationship may not be symmetrical, more talking at one end will result in more drugs at the other.

Is our message, then, *don't worry and do nothing*? Certainly not. It is clear that some parental impairment may heighten the risk of negative outcomes for children, even with the presence of effective support services. However, two elements appear necessary for the impact on the child to cause significant harm. Firstly, the parental incapacity must be compounded by additional environmental adversities and particularly by a parenting style of low warmth and high criticism, and by marital conflict. Secondly, the parental incapacity must be considerable, with parental mental illness being a crucial factor. Little evidence exists of significant psycho-social damage to children resulting from exposure to the disability or illness of siblings; in fact, with the exception again of extreme examples, the psycho-social *benefits* to children of sibling care appear to be equal to any detected deficits.

Conclusion

> People classified in a certain way tend to conform or to grow into the ways they are described.
>
> (Hacking, 1995.)

While the situation of children living with disabled parents is by no means the only dimension of child welfare practice where the rights of children can collide with the rights of those who care for them, it is clear that we have different degrees of concern with the welfare of the well and with the welfare of the sick. Our preoccupation with the impact of the sick on the well, the problems caused to healthy organisms by diseased, impaired or disturbed others, and how we can moderate or eliminate their impact, illustrate the different values that we attach to health status. Where parental disability or

illness occasions 'caring', which impairs, or has the potential to impair, a child's health and development, we are obliged, under section 17(10) of the 1989 Children Act, to consider an appropriate intervention. However, it is clear that the *direct* association between family disability and illness, and diminished levels of child wellbeing is no more than moderate; additional factors are necessary to endanger child health. There is also persuasive evidence that salutogenic approaches to health gain are greatly under-utilised by child welfare services and furthermore, that children's health may be actively degraded by an excessive focus on identifying and neutralising potential risk factors.

The construction by professionals of a 'young carer' identity is only partially related to the way in which young people themselves perceive their roles. The imputation of a sick or victim role to a person, or class of people, has considerable contemporary resonance. The pathologising of a range of conditions previously treated as part of the normative range of human behaviour, and the corresponding broadening of definitional bases are increasingly common in both health and social care (Summerfield, 2000; 2002). The 'young carer' phenomenon, aside from any specific characteristics it possesses, is part of an overall Western cultural trend of growth in the accepted range of potential traumatic stressors. Concern about caregiving by children has become almost exclusively associated with parental incapacity rather, as in earlier times, economic necessity. This concern has emerged within the context of a growing emphasis on children's rights, the detection of previously undiscovered continents of child distress, their subsequent colonisation by health and social welfare agencies, and an intensified belief in children's vulnerability.

That, in many cases, severe parental incapacity, especially when compounded by poverty, lack of support from relatives and inadequate statutory support results in distress and inappropriate demands on children is incontestable, and is certainly not disputed here. Even if severe long term harm to children is unlikely, this is no excuse for not paying attention to current suffering. However, our conclusion must be that some professional stocktaking is urgently required. Problematising phenomena previously thought of as 'normal', or promoting moderate difficulties as major ones, has not, to date, resulted in detectable improvements in children's heath and wellbeing. Rather than seek to widen the range and number of children to whom a label may be applied, an approach more conscious of the potential dangers of offering an adult-generated identity to children seems advisable. We have no knowledge, to date, of the distal effect of offering children a powerful social identity at a tender age. Will children's future life trajectories, their educational, vocational and social achievements, as well as their health and wellbeing, be enhanced or impeded by early social labelling?

We simply do not know, and are unlikely to learn more until longitudinal data are available. Until our knowledge base broadens and deepens, the Hippocratic exhortation to do no harm should assume a higher profile in the consciousness of those commissioning, managing and delivering support services to disabled children and their families. In the meantime, the welfare of children may be better served by the more parsimonious application of professional labels, more emphasis on the recuperative powers of children and their ability to cope with and even benefit from adversities, and a more honest appraisal of whether our sentimentalisation of childhood is part of the solution – or part of the problem.

Appendix 1

Health Questionnaire (Junior)

School _____   Year _____

Thank you for helping us. We are trying to find out how many children in [town] need extra help at home.

Don't write down your name.

All you have to do is fill in your age and tick the boxes.

1. How old are you?   ____

2. Which are you   A boy   ____
                                             A girl   ____

3. Who else lives in your house?   Mum   ____
                                             Dad   ____
                                             Brother   ____
                                             Sister   ____
                                             Grandparent   ____

4. How often do you...?

	Most of the time	Some of the time	None of the time
N12 want to be by yourself	☐	☐	☐
N13 want a rest from doing things	☐	☐	☐
N14 not want to go to school	☐	☐	☐
N15 not want to go home from school	☐	☐	☐

5.   Do you think that...?

	Agree a lot	Agree a bit	Don't agree
N16 if you try hard things will work out for the best	☐	☐	☐
N17 I can do what I want most of the time	☐	☐	☐
N18 I worry a lot about other people	☐	☐	☐

6.   How often do you...?

	Most of the time	Some of the time	None of the time
N19 feel happy	☐	☐	☐
N20 worry about someone who is ill	☐	☐	☐
N21 feel lonely	☐	☐	☐
N22 feel unhappy	☐	☐	☐
N23 have fun	☐	☐	☐

7.   How often do you...?

	A lot	A bit	Never
N24 tidy the house	☐	☐	☐
N25 do the washing up	☐	☐	☐
look after brothers or sisters	☐	☐	☐
do things for a grown up who is ill	☐	☐	☐

8.   If you could have ONE wish come true, what would it be?

_____

_____

Thank you very much for your help.

Health Questionnaire (Senior)

School _____   Year _____

Thank you for helping us. We are trying to find out how many young people in [town] need extra help at home. We are collecting information from a lot of schools. Some of the questions may seem a bit personal. That's why we don't want to know your name.

All you have to do is fill in your age and tick the boxes.

1.   How old are you?   ____

2.   Which are you?   A boy   ____
                                              A girl   ____

3.   Who else lives in your house?   Mum   ____
                                             Dad   ____
                                             Brother(s)   ____
                                             Sister(s)   ____
                                             Grandparent ____
                                             Other   ____

4.   How often in the past four weeks have you...?

	All the time	Most of the time	Some of the time	None of the time
N11 had a hard time paying attention in school	☐	☐	☐	☐
N12 wanted to be by yourself	☐	☐	☐	☐
N13 wanted a rest from having to do things	☐	☐	☐	☐
N14 not wanted to go to school	☐	☐	☐	☐
N15 not wanted to go home from school	☐	☐	☐	☐

5.   How much do you agree...?

	Agree a lot	Agree a bit	Don't agree at all
N16 if you try hard things will work out for the best	☐	☐	☐
N17 I'm in charge of my own life	☐	☐	☐
N18 I can do what I want most of the time	☐	☐	☐
N19 sometimes I feel jealous of my friends	☐	☐	☐
N20 I worry a lot about other people	☐	☐	☐

6. How often in the past 4 weeks did you...?

	All the time	Most of the time	Some of the time	None of the time
N21 feel sad	☐	☐	☐	☐
N22 feel happy	☐	☐	☐	☐
N23 worry about someone who is poorly	☐	☐	☐	☐
N24 feel lonely	☐	☐	☐	☐
N25 feel unhappy	☐	☐	☐	☐
N26 have fun	☐	☐	☐	☐
N27 have trouble sleeping	☐	☐	☐	☐
N28 feel good about yourself	☐	☐	☐	☐

7.   Do you do any jobs for money?   Yes   _____
                                           No   _____

If you said YES, what kind of job is it?

newspaper round   _____
milk round   _____
work in shop   _____
helping at home   _____
other   _____

8.   Some young people help with...

	This is a lot like me	This is a bit like me	This is not like me
N35 tidying the house	☐	☐	☐
N36 doing the washing up	☐	☐	☐
looking after brothers or sisters	☐	☐	☐
looking after a grown up who is poorly	☐	☐	☐

9.   If you could have ONE wish come true, what would it be?

_____

_____

Thank you very much for your help.

Bibliography

Ackerman, R.J. and Gondolf, E.W. (1991) Adult Children of Alcoholics: The Effects of Background and Treatment of ACOA Symptoms. *International Journal of Addiction*, 26(11): p1159–72.

Ahmad, W.I.U. (1996) Family Obligations and Social Change Among Asian Communities. In Ahmad, W.I.U. and Atkin, K. (Eds.) *'Race' and Community Care.* Buckingham: Open University Press.

Albert, S.M. (1990) Care Giving as a Cultural System: Conceptions of Filial Obligation and Parental Dependency in Urban America. *American Anthropologist*, 92(2): p319–31.

Alderson, P. (1995) *Listening to Children: Children, Ethics and Social Research.* Barkingside, Barnardo's.

Aldridge, J. and Becker, S. (1993a) *Children Who Care: Inside the World of Young Carers.* Loughborough University, Department of Social Sciences.

Aldridge, J. and Becker, S. (1993b) Children as Carers. *Archives of Disease in Childhood*, 69: p459–62.

Aldridge, J. and Becker, S. (1994a) *My Child, My Carer: The Parent's Perspective.* Loughborough: Loughborough University Department of Social Sciences.

Aldridge, J. and Becker, S. (1994b) *A Friend Indeed: The Case for Befriending Young Carers.* Loughborough: Loughborough University Young Carers Research Group.

Aldridge, J. and Becker, S. (1996a) *Befriending Young Carers: A Pilot Study.* Loughborough: Loughborough University Department of Social Sciences and Calouste Gulbenkian Foundation.

Aldridge, J. and Becker, S. (1998) *The National Handbook of Young Carers' Projects.* London: Carers National Association.

Aldridge, J. and Becker, S. (1999) Children as Carers: The Impact of Parental Illness and Disability on Children's Caring Roles. *Journal of Family Therapy*, 21: p303–20.

Alexander, H. (1995) *Young Carers and HIV.* Edinburgh: Children in Scotland.

Alexander, P.C. (1992) Application of Attachment Theory to the Study of Sexual Abuse. *Journal of Consulting Clinical Psychology*, 60(2): p182–95.

Armistead, L., Klein, K. and Forehand, R. (1995) Parental Physical Illness and Child Functioning. *Clinical Psychology Review*, 15(5): p409–22.

Arnaud, S.H. (1959) Some Psychological Characteristics of Children of Multiple Sclerotics. *Psychosomatic Medicine*, 21: p8–22.

Astil, D. (1998) Young Carers Research 'Youcare 98'. *Journal of Young Carers Work*, 1:, p31–2.

Atkin, K, and Rollings, J. (1996) Looking After Their Own? Family Care Giving Among Asian and Afro-Caribbean Communities. In Ahmad, W.I.U. and Atkin, K. (Eds.) *'Race' and Community Care.* Buckingham: Open University Press.

Audit Commission (1999) *Children in Mind: Child and Adolescent Mental Health Services.* London, Audit Commission for Local Authorities and The National Health Service in England and Wales.

Bacciagaluppi, M. (1985) Inversion of Parent-Child Relationships: A Contribution to Attachment Theory. *British Journal of Medical Psychology*, 58(4): p369–73.

Banks, P., Cogan, N., Deeley, S., Hill, M., Riddell, S. and Tisdall, K. (2001) Seeing the Invisible Children and Young People Affected by Disability. *Disability and Society*, 16(6): p797–814.

Barnes, J., Kroll, L., Lee, J., Jones, A. and Stein, A. (1998) Communication About Parental Illness With Children Who Have Learning Disabilities and Behavioural Problems: Three Case Studies. *Child: Health, Care and Development*, 24(6): p441–56.

Barrett, M.L., Berney, T.P., Bhate, S., Famuyiwa, O.O., Fundudis, T., Kolvin, I. and Tyrer, S. (1991) Diagnosing Childhood Depression: Who Should Be Interviewed - Parent or Child? *British Journal of Psychiatry*, 159 (Supplement 11): p22–8.

Barrowclough, C., Tarrier, N., Lewis, S., Sellwood, W., Mainwaring, J., Quinn, J. and Hamlin, C. (1999) Randomised Controlled Effectiveness Trial of a Needs-Based Psycho-Social Intervention Service for Carers of People with Schizophrenia. *British Journal of Psychiatry*, 174: p505–11.

Barthes, R. (1972) Mythologies. London: Vintage.

Baskett, L.M. and Johnson, S.M. (1982) The Young Child's Interactions With Parents Versus Siblings: A Behavioural Analysis. *Child Development*, 53: p643–50.

Baumgarten, M., Battista, R.N., Infante-Rivard, C., Finley, J.A., Becker, R. and Gaythier, S. (1992) The Psychological and Physical Health of Family Members Caring for an Elderly Person with Dementia. *Journal of Clinical Epidemiology*, 45: p61–70.

Bayley, M. (1997) *What Price Friendship? Encouraging the Relationships of People with Learning Disabilities.* Minehead: Hexagon Publishing.

Beach, D. (1997) Family Caregiving: The Positive Impact on Adolescent Relationships. *Gerontologist*, 37: p233–8.

Beardslee, W.R., Bemporad, J., Keller, M. and Klerman, G. (1983) Children of Parents With Major Affective Disorder: A Review. *American Journal of Psychiatry*, 140(7): p825–31.

Beardslee, W.R., Keller, M.B., Lavori, P.W., Staley, J. and Sacks, N. (1993) The Impact of Parental Affective Disorder on Depression in Off-Spring: A Longitudinal Follow-Up in a Non-referred Sample. *Journal of The American Academy of Child and Adolescent Psychiatry*, 32(4): p723–30.

Beardslee, W.R., Versage, E.M., Wright; E.J., Salt, P., Rothberg, P.C., Drezner, K. and Gladstone, T.R. (1997a) Examination of Preventive Interventions for Families With Depression: Evidence of Change. *Developmental Psychopathology*, 9: p109–30.

Beardslee, W.R., Wright, E.J., Salt, P., Drezner, K., Gladstone, T.R., Versage, E.M. and Rothberg, P.C. (1997b) Examination of Children's Responses to Two Preventive Intervention Strategies over Time. *Journal of the American Academy of Child and Adolescent Psychiatry*, 36: p196–204.

Beardslee, W.R., Versage, E.M. and Gladstone, T.R. (1998) Children of Affectively Ill Parents: A Review of the Past 10 Years. *Journal of the American Academy of Child and Adolescent Psychiatry*, 37(11): p1134–41.

Beck, U. (1992) *Risk Society: Towards a New Modernity*. London: Sage.

Becker, S. (1999) Research Review. *Journal of Young Carers Work*, 3: October; p26–33.

Becker, S., Aldridge, J. and Dearden, C. (1998) *Young Carers and Their Families*. Oxford: Blackwell Science Ltd.

Becker, S., Dearden, C. and Aldridge, J. (2000) Young Carers in the UK: Research, Policy and Practice. *Research, Policy and Planning*, 18(2): p13–22.

Begg, N. and Gregor, S. (1999) Meningitis in Wales. *British Medical Journal*, 318: p544.

Beishon, S., Modood, T. and Virdee, S. (1998) *Ethnic Minority Families*. Grantham: Policy Studies Institute.

Bekir, P., Mclellan, T., Childress, A. and Gariti, P. (1993) Role Reversals in Families of Substance Misusers: A Trans-Generational Phenomenon. *International Journal of the Addictions*, 28(7): p613–30.

Bennet, L.A., Wolin, S.J., Reiss, D. and Teitelbaum, M.A. (1987) Couples at Risk for Transmission of Alcoholism: Protective Influences. *Family Process*, 26: p111–29.

Berkman, L.F. and Syme, S.L. (1979) Social Networks, Host Resistance and Mortality: A Nine Year Follow up of Almeda County Residents. *American Journal of Epidemiology*, 109: p186.

Bibby, A. and Becker, S. (Eds.) (2000) *Young Carers in Their Own Words*. London: Calouste Gulbenkian Foundation.

Bifulco, A. and Moran, P. (1998) *Wednesday's Child: Research Into Women's Experience of Neglect and Abuse in Childhood and Adult Depression*. London: Routledge.

Billings, A. and Moos, R. (1985) Children of Parents With Unipolar Depression: A Controlled 1 Year Follow up Study. *Journal of Abnormal Child Psychology*, 14: p149–66.

Bilsborrow, S. (1992) 'You Grow up Fast as Well...' Young Carers on Merseyside. Ilford: Barnardo's.

Blackford, K.A. (1999) A Child Growing Up with a Parent who has Multiple Sclerosis: Theories and Experiences. *Disability and Society*, 14(5): p673–85.

Bleuler, M. (1978) *The Schizophrenic Disorders: Long Term Patient and Family Studies*. New Haven: Yale University Press.

Blyth, E. and Milner, J. (1997) *Social Work With Children: The Educational Perspective*. Longman.

Booth, T. and Booth, W. (1993) Parenting With Learning Disabilities: Lessons for Practitioners. *British Journal of Social Work*, 23: p459–80.

Booth, T. and Booth, W. (1994) *Parenting Under Pressure: Mothers and Fathers With Learning Disabilities*. Milton Keynes: Open University Press.

Booth, T. and Booth, W. (1997) *Exceptional Childhoods, Unexceptional Children: Growing Up With Parents Who Have Learning Difficulties*. York: Family Policy Studies Centre/Joseph Rowntree Foundation.

Boszormenyi-Nagy, I. (1965) A Theory of Relationships: Experience and Transaction. In Boszormenyi-Nagy, I. and Framo, J.L. (Eds.) *Intensive Family Therapy: Theoretical and Practical Aspects*. New York: Harper and Row.

Boszormenyi-Nagy, I. and Spark, G.M. (1973) *Invisible Loyalties: Reciprocity in Inter-Generational Family Therapy*. New York: Harper-Row.

Boszormenyi-Nagy, I. and Krasner, B.R. (1986) *Between Give and Take*. New York: Brunner-Mazel.

Bowlby, J. (1971) *Attachment and Loss, Volume 1: Attachment*. Harmondsworth: Penguin.

Boyden, J., Ling, B. and Myers, W. (1998) *What Works for Working Children*. Stockholm: Radda Barnen/UNICEF.

Boyle, D. (1994) New Identities: The Changing Profile of Patients With Cancer, Their Families and Their Professional Caregivers. *Oncology Nursing Forum*, 21: p57–61.

Boyle, M.H. and Pickles, A. (1997) Maternal Depressive Symptoms and Ratings of Emotional Disorder Symptoms in Children and Adolescents. *Journal of Child Psychology and Psychiatry*, 38(8): p981–92.

Bradburn, J., Maher, J., Adewuyi-Dalton, R., Grunfeld, E., Lancaster, T. and Mant, D. (1995) Developing Clinical Trial Protocols: The Use of Patient Focus Groups. *Psycho-Oncology*, 4: p107–12.

Bradshaw, J. and Miller, J. (1991) *Lone Parents in The UK*. London: HMSO.

Breslau, N., Weitzman, M. and Messenger, K. (1981) Psychological Functioning of Siblings of Disabled Children. *Pediatrics*, 67: p344–53.

Brisby, T., Baker, S. and Hedderwick, T. (1997) *Under The Influence: Coping with Parents who Drink Too Much*. London: Alcohol Concern.

Brody, E.M., Litvin, S.J., Hoffman, C. and Kleban, M.H. (1995) Marital Status of Caregiving Daughters and Co-Residence with Dependent Parents. *Gerontologist*, 35: p75–85.

Brown, D. (1981) All in the Family. *Disabled USA*, 4(3): p30–5.

Brown, S. (1991) Adult Children of Alcoholics: The History of A Social Movement and Its Impact on Clinical Theory and Practice. *Recent Developments in Alcoholism*, 9: p267–285.

Brown, G. and Harris, J. (1978) *Social Origins of Depression*. London: Tavistock.

Bruck, M., Ceci, S.J. and Hembrooke, H. (1998) Reliability and Credibility of Young Children's Reports: From Research to Policy and Practice. *American Psychologist*, 53(2): p136–51.

Bryant, B.K. (1992) Sibling Caretaking: Providing Emotional Support During Middle Childhood. In Boer, F. and Dunn, J. (Eds.) *Children's Sibling Relationships: Developmental and Clinical Issues*. Hillsdale, NJ: Erlbaum.

Bukatko, D. and Daehler, M.W. (1995) *Child Development: A Thematic Approach*. Boston, MA: Houghton Mifflin Company.

Burton, S.L. and Parks, A.L. (1994) Self-Esteem, Locus of Control and Career Aspirations of College-Age Siblings of Individuals With Disabilities. *Social Work Research*, 18(3): p178–85.

Bury, M. (2000) A Comment on the ICIDH-2. *Disability and Society*, 15(7): p1073–7.

Butler, S. and Kirwan, G. (1999) The Icarus Project: Report on Luxembourg Seminar of March 1999. *Social Work in Europe*, 6(2): p72–4.

Cachia, P., Zammit, M. and Macelli, N. (1998) The Young Carer in Malta: Some Early Thinking About The Child as Carer in a Small Mediterranean State. *Journal of Young Carers Work*, 1: p10–12.

Calder, M. (2002) A Framework for Conducting Risk Assessment. *Child Care in Practice*, 8(1): p7–18.

Candappa, M. and Egharevba, I. (2000) *'Extraordinary Childhoods': The Social Lives of Refugee Children*. University of Hull, ESRC Children 5–16 Research Briefing.

Caspi, A., Elder, G.H. and Herbener, E.S. (1990) Childhood Personality and the Prediction of Life-Course Patterns. in Robins, L.N. and Rutter, M. (Eds.) *Straight and Devious Pathways from Childhood to Adulthood*. Cambridge: Cambridge University Press.

Cassino, C., Auerbach, M., Kammerman, S., Birgfield, E., Bordman, I., Ciotoli, C. and Reibman, J. (1997) Effect of Maternal Asthma on Performance of Parenting Tasks and Children's School Attendance. *Journal of Asthma*, 34(6): p499–507.

Challener, B. (Ed.) (1997) *Stories of Resilience in Childhood*. New York: Garland.

Chalmers, I. (1983) Scientific Enquiry and Authoritarianism in Perinatal Care and Education. *Birth*, 10(3): p151–66.

Childline (1997) *Beyond The Limit: Children Who Live With Alcohol Abuse*. London.

Claflin, C.J. and Barbarin, O.A. (1991) Does 'Telling' Less Protect More? Relationships Among Age, Information Disclosure, and What Children With Cancer See and Feel. *Journal of Pediatric Psychology*, 16(2): p169–91.

Clark, A. and Harrington, R. (1999) On Diagnosing Rare Disorders Rarely: Appropriate Use of Screening Instruments. *Journal of Child Psychology and Psychiatry*, 40(2): p287–90.

Coates, D.L., Vietze, P.M. and Gray, D.B. (1985) Methodological Issues in Studying Children of Disabled Parents. In Thurman, S.K. (Ed.) *Children of Handicapped Parents: Research and Clinical Perspectives*. New York: Academic Press.

Cochrane, A. (1972) *Effectiveness and Efficiency: Random Reflections on Health Services*. Nuffield Provincial Hospital Trust, Cambridge University Press.

Cooper, E.T. (1984) A Pilot Study on The Effects of The Diagnosis of Lung Cancer on Family Relationships. *Cancer Nursing*, 7: p301–8.

Cowen, E. and Work, W. (1988) Resilient Children, Psychological Wellness, and Primary Prevention. *American Journal of Community Psychology*, 16: p591–607.

Cowling, V. (1996) Meeting the Support Needs of Families With Dependent Children Where the Parent Has a Mental Illness. *Australian Institute of Family Studies*, 45: Spring/Summer; p22–5.

Cowling, V. (Ed.) (1999) *Children of Parents with Mental Illness*. Australian Council for Educational Research.

Cox, A. (1988) Maternal Depression and Impact on Children's Development. *Archives of Disease in Childhood*, 63: p90–5.

Crabtree, H. and Warner, L. (1999) *Too Much to Take on: A Report on Young Carers and Bullying*. London: Princess Royal Trust for Carers.

Craft, M.J., Lakin, J.A., Oppliger, R.A., Clancy, G.M. and Vanderlinden, D.W. (1990) Siblings as Change Agents for Promoting the Functional Status of Children With Cerebral Palsy. *Developmental Medicine and Child Neurology*, 32(12): p1049–57

Crow, L. (1996) Including All of Our Lives: Renewing the Social Model of Disability. in Barnes, C. and Mercer, G. (Eds.) *Exploring the Divide: Illness and Disability*. Leeds: The Disability Press.

Cytryn, L., Mcknew, D., Zahn-Waxler, C. and Gershon, E. (1984) Developmental Issues in Risk Research: The Offspring of Affectively Ill Parents. In Rutter, M., Izard, C. and Read, P. (Eds.) *Depression in Children: Developmental Perspectives*. New York: Guilford Press.

Davie, R., Upton, G. and Varma V. (Eds.) (1996) *The Voice of the Child: A Handbook for Professionals*. London: Falmer Press.

Davies, L.K. (1993) Comparison of Dependent-Care Activities for Well Siblings of Children With Cystic Fibrosis and Well Siblings in Families Without Children With Chronic Illness. *Issues in Comprehensive Pediatric Nursing*, 16(2): p91–8.

Davin, A. (1996) *Growing Up Poor: Home, School and Street in London 1870–1914.* London: River Oram Press.

Deacon, D. (1999) Young Carers and Old Hacks. *Journal of Young Carers Work,* 2: p9–11.

Dearden, C., Aldridge, J., Newton, B. and Becker, S. (1994) *Getting It Right for Young Carers: A Training Pack for Professionals.* Loughborough University, Department of Social Sciences/Crossroads.

Dearden, C. and Becker, S. (1995) *The National Directory of Young Carers' Projects and Initiatives.* Loughborough University, Young Carers Research Group in association with Carers National Association.

Dearden, C. and Becker, S. (1996) *Young Carers at the Crossroads: An Evaluation of the Nottingham Young Carers' Project.* Department of Social Sciences, Loughborough University, Young Carers Research Group, in association with Crossroads.

Dearden, C. and Becker, S. (1997) Protecting Young Carers: Legislative Tensions and Opportunities in Britain. *Journal of Social Welfare and Family Law,* 19(2): p123–38.

Dearden, C. and Becker, S. (1998) *Young Carers in the UK.* Young Carers Research Group/Carers National Association. London: Carers National Association.

Dearden, C. and Becker, S. (1999) The Experiences of Young Carers in the UK: The Mental Health Issues. *Mental Health Care,* 21(8): p273–6.

Dearden, C. and Becker, S. (2000) *Young Carers Transitions into Adulthood.* York: Joseph Rowntree Foundation.

Dearden, C., Becker, S. and Aldridge, J. (1995) Children Who Care: A Case for Nursing Intervention? *British Journal of Nursing,* 4(12): p698–701.

Dekker, J.J. (2000) The Century of The Child Revisited. *International Journal of Human Rights,* 8: p133–50.

Demeyer, M.K. (1979) Comments on 'Siblings of Autistic Children'. *Journal of Autism and Developmental Disorders,* 9: p296–8.

Department of Health (1995) *Child Protection: Messages From Research.* London: HMSO.

Department of Health (1996) *Carers (Recognition and Services) Act: Policy Guidance and Practice Guide.* London: Department of Health.

Department of Health (1997) *Health and Personal Social Services Statistics for England.* London: Department of Health.

Department of Health (1998a) *Working Together to Safeguard Children. New Government Proposals for Inter-Agency Co-operation: Consultation Paper.* Wetherby: Department of Health.

Department of Health (1998b) *Modernising Social Services.* London: The Stationery Office, Cm. 4169.

Department of Health (1999a) *Caring About Carers: A National Strategy for Carers.* London: Department of Health.

Department of Health (1999b) *Our Healthier Nation: A Contract for Health.* London: The Stationery Office.

Department of Health (1999c) *Framework for Assessment of Children in Need and Their Families* (Consultation Draft) Social Care Group. London: Department of Health.

Department of Health (January 2000) *The Children Act Report 1995–1999.* Cm. 4579.

Derouin, D. and Jessee, P.O. (1996) Impact of a Chronic Illness in Childhood: Siblings' Perceptions, *Issues in Comprehensive Pediatric Nursing,* 19(2): p135–47.

Dhooper, S. (1983) Family Coping with the Crisis of Heart Attack. *Social Work Health Care,* 9: p15–31.

Dineen, T. (2000) Manufacturing Victims: What the Psychology Industry is Doing to People. London: Constable.

Dix, T.H. and Grusec, J.E. (1985) Parent Attribution Processes in the Socialization of Children. In Sigel, I.E. (Ed.) *Parental Belief Systems: The Psychological Consequences for Children.* Hillsdale, NJ: Erlbaum.

Dodge, K.A. (1990) Developmental Psychopathology in Children of Depressed Mothers. *Developmental Psychology,* 26(1): p3–6.

Doyal, L. and Gough, I. (1991) *A Theory of Human Need.* Basingstoke: Macmillan Education.

Dominelli, L. (1988) *Anti-Racist Social Work.* Basingstoke: Macmillan.

D'Orban, P. (1979) Women Who Kill Their Children. *British Journal of Psychiatry,* 134: p560–571.

Douglas, J.W.B. and Ross, J. (1965) The Effects of Absence on Primary School Attendance. British *Journal of Educational Psychology,* 35: p18–40.

Dweck, C.S. and Elliot, E.S. (1983) Achievement Motivation. in Hetherington, E.M. (Ed.) *Handbook of Child Psychology, Vol. 4: Socialization, Personality and Development.* New York: Wiley.

Drotar, D. (1994) Impact of Parental Health Problems on Children: Concepts, Methods and Unanswered Questions. *Journal of Pediatric Psychology,* 19(5): p525–36.

Drotar, D. and Crawford, P. (1985) Psychological Adaptation of Siblings of Chronically Ill Children: Research and Practice Implications. *Journal of Developmental and Behavioural Pediatrics,* 6(6): p355–62.

Dulmus, C. and Wodarski, J. (1997) Prevention of Childhood Mental Disorders: Hope and a Vision for the Future. *Child and Adolescent Social Work Journal,* 14: p1811–98.

Dunn, J. (1991) Sibling Influences. In Lewis, M. and Feinman, S. (Eds.) *Social Influences and Socialization in Infancy.* New York: Plenum Press.

Durkin, K. (1995) *Developmental Social Psychology: From Infancy to Old Age.* Oxford: Blackwell.

Edwards, A. (1997) Young Carers and their Parents with Long Term Psychiatric Disorders. In *Keeping Children in Mind: Balancing Children's Needs with Parents' Mental Health.* Report of The 12th Annual Conference hosted by the Michael Sieff Foundation, September.

Eiser, C. (1994) Making Sense of Chronic Disease. *Journal of Child Psychology and Psychiatry*, 35: p1373–90.

Elder, G. (1974) *Children of the Great Depression*. Chicago: University of Chicago Press.

Ellman, J.P. (1996) Analyst and Patient at Midlife. *Psychoanalytical Quarterly*, 65: p357–371.

Emery, R., Weintraub, S. and Neale, J. (1982) Effects of Marital Discord on the School Behavior of Children of Schizophrenic, Affectively Disordered and Normal Parents. *Journal of Abnormal Child Psychology*, 10: p215–28.

Ervin-Tripp, S. (1989) Sisters and Brothers. In Zukow, P.G. (Ed.) *Sibling Interaction Across Cultures: Theoretical and Methodological Issues*. New York: Springer-Verlag.

Etzioni, A. (1995) *The Spirit of Community: Rights, Responsibilities and the Communitarian Agenda*. London: Fontana.

Falkov, A. (1996) Parental Psychiatric Disorder and Child Maltreatment: Part 1: Context and Historical Overview. *Highlight* No.148. London: National Children's Bureau and Barnardo's.

Falkov, A. (1998) *Crossing Bridges: Training Resources for Working with Mentally Ill Parents and their Children*. Brighton: Pavilion Press.

Fallon, T. Jr. and Schwab-Stone, M. (1994) Determinants of Reliability in Psychiatric Surveys of Children Aged 6-12. *Journal of Child Psychology and Psychiatry*, 35(8): p1391–1408.

Farmer, R.L., Walsh, J. and Bentley, K.J. (1998) Schizophrenia. In Thyer, B. and Wodarski, J.S. (Eds.) *Handbook of Empirical Social Work Practice, Vol. 1: Mental Disorders*. New York: John Wiley.

Farren, C.J., Keane-Hagerty, E., Salloway, S., Kupferer, S. and Wilken, C.S. (1991) Finding Meaning: An Alternative Paradigm for Alzheimer's Disease Family Caregivers. *Gerontologist*, 31: p483–9.

Feldman, M. (1986) Research on Parenting by Mentally Retarded Persons. *Psychiatric Clinics of North America*, 9(4): p777–96.

Feldman, M. and Walton-Allen, N. (1998) Effects of Maternal Mental Retardation and Poverty on Intellectual, Academic and Behavioural Status of School-Age Children. *American Journal of Mental Retardation*, 101: p352–64.

Fendrich, M., Warner, V. and Weissman, M. (1990) Family Risk Factors, Parental Depression and Psychopathology in Offspring. *Developmental Psychology*, 26: p40–50.

Ferenczi, S. (1928) The Adaptation of the Family to the Child. In Balint, M. (Ed.) *Final Contributions to the Problems and Methods of Psychoanalysis*. London: Hogarth Press.

Ferrari, M. (1984) Chronic Illness: Psychosocial Effects on Siblings 1: Chronically Ill Boys. *Journal of Child Psychiatry and Psychology*, 25(3): p459–476.

Finch, J. (1989) *Family Obligations and Social Change*. Cambridge: Polity Press.

Fisher, D. (1998) Young Carers in Australia. *Journal of Young Carers Work*, 1: p13–15.

Fisman, S., Wolf, L., Ellison, D., Gillis, B., Freman, T. and Szatmari, P. (1996) Risk and Protective Factors Affecting The Adjustment of Siblings of Children With Chronic Disabilities. *Journal of The American Academy of Child and Adolescent Psychiatry*, 35(11): p1532–41.

Fleming, J.E., Offord, D.R. and Boyle, M.H. (1989) Prevalence of Childhood and Adolescent Depression in the Community: Ontario Child Health Study. *British Journal of Psychiatry*, 155: p647–54.

Fogelman, K. and Richardson, K. (1974) School Attendance: Some Results From the National Child Development Study. In Turner, B. (Ed.) *Truancy*. London: Ward Lock.

Folkman, S. and Lazarus, R.S. (1980) An Analysis of Coping in a Middle-aged Community Sample. *Journal of Health and Social Behaviour*, 21: p219–39.

Fox, N.J. (1995) Professional Models of School Absence Associated with Home Responsibilities, *British Journal of Sociology of Education*, 16(2): p221–42.

Frank, J., Tatum, C. and Tucker, S. (1999) *On Small Shoulders: Learning from the Experiences of Former Young Carers*. London: The Children's Society.

Fraser, M. (Ed.) (1998) *Risk and Resilience in Childhood: An Ecological Perspective*. Washington DC: NASW Press.

Freedman, B. (1996) Respectful Service and Reverent Obedience: A Jewish View on Making Decisions for Incompetent Parents. *Hastings Center Report*, 26: p31–7.

Freedman, B. and Weijer, C. (Eds.) (1999) *Duty and Healing: Foundations of a Jewish Bio-ethic*. New York: Routledge.

Freeman-Longo, R.E. (1996) Feel Good Legislation: Prevention or Calamity. *Child Abuse and Neglect*, 20: p95–101.

Freud, A. (1965) *Normality and Pathology in Childhood*. New York: International Universities Press.

Fruin, D. (1998) *A Matter of Chance for Carers? Inspection of Local Authority Support for Carers*. Wetherby: Social Services Inspectorate/ Department of Health.

Furedi, F. (1998) *Culture of Fear: Risk-Taking and the Morality of Low Expectation*. London: Cassell.

Furniss, M.J. (Ed.) (1998) *Evidence-based Practice: A Guide to Effective Practice*. London: Home Office Publications Unit.

Gallant, W.A., Gorey, K.M., Gallant, M.D., Perry J.L. and Ryan, P.K. (1998) The Association of Personality Characteristics with Parenting Problems Among Alcoholic Couples. *American Journal of Drug and Alcohol Abuse*, 24: p119–29.

Gallo, A.M., Breitmayer, B.J., Knafl, K.A. and Zoeller, L.H. (1992) Well Siblings of Children with Chronic Illness: Parents' Reports of their Psychological Adjustment. *Pediatric Nursing*, 18(1): p23–7.

Galloway, D. (1980) Problems of Assessment and

Management of Persistent Absenteeism From School. In Hersov, L. and Beg, I. (Eds.) *Persistent Absenteeism From School*. Chichester: Wiley.

Gambrill, E. (1990) *Critical Thinking in Clinical Practice*. San Francisco: Jossey-Bass.

Garley, D., Gallop, R., Johnston, N. and Pipitone, J. (1997) Children of the Mentally Ill: A Qualitative Focus Group Approach. *Journal of Psychiatric Mental Health Nursing*, 4(2): p97–103.

Garmezy, N. (1985) Stress-Resistant Children: The Search for Protective Factors. In *Recent Research in Developmental Psychopathology, Book Supplement No. 4 to Journal of Child Psychology and Psychiatry*. Oxford: Pergamon Press.

Garmezy, N. and Devine, V. (1984) Project Competence: The Minnesota Studies of Children Vulnerable to Psychopathology. In Watt, N., Anthony, E., Wynne, L. and Rolf, J. (Eds.) *Children at Risk From Schizophrenia*. New York: Cambridge University Press.

Garratt, D., Roche, J. and Tucker, S. (1997) *Changing Experiences of Youth*. London: Sage/Open University.

Gates, M.F. and Lackey, N.R. (1998) Youngsters Caring for Adults With Cancer. *Image: Journal of Nursing Scholarship*, 30(1): p11–1.

Gath, A. (1973) The School Age Siblings of Mongol Children. *British Journal of Psychiatry*, 123: p161–7.

Gath, A. (1992) The Brothers and Sisters of Mentally Retarded Children. In Boer, F. and Dunn, J. (Eds.) *Children's Sibling Relationships: Developmental and Clinical Issues*. Hillsdale, NJ: Laurence Erlbaum.

Geddes, J. (1999) Suicide and Homicide by People with Mental Illness. *British Medical Journal*, 318: p1225–6.

Gibbs, L. and Gambrill, E. (1996) *Critical Thinking for Social Workers*. Thousand Oaks, CA: Pine Forge Press.

Gilligan, R. (1997) Beyond Permanence? The Importance of Resilience in Child Placement Practice and Planning. *Adoption and Fostering*, 21(1): p12–20.

Gilligan, R. (2000) Adversity, Resilience and Young People: The Protective Value of Positive School and Spare Time Experiences. *Children and Society*, 14: p37–47.

Glass, D.D. (1985) Onset of Disability in a Parent: Impact on Child and Family. In Thurman, S.K. (Ed.) *Children of Handicapped Parents: Research and Clinical Perspectives*. New York: Academic Press.

Goglia, L.R., Jurkovic, G.J., Burt, A.M. and Burge-Calloway, K.G. (1992) Generational Boundary Distortions by Adult Children of Alcoholics: Child-As-Parent and Child-As-Mate. *American Journal of Family Therapy*, 20(4): p291–9.

Goldman, J. and Coane, J. (1977) Family Therapy After the Divorce: Developing a Strategy. *Family Process*, 16(3): p357–62.

Goodinge, S. (2000) *A Jigsaw of Services: Inspection of Services to Support Disabled Parents in their Parenting Role*. London: Department of Health.

Goodman, C. (1984) The PACE Family Treatment and Education Programme: A Public Health Approach to Parental Competence and Promotion of Mental Health. In Cohler, B.J. and Musick, J.S. (Eds.) Intervention Among Psychiatrically Impaired Parents and their Young Children. *New Directions for Mental Health Services*, No. 24. San Francisco: Jossey-Bass Inc.

Goodman, S.H. (1984) Children of Disturbed Parents: A Research-Based Model for Intervention. In Cohler, B.J. and Musick, J.S. (Eds.) Intervention Among Psychiatrically Impaired Parents and their Young Children. *New Directions for Mental Health Services*, No. 24. San Francisco: Jossey-Bass Inc.

Gopfert, M., Webster, J. and Seeman, M. (1996) *Parental Psychiatric Disorder: Distressed Parents and their Families*. Cambridge: Cambridge University Press.

Gorey, K.M. (1996) Effectiveness of Social Work Intervention Research: Internal Versus External Evaluations. *Social Work Research*, 20(2): p119–128.

Graham, P. and George, S. (1972) Children's Responses to Parental Illness. *Journal of Psychosomatic Research*, 16: p251–5.

Grant, K.E. and Compas, B.E. (1994) Stress and Anxious-Depressed Symptoms of Anxiety/Depression Among Adolescents: Searching for Mechanisms of Risk. *Journal of Consulting and Clinical Psychology*, 63: p1015–21.

Greenberg, M.A., Wortman, C.B. and Stone, A.A. (1996) Emotional Expression and Physical Health: Revising Traumatic Memories or Fostering Self Regulation? *Journal of Personality and Social Psychology*, 71: p588–602.

Greenhalgh, T. and Hurwitz, B. (1999) Why Study Narrative? *British Medical Journal*, 318: p48–50.

Greening, K. (1992) The 'Bear Essentials' Program: Helping Young Children and their Families Cope When a Parent has Cancer. *Journal of Psychosocial Oncology*, 10: p47–61.

Greer, B.G. (1985) Children of Physically Disabled Parents: Some Thoughts, Facts and Hypotheses. In Thurman, S.K. (Ed.) *Children of Handicapped Parents: Research and Clinical Perspectives*, p131–44. New York: Academic Press.

Gregg, P., Harkess, S. and Machin, S. (1999) *Child Development and Family Income*. York: Joseph Rowntree Foundation.

Grimshaw, R. (1991) *Children of Parents with Parkinson's Disease: A Research Report for the Parkinson's Disease Society*. London: National Children's Bureau.

Gupta, R. (1999) The Revised Caregiver Burden Scale: A Preliminary Evaluation. *Research on Social Work Practice*, 9(4): p508–20.

Hacking, I. (1995) *Rewriting the Soul: Multiple Personality and the Sciences of Memory*. Princeton, NJ: Princeton University Press.

Hacking, I. (1999) *Mad Travellers: Reflections of the Reality of Transient Mental Illnesses*. University Press of Virginia.

Hall, A. (1996) Parental Disorder and the Developing Child. In Gopfert, M., Webster, J. and Seeman, M. (Eds.) *Parental Psychiatric Disorder: Distressed Parents and their Families.* Cambridge: Cambridge University Press.

Halmos, P. (1965) *The Faith of the Counsellors.* London: Constable.

Hammen, C., Gordon, D., Burge, D., Adrian, C., Jaenicke, C. and Hiroto, D. (1987) Maternal Affective Disorders, Illness and Stress: Risk for Children's Psychopathology. *American Journal of Psychiatry,* 144(6): p736–41.

Hammen, C. (1997) Children of Depressed Parents: The Stress Context. In Wolchik, S.A. and Sandler, I.N. (Eds.) *Handbook of Children's Coping: Linking Theory and Practice.* New York: Plenum Press.

Hantrais, L. and Becker, S. (1995) Young Carers in Europe: A Comparative Perspective. In Becker, S. (Ed.) *Young Carers in Europe: An Exploratory Cross-National Study in Britain, France, Sweden and Germany.* Loughborough University, Young Carers Research Group in association with the European Research Centre.

Hansbro, J., Bridgewood, A. with Morgan, A. and Hickman, M. (1997) *Health in England 1996: What People Know, What People Think, What People Do.* Office of National Statistics. London: The Stationery Office.

Harden, J. (2000) There's No Place Like Home: The Public/Private Distinction in Children's Theorizing of Risk and Safety. *Childhood,* 7(1): p43–59.

Harden, J., Backett-Milburn, K., Scott, S. and Jackson, S. (2000) Scary Faces, Scary Places: Children's Perceptions of Risk and Safety. *Health Education Journal,* 59: p12–22.

Harrington, R. (1996) The 'Railway Spine' Diagnosis and Victorian Responses to Post Traumatic Shock Disorder. *Journal of Psychosomatic Research,* 40: p11–14.

Harris, A. with Cox, E. and Smith, C. (1971) *Handicapped and Impaired in Great Britain,* Part 1. London: HMSO.

Harris, M.J., Milich, R., Corbitt, E.M., Hoover, D.W. and Brady, M. (1992) Self-Fulfilling Effects of Stigmatizing Information on Children's Social Interactions. *Journal of Personality and Social Psychology,* 63: p41–50.

Harris, P.B. (1998) Listening to Caregiving Sons: Misunderstood Realities. *Gerontologist,* 38: p342–52.

Harrison, R.S., Boyle, S.W. and Farley, O.W. (1999) Evaluating The Outcomes of Family-based Intervention for Troubled Children: A Pretest-Posttest Study. *Research on Social Work Practice,* 9(6): p640–55.

Hatton, C., Azmi, S., Caine, A. and Emerson, E. (1998) Informal Carers of Adolescents and Adults with Learning Difficulties From the South Asian Communities: Family Circumstances, Service Support and Carer Stress. *British Journal of Social Work,* 28: p821–37.

Hawker, S.J. and Boulton, M.J. (2000) Twenty Years Research on Peer Victimization and Psychosocial Maladjustment: A Meta-Analytical Review of Cross-Sectional Studies. *Journal of Child Psychology and Psychiatry,* 41(4): p441–55.

Heath, I. (1999) Commentary: There Must be Limits to the Medicalisation of Human Distress. *British Medical Journal,* 318: p439–40.

.Heller, S.S., Larrieu, J.A., D'Imperio, R. and Boris N.W. (1999) Research on Resilience to Child Maltreatment: Some Empirical Considerations. *Child Abuse and Neglect,* 23(4): p321–338.

Hendessi, M. (1996) *Report of the Survey of Young Carers in Hammersmith and Fulham.* Hammersmith and Fulham Social Services for Caring for Carers Association.

Hetherington, E.M. (1989) Coping with Family Transitions: Winners, Losers and Survivors. *Child Development,* 60: p1–14.

Hetherington, E.M., Cox, M. and Cox, R. (1982) Effects of Divorce on Parents and Children. In Lamb, M. (Ed.) *Nontraditional Families.* Hillsdale NJ: Erlbaum.

Hill, S. (1999) The Physical Effects of Caring on Children. *Journal of Young Carers Work,* 3: p6–7.

Hindle, D. (1998) Growing Up With a Parent who has a Chronic Mental Illness: One Child's Perspective. *Child and Family Social Work,* 3: p259–66.

Hinrichsen, G.A., Hernandez, N., and Pollock, S. (1992) Difficulties and Rewards in Family Care of the Depressed Older Adult. *Gerontologist,* 32: p486–92.

Hirsch, B.J., Moos, R.H. and Reischl, T.M. (1985) Psychosocial Adjustment of Adolescent Children of a Depressed, Arthritic or Normal Parent. *Journal of Abnormal Psychology,* 94(2): p154–64.

Hodgkin, R. and Newell, P. (1996) *Effective Government Structures for Children: Report of a Gulbenkian Foundation Inquiry.* London: Calouste Gulbenkian Foundation.

House, J.S., Landis, K. and Umberston, D. (1988) Social Relationships and Health. *Science,* 24: p540–5.

Huff, D. (1981) *How to Lie with Statistics.* Harmondsworth: Penguin.

Hughes, A. (1999) Befriending: A Note of Caution. *British Journal of Learning Disabilities,* 27: p88–92.

Hughes, R. (1993) *The Culture of Complaint: The Fraying of America.* Oxford: Oxford University Press.

Hugman, R. and Phillips, N. (1993) 'Like Bees Round A Honeypot': Social Work Responses to Parents With Mental Health Needs. *Practice,* 6(3): p193–205.

Hunt, A. with Fox, J. and Morgan, M. (1973) *Families and their Needs with Particular Reference to One-Parent Families* (Vol. II, Tables) London: OPCS Social Survey Division, HMSO.

Imrie, J. and Coombs, Y. (1995) *No Time to Waste: The Scale and Dimensions of the Problem of Children Affected by HIV/AIDS in The UK.* Ilford: Barnardo's.

Iredale, R. and Cleverly, A. (1998) Research Note: Education and Training in Genetics in Social Work Programmes Across the United Kingdom. *British Journal of Social Work,* 28: p961–8.

Jackson, S. and Martin, P.Y. (1998) Surviving the Care

System: Education and Resilience. *Journal of Adolescence*, 21: p569–83.

James, A., Jenks, C. and Prout, A. (1998) Theorising Childhood. Cambridge: Polity Press.

Jenkins, S. and Wingate, C. (1994) Who Cares for Young Carers? *British Medical Journal*, 308: p733–4.

Jenks, C. (1994) Child Abuse in the Postmodern Context: An Issue of Social Identity. *Childhood*, 2: p111–21.

Johnson, C.L. and Irvin, F.S. (1983) Depressive Potentials: Interface Between Adolescence and Midlife Transition. In Morrison, H.L. (Ed.) *Children of Depressed Parents: Risk, Identification and Intervention.* New York: Grune and Stratton.

Johnson, J.L. and Tiegel, S. (1991) Treating Adults Raised by Alcoholic Parents. *Recent Developments in Alcoholism*, 9: p347–59.

Johnson, J.L. and Leff, M. (1999) Children of Substance Abusers: Overview of Research Findings. *Pediatrics*, 103(5, Pt. 2): p1085–99.

Johnson, Z., Howell, F. and Molloy, B. (1993) 'Community Mothers' Programme: Randomised Controlled Trial of Non-Professional Intervention in Parenting. *British Medical Journal*, 306: p1449–52.

Johnston, M., Martin, D., Martin, M. and Gumaer, J. (1992) Long Term Parental Illness and Children: Perils and Promises. *The School Counselor*, 39: p225–31.

Jones, A., Jeyasingham, D. and Rajasooriya, S. (2002) *Invisible Families: The Strengths and Needs of Black Families in Which Young People Have Caring Responsibilities.* Bristol: The Policy Press/Joseph Rowntree Foundation.

Jones, R.A. and Wells, M. (1996) An Empirical Study of Parentification and Personality. *American Journal of Family Therapy*, 24(2): p145–52.

Jung, C.G. (1933) *Modern Man in Search of a Soul.* London: Lund Humphries.

Jurkovic, G.J. (1997) *Lost Childhoods: The Plight of the Parentified Child.* New York: Brunner/Mazel.

Kashani, J.H., Burk, J.P. and Reid, J.C. (1985a) Depressed Children of Depressed Parents. *Canadian Journal of Psychiatry*, 30(4): p265–9.

Kashani, J.H., Burk, J.P., Horwitz, B. and Reid, J.C. (1985b) Differential Effect of Subtype of Parental Major Affective Disorder on Children. *Psychiatry Research*, 15(3): p195–204.

Katz, M. (1997) *On Playing a Poor Hand Well: Insights from the Lives of Those Who Have Overcome Childhood Risks and Adversities.* London: Norton.

Kazdin, A.E. and Petti, J.A. (1983) Self Report and Interview Measures of Childhood and Adolescent Depression. *Journal of Child Psychology and Psychiatry*, 23: p437–58.

Keith, L. and Morris, J. (1995) 'Easy Targets: A Disability Rights Perspective on the 'Children as Carers' Debate'. *Critical Social Policy*, 44/45: Autumn; p36–57.

Keller, M.B., Beardslee, W.R., Dorer, D.J., Lavori, P.W.,

Samuelson, H. and Klerman, G.R. (1986) Impact of Severity and Chronicity of Parental Affective Illness on Adaptive Functioning and Psychopathology in Children. *Archives of General Psychiatry*, 43(10): p930–7.

Kessler, D., Lloyd, K., Lewis, G., Gray, D.P. and Health, I. (1999) Cross-Sectional Study of Symptom Attribution and Recognition of Depression and Anxiety in Primary Care. *British Medical Journal*, 318: p436–40.

Kiernan, K. (1996) Lone Motherhood, Employment and Outcomes for Children. *International Journal of Law, Policy and the Family*, 10: p233–49.

Kleinman, A. (1988) *The Illness Narratives.* New York: Basic Books.

Kotchick, B., Summers, P., Forehand, R. and Steele, R.G. (1997) The Role of Parental and Extrafamilial Social Support in the Psychosocial Adjustment of Children with a Chronically Ill Father. *Behavior Modification*, 21(4): p409–32.

Kovacs, M. (1985) The Interview Schedule for Children (ISC) *Psychopharmacology Bulletin*, 21: p991–4.

Lackey, N.R. and Gates, M.F. (1997) Combining the Analyses of Three Qualitative Data Sets in Studying Young Caregivers. *Journal of Advanced Nursing*, 26: p664–71.

Lackey, N.R. and Gates, M.F. (2001) Adults' Recollections of their Experiences as Young Care Givers of Family Members with Chronic Physical Illnesses. *Journal of Advanced Nursing*, 34(3): p320–8.

Landgraf, J.M., Abetz, L. and Ware, J.E. (1996) *The CHQ User's Manual* (1st edn.) Boston, MA: The Health Institute, New England Medical Center.

Landgraf, J.M., Maunsell, E., Speechley, K.N., Bullinger, M., Campbell, S., Abetz, L. and Ware, J.E. (1998) Canadian-French, German and UK Versions of the Child Health Questionnaire: Methodology and Preliminary Item Scaling Results. *Quality of Life Research*, 7(5): p433–5.

La Greca, A. and Varni, J. (1993) Interventions in Pediatric Psychology: A Look Towards the Future. *Journal of Pediatric Psychology*, 18: p667–80.

Lange, S.M. (1996) *The Impact of Parental Illness on Children.* Fordham University, USA, Unpublished Phd Thesis, Vol. 57/05-B (Dissertation Abstracts Online, DIALOG File 35, 1998 UMI)

La Palme, M., Hodgins, S. and Laroche, C. (1997) Children of Parents with Bipolar Disorder: A Meta-Analysis of Risk for Mental Disorders. *Canadian Journal of Psychiatry*, 42(6): p623–31.

La Roche, C. (1989) Children of Parents with Major Affective Disorders: A Review of the Past 5 Years. *Psychiatric Clinics of North America*, 12(4): p919–32.

Lavigueur, J.V. and Ryan, M. (1979) Psychological Adjustment of Siblings of Children with Chronic Illness. *Pediatrics*, 63: p616–27.

Laws, S. (1998) *Hear Me! Consulting with Young People on Mental Health Services.* London: Mental Health Foundation.

Laybourn, A., Brown, J. and Hill, M. (1996) *Hurting on the*

Inside: Children's Experiences of Parental Alcohol Abuse. Aldershot: Avebury.

Lazarus, R.S. and Folkman, S. (1984) *Stress, Appraisal and Coping.* New York: Springer.

Le Clere, F.B. and Kowalewski, B.M. (1994) Disability in the Family: The Effects on Children's wellbeing. *Journal of Marriage and the Family*, 56: p457–68.

Lefley, H.P. (1996) *Family Caregiving in Mental Illness.* Family Caregiver Applications Series, Vol. 7. Thousand Oaks, CA: Sage.

Leonard, B.J. (1991) Siblings of Chronically Ill Children: A Question of Vulnerability Versus Resilience. *Pediatric Annals*, 20(9): p505–6.

Levin, E., Kearney, P. and Rosen, G. (2000) Fitting it Together. *Community Care*, 3–9 August: p24–5.

Lewandowski, L.A. (1992) Needs of Children During the Critical Illness of a Parent or Sibling. *Critical Care Nursing Clinics of North America*, 4: p573–85.

Lewinsohn, P.M., Clarke, G.N., Hops, H. and Andrews, J. (1994) Major Depression in Community Adolescents: Age of Onset, Duration and Time to Recurrence. *Journal of The American Academy of Child and Adolescent Psychiatry*, 33: p385–401.

Lewis, J. (1999) Research Into the Concept of Resilience as a Basis for the Curriculum for Children With EBD. *Emotional and Behavioural Difficulties*, 4(2): p11–22.

Lewis, J. and Meredith, B. (1988) *Daughters who Care: Daughters Caring for Mothers at Home.* London: Routledge.

Lewis, R., Ellison, E. and Woods, J. (1985) The Impact of Breast Cancer on the Family. *Seminars in Oncological Nursing*, 1: p206–13.

Lewis, V. and Creighton, S. (1999) Parental Mental Health as a Child Protection Issue: Data from the NSPCC National Child Protection Helpline. *Child Abuse Review*, 8: p152–63.

Llewellyn, G. (1994) Generic Family Support Services: Are Parents with Learning Disability Catered For? *Mental Handicap Research*, 7(1): p64–77.

Lobato, D. (1983) Siblings of Handicapped Children: A Review. *Journal of Autism and Developmental Disorder*, 13(4): p347–64.

London Borough of Enfield Research and Development Project (1994/5) *Young Carers and Education.* Enfield: Department of Education.

Lucas, L.E., Montgomery, S.H., Richardson, D.A. and Rivers, P.A. (1984) Impact Project: Reducing the Risk of Mental Illness to Children of Distressed Mothers. In Cohler, B.J. and Musick, J.S. (Eds.) *Intervention Among Psychiatrically Impaired Parents and their Young Children.* New Directions for Mental Health Services, No. 24. San Francisco: Jossey-Bass Inc.

Lutenbacher, M. and Hall, L.A. (1998) The Effects of Maternal Psychosocial Factors on Parenting Attitudes of Low Income, Single Mothers with Young Children. *Nursing Research*, 47: p25–34.

Lyall, J. (1989) Stolen Youth. *Nursing Times*, 85: p16–17.

McClelland, D.C. (1961) *The Achieving Society.* New York.

McCord, J. (1978) A Thirty Year Follow-up of Treatment Effects. *American Psychologist*, 33: p284–9.

McCowan, C., Bryce, F.P., Neville, R.G., Crombie, I.K. and Clark, R.A. (1996) School Absence: A Valid Morbidity Marker for Asthma? *Health Bulletin* (Edinburgh), 54(4): p307–13.

MacDonald, G. (1997) Social Work: Beyond Control? In Maynard, A. and Chalmers, I. (Eds.) *Non-random Reflections on Health Services Research.* London: BMJ Publishing Group.

MacDonald, G., Sheldon, B. and Gillespie, J. (1992) Contemporary Studies of the Effectiveness of Social Work. *British Journal of Social Work*, 22(6): p615–43.

MacDonald, G. and Roberts, H. (1995) *What Works in the Early Years?* Ilford: Barnardo's.

McGaw, S. and Sturmey, P. (1994) Assessing Parents with Learning Disabilities: The Parental Skills Model. *Child Abuse Review*, 3: p36–51.

McGaw, S. (1997) Practical Support for Parents with Learning Disabilities. In O'Hara, J. and Sperlinger, A. (Eds.) *Adults with Learning Disabilities: A Practical Approach.* Chichester: John Wiley and Sons.

McGaw, S. (2000) *What Works for Parents with Learning Disabilities.* Ilford: Barnardo's.

McHale, S., Bartko, W., Crouter, A. and Perry-Jenkins, M. (1990) Children's Housework and Psychosocial Development: The Mediating Effects of Parents' Sex-Role Behaviors and Attitudes. *Child Development*, 61: p1413–26.

McHale, S. and Harris, V. (1992) Children's Experiences with Disabled and Nondisabled Siblings: Links with Personal Adjustment and Relationship Evaluations. In Boer, F. and Dunn, J. (Eds.) *Children's Sibling Relationships: Developmental and Clinical Issues.* Hillsdale, NJ: Laurence Erlbaum.

McHugh, M. (1999) *Special Siblings: Growing up with Someone with a Disability.* New York: Hyperion.

Magen, R.H. and Glajchen, M. (1999) Cancer Support Groups: Client Outcome and the Context of Group Process. *Research on Social Work Practice*, 9(5): p541–54.

Mahon, A. and Higgins, J. (1995) *'A Life of Our Own' Young Carers: An Evaluation of Three RHA Funded Projects in Merseyside.* Manchester: University of Manchester Health Services Management Unit.

Mander, A.J., Horton, B. and Hoare, P. (1987) The Effect of Maternal Psychotic Illness on a Child. *British Journal of Psychiatry*, 151: p548–50.

Mari, J.J. and Streiner, D. (1997) *Family Intervention for Schizophrenia* (Issue 3) The Oxford: Cochrane Library.

Marlowe, J. (1996) Helpers, Helplessness and Self-Help: Shaping the Silence: A Personal Account. In Gopfert, M., Webster, J. and Seeman, M. (Eds.) *Parental Psychiatric Disorder: Distressed Parents and their Families.* Cambridge: Cambridge University Press.

Marsh, D. and Simpkins, R. (1997) *Troubled Journey: Coming to Terms with the Mental Illness of a Sibling or Parent.* New York: Tarcher/Putnam.

Marshall, P.A. and O'Keefe, J.P. (1995) Medical Students' First Person Narratives of a Patient's Story of AIDS. *Social Science and Medicine*, 40(1): p67–76.

De Mause, L. (1976) The Evolution of Childhood. in De Mause, L. (Ed.) *The History of Childhood.* London: Souvenir Press.

Meltzer, H., Gill, B., Petticrew, M. and Hinds, K. (1995) *The Prevalence of Psychiatric Morbidity Among Adults Living in Private Households.* OPCS Surveys of Psychiatric Morbidity in Great Britain, Report 1. London: HMSO.

Mental Health Foundation (1999) *Bright Futures: Promoting Children and Young People's Mental Health.* London: Mental Health Foundation.

Meredith, H. (1991a) Young Carers: The Unacceptable Face of Community Care. *Social Work and Social Sciences Review*, 3 (Supplement): p47–51.

Meredith, H. (1991b) Young Carers. *Contact*, Summer: p14–15.

Meyer, D. (Ed.) (1997) *Views From Our Shoes: Growing up with a Brother or Sister with Special Needs.* Bethesda, MD: Woodbine House.

Minty, B. (1995) Social Work's Five Deadly Sins. *Social Work and Social Sciences Review*, 6(1): p48–63.

Minuchin, S. (1974) *Families and Family Therapy.* Cambridge, MA: Harvard University Press.

Modood, T., Beishon, S. and Virdee, S. (1994) *Changing Ethnic Identities.* London: Policy Studies Institute.

Moffat, F. (1997) Raising The Profile. *Community Care*, 24–30 July: p22.

Mok, J. and Cooper, S. (1997) The Needs of Children whose Mothers have HIV Infection. *Archives of Disability in Childhood*, 77: p483–487.

Monahan, D.J. and Hooker, K. (1997) Caregiving and Social Support in Two Illness Groups. Social Work, 42(3): p278–87.

Moore, S. and Parsons, J. (2000) A Research Agenda for Adolescent Risk Taking: Where Do We Go From Here? (Editorial) *Journal of Adolescence*, 23: p371–6.

Morrow, V. (1994) Responsible Children? Aspects of Children's Work and Employment Outside School in Contemporary UK. In Mayall, B. (Ed.) *Children's Childhoods: Observed and Experienced.* London: Falmer Press.

Morrow, V. (1996) Rethinking Childhood Dependency: Children's Contributions to the Domestic Economy. *The Sociological Review*, 44(1): p58–77.

Morrow, V. (1999) 'We Are People Too': Children's and Young People's Perspectives on Children's Rights and Decision Making in England. *International Journal of Children's Rights*, 7(2): p149–67.

Morris, J. (1997) A Response to Aldridge and Becker Disability Rights and the Denial of Young Carers: The Dangers of Zero-Sum Arguments. *Critical Social Policy*, 17: p133-5.

Mounteney, J. (1998) Children of Drug Using Parents. NCB/Barnardo's *Highlight* No. 163. London: National Children's Bureau.

Moynihan, C., Bliss, J.M., Davidson, J., Burchell, L. and Horwich, A. (1998) Evaluation of Adjuvant Psychological Therapy in Patients with Testicular Cancer: Randomised Controlled Trial. *British Medical Journal*, 316: p429–35.

Mrazek, P.J. and Mrazek, D.A. (1987) Resilience in Child Maltreatment Victims: A Conceptual Exploration. *Child Abuse and Neglect*, 11: p357–66.

Murray, B.L. (1998) Perceptions of Adolescents Living with Parental Alcoholism. *Journal of Psychiatric Mental Health Nursing*, 5(6): p525–34.

Murray, L. (1992) The Impact of Post-Natal Depression on Infant Development. *Journal of Child Psychology and Psychiatry*, 33: p543–61.

National Assembly of Wales (1999) *Welsh Health Survey 1998: Report of 2nd Welsh Health Survey.* Cardiff, Government Statistical Service.

NCH - Action for Children (1999) '*Factfile*'. London: NCH.

Natural Children's Support Group (1990) *Children Who Foster.* Leeds: Vera Publications.

Neff, J.A. (1994) Adult Children of Alcoholic or Mentally Ill Parents: Alcohol Consumption and Psychological Distress in a Tri-Ethnic Community Study. *Addictive Behaviors*, 19(2): p185–97.

Nelson, E., Sloper, P., Charlton, A. and While, D. (1994) Children who have a Parent with Cancer: A Pilot Study. *Journal of Cancer Education*, 9(1): p30–6.

Nevitt, D. (1977) Demand and Need. In Heisler, H. (Ed.) *Foundations of Social Administration.* Basingstoke: Macmillan.

Newman, T. (1996) Rights, Rites and Responsibilities. In Roberts, H. and Sachdev, D. (Eds.) *Young People's Social Attitudes: Having their Say - The Views of 12–19 Year Olds.* Ilford: Barnardo's and Social Community Planning Research.

Newman, T. (2000) Workers and Helpers: Perspectives on Children's Labour 1899–1999. *British Journal of Social Work*, 30: p323–38.

Newman, T. (In Press 2002) *Children and Resilience: A Review of Effective Strategies for Child Care Services.* Exeter: University of Exeter, Centre for Evidence-based Social Services.

Newton, B. and Becker, S. (1996) *Young Carers in Southwark: The Hidden Face of Community Care.* London Borough of Southwark Social Services Department. Loughborough University Young Carers Group.

Nixon, S.P., Maunsell, E., Desmeules, M., Schanzer, D., Landgraf, J.M., Feeny, D.H. and Barrera, M.E. (1999) Mutual Concurrent Validity of the Child Health Questionnaire and the Health Utilities Index: An

Exploratory Analysis Using Survivors of Childhood Cancer. *International Journal of Cancer* (Supplement), 83 (S12): p95–105.

Oakley, A. (1993) *Social Support and Maternity and Child Health Care*. Salford: Public Health Resource Centre.

Office for National Statistics (1997) *Population Trends*. London: The Stationery Office.

Office for National Statistics (1998a) *1996 General Household Survey*. London: The Stationery Office.

Office for National Statistics (1998b) *Social Trends 28*. London: The Stationery Office.

Office for National Statistics (6th August, 1999) *Personal Communication*. London: The Stationery Office.

Office for National Statistics (2000a) *Population Trends*. London: The Stationery Office.

Office for National Statistics (2000b) *Living in Britain: Results from the 1998 General Household Survey*. London: The Stationery Office.

Office for National Statistics (2000c) *Mental Health of Children and Adolescents in Great Britain*. London: The Stationery Office.

Oliver, M. (1998) Theories of Disability Health Practice and Research. *British Medical Journal*, 317: p1446–9.

Olsen, R. (1996) Young Carers: Challenging the Facts and Politics of Research into Children and Caring. *Disability and Society*, 11(1): p41–54.

Olsen, R. (1997) *Young Carers in Leicestershire: Estimating Numbers and Characteristics Using a School Based Survey*. Leicester: University of Leicester, Nuffield Community Care Studies Unit.

Olsen, R. (2000) Families Under the Microscope: Parallels Between the Young Carers Debate of the 1990s and the Transformation of Childhood in the Late Nineteenth Century. *Disability and Society*, 14: p384–94.

Olson, M. and Gariti, P. (1993) Symbolic Loss in Horizontal Relating: Defining the Role of Parentification in Addictive/Destructive Relationships. *Contemporary Family Therapy*, 15(3): p197–208.

O'Neill, A. (1988) *Young Carers: The Tameside Research*. Tameside: Tameside Metropolitan Borough Council.

Orvaschel, H., Weissman, M.M. and Kidd, K.K. (1980) Children and Depression – The Children of Depressed Parents; The Childhood of Depressed Parents; Depression in Children. *Journal of Affective Disorders*, 2(1): p1–16.

Page, R. (1988) *Report on The Initial Survey Investigating the Number of Young Carers in Sandwell Secondary Schools*. Sandwell Caring for Carers Project/Sandwell MBC Education Department.

Palmer, N. (1997) Resilience in Adult Children of Alcoholics. *Health and Social Work*, 22(3): p201–9.

Parcel, G.S., Gilman, S.C., Nader, P.R. and Bunce, H. (1979) A Comparison of Absentee Rates of Elementary Schoolchildren with Asthma and Non-asthmatic Schoolmates. *Pediatrics*, 64(6): p878–81.

Parker, G. and Olsen, R. (1995) *A Sideways Glance at Young Carers*. Paper Presented at a Social Services Inspectorate Conference, Leicester, June 27th.

Part, D. (1993) Fostering as Seen by the Carers' Children. *Adoption and Fostering*, 17(1): p26–31.

Pearlin, L.I. (1983) Role Strains and Personal Stress. In Kaplan, H.B. (Ed.) *Psychosocial Stress: Trends in Theory and Research*. New York: Academic Press.

Phipps, S. and Srivastava, D. (1997) Repressive Adaption in Children with Cancer: It May Be Better Not to Know. *Journal of Pediatrics*, 130: p257–65.

Pilkington, B. and Kremer, J. (1995) A Review of the Epidemiological Research on Child Sexual Abuse: Clinical Samples. *Child Abuse Review*, 4: p191–205.

Pilling, D. (1990) *Escape from Disadvantage*. Basingstoke: Falmer Press.

People Science Intelligence Unit Ltd. (2000) *Asian Community Report 1999–2000*. London: People Science Intelligence Unit.

Policy Studies Institute (1994) *Fourth Survey of Ethnic Minorities*. London: PSI.

Pollock, L. (1983) *Forgotten Children: Parent-Child Relationships from 1500 to 1900*. Cambridge: Cambridge University Press.

Post, P. and Robinson B.E. (1998) A Comparison of School-Aged Children of Alcoholic and Non-Alcoholic Parents on Anxiety, Self-esteem and Locus of Control. *School Counsellor*, 5: p23–9.

Pound, A. (1982) Attachment and Maternal Depression. In Murray Parkes, C. and Stevenson-Hinde, J. (Eds.) *The Place of Attachment in Human Behaviour*. London: Tavistock.

Pound, A. (1996) Parental Affective Disorder and Childhood Disturbance. In Gopfert, M., Webster, J. and Seeman, M. (Eds.) *Parental Psychiatric Disorder: Distressed Parents and their Families*. Cambridge: Cambridge University Press.

Powell, T. and Ogle, P. (1985) *Brothers and Sisters: A Special Part of Exceptional Families*. Baltimore, MD: Paul H. Brookes.

Power, P. (1977) The Adolescent's Reaction to Chronic Illness of a Parent: Some Implications for Family Counselling. *International Journal of Family Counselling*, 5: p70–8.

Prescott-Clarke, P. and Primatesta, P. (Eds.) (1998) *Health Survey for England: The Health of Young People 95-97*. Social and Community Planning Research/Department of Epidemiology and Public Health, University College London. London: The Stationery Office.

Puura, K., Almqvist, F., Piha, J., Moilanen, I., Tamminen, T., Kumpulainen, K., Rasanen, E. and Koivisto, A. (1998) Children with Symptoms of Depression: What Do Adults See? *Journal of Child Psychology and Psychiatry*, 39(4): p577–85.

Rachman, S.J. (1978) *Fear and Courage*. San Francisco, CA: Freeman.

Radke-Yarrow, M. (1989) Family Environments of Depressed and Well Parents and their Children: Issues of Research Methods. In Patterson, G. (Ed.) *Aggression and Depression in Family Interactions.* Hillsdale, NJ: Erlbaum.

Radke-Yarrow, M., Nottelmann, E., Belmont, B. and Welsh, J. (1993) Affective Interactions of Depressed and Non-depressed Mothers and their Children. *Journal of Abnormal Child Psychology,* 21: p683–95.

Radke-Yarrow, M., Zahn-Waxler, C., Richardson, D.T., Susman, A. and Martinez, P. (1994) Caring Behaviour in Children of Clinically Depressed and Well Mothers. *Child Development,* 65(5): p1405–14.

Raphael, B. (1993) Adolescent Resilience: The Potential Impact of Personal Development in Schools. *Journal of Paediatric Child Health,* 29: Supplement 1; p31–6.

Ray, N.K., Rubenstein, H. and Russo, N.J. (1994) Understanding the Parents who are Mentally Retarded: Guidelines for Family Preservation Programs. *Child Welfare,* 73(6): p725–43.

Reed, J.A. (1995) Young Carers. NCB/Barnardo's *Highlight* No. 137. London: National Children's Bureau.

Rende, R. and Plomin, R. (1993) Families at Risk from Psychopathology: Who Becomes Affected and Why? *Development and Psychopathology,* 5(4): p529–40.

Renouf, A.G. and Kovacs, M. (1994) Concordance Between Mothers' Reports and Children's Self-Reports of Depressive Symptoms: A Longitudinal Study. *Journal of the American Academy of Child and Adolescent Psychiatry,* 33(2): p208–16.

Rheingold, H.L. (1982) Little Children's Participation in the Work of Adults: A Nascent Pro-Social Behavior. *Child Development,* 53: p114–25.

Rice, E., Ekdahl, M. and Miller, L. (1971) *Children of Mentally Ill Parents: Problems in Child Care.* New York: Behavioral Publications.

Richman, N., Stevenson, J. and Graham, P. (1982) *Pre-school to School: A Behavioural Study.* London: Academic Press.

Roberts, D. (1996) The Child Grown up: 'On Being and Becoming Mindless': A Personal Account. In Gopfert, M., Webster, J. and Seeman, M. (Eds.) *Parental Psychiatric Disorder: Distressed Parents and their Families.* Cambridge: Cambridge University Press.

Robins, L. (1995) Sociocultural Trends Affecting the Prevalence of Adolescent Problems. In Rutter, M. (Ed.) *Psychosocial Disturbances in Young People: Challenges for Prevention.* Cambridge: Cambridge University Press.

Robinson, B.E. and Rhoden, J.L. (1998) *Working with Children of Alcoholics: The Practitioner's Handbook.* Thousand Oaks, CA: Sage.

Robson, E. (2000) Invisible Carers: Young People in Zimbabwe's Home-Based Healthcare. *Area,* 32(1): p59–69.

Robson, E. and Ansell, N. (2000) Young Carers in Southern Africa: Exploring Stories From Zimbabwean School Students. In Holloway, S.L. and Valentine, G. (Eds.)

Children's Geographies: Playing, Living, Learning. London: Routledge.

Rolland, J. (1987) Chronic Illness and the Life Cycle: A Conceptual Framework.. *Family Process,* 26: p203–21

Romano, M. (1976) Preparing Children for Parental Disability. *Social Work in Health Care,* 1(3): p309–15.

Roosa, M.W., Wolchik, S.A. and Sandler, I.S. (1997) Preventing the Negative Effects of Common Stressors: Current Status and Future Directions. In Wolchik, S.A. and Sandler, I.N. (Eds.) (1997) *Handbook of Children's Coping: Linking Theory and Intervention.* New York: Plenum Press.

Rosen, A., Proctor, E.K. and Staudt, M.M. (1999) Social Work Research and the Quest for Effective Practice. *Social Work Research,* 23(1): p4–14.

Roth, A. and Fonagy, P. (1996) *What Works for Whom? A Critical Review of Psychotherapy Research.* New York: Guildford Press.

Rowlands, J. (1997) A Better Way to Define Needs. *Children's Services News,* July.

Roy, R. (1991) Consequences of Parental Illness on Children: A Review. *Social Work and Social Science Review,* 2(2): p109–21.

Ruppert, S. and Bagedahl-Strindlund, M. (2001) Children of Parapartum Mentally Ill Mothers: A Follow-up Study. *Psychopathology,* 34: p174–8.

Rutter, M. (1966) *Children of Sick Parents: An Environmental and Psychiatric Study.* London: Oxford University Press.

Rutter, M. (1985) Resilience in the Face of Adversity: Protective Factors and Resistance to Psychiatric Disorders. *British Journal of Psychiatry,* 147: p589–611.

Rutter, M. (1999) Resilience Concepts and Findings: Implications for Family Therapy. *Journal of Family Therapy,* 21: p119–44.

Rutter, M. and Quinton, D. (1984) Parental Psychiatric Disorder: Effects on Children. *Psychological Medicine,* 14: p853–80.

Rutter, M. and Smith, D.J. (Eds.) (1995) *Psychosocial Disorders in Young People.* Chichester: John Wiley.

Rydelius, P. (1997) Annotation: Are Children of Alcoholics a Clinical Concern for Child and Adolescent Psychiatrists of Today? *Journal of Child Psychology and Psychiatry,* 38(6): p615–24.

Saleebey, D. (1996) The Strengths Perspective in Social Work Practice: Extensions and Cautions. *Social Work,* 41: p296–305.

Salmon, G., James, A. and Smith, D.M. (1998) Bullying in Schools: Self Reported Anxiety, Depression and Self Esteem in Secondary School Children. *British Medical Journal,* 317: p924–5.

Sandler, I.N., Miller, P., Short, J. and Wolchik, S.A. (1989) Social Support as a Protective Factor for Children in Stress. In Belle, D. (Ed.) *Children's Social Networks and Social Supports.* New York: John Wiley and Sons.

Sandler, I.N., Wolchik, S.A., Mackinnon, D., Ayers, T.S. and

Roosa, M.W. (1997) Developing Linkages Between Theory and Intervention in Stress and Coping Processes. In Wolchik, S.A. and Sandler, I.N. (Eds.) *Handbook of Children's Coping: Linking Theory and Intervention*. New York: Plenum Press.

Saxena, S., Majeed, A. and Jones, M. (1999) Socio-economic Differences in Childhood Consultation Rates in General Practice in England and Wales: Prospective Cohort Study. *British Medical Journal*, 318: p642–6.

Sayce, L. (1999) Parenting as a Civil Right: Supporting Service Users who Choose to have Children. In Weir, A. and Douglas, A. (Eds.) *Child Protection and Adult Mental Health: Conflict of Interest?* Oxford: Butterworth-Heinemann.

Scarr, S. and McCartney, K. (1983) How People Make their Own Environments: A Theory of Genotype Environmental Effects. *Child Development*, 54: p424–35.

Schmideberg, M. (1948) Parents as Children. *Psychiatric Quarterly Supplement*, 22: p207–18.

Schuckit, M.A. (1991) A 10 Year Follow up of Sons of Alcoholics: Preliminary Results. *Alcohol* (Alcohol Supplement), 1: p147–9.

Schwab-Stone, M., Fallon, T., Briggs, M. and Crowther, B. (1994) Reliability of Diagnostic Reporting for Children Aged 6–11 Years: A Test, Re-Test Study of the Diagnostic Interview Schedule for Children: Revised. *American Journal of Psychiatry*, 151: p1048–54.

Scottish Office Social Work Services Group (1997) *The Children (Scotland) Act 1995, Regulations and Guidance. 1: Support and Protection for Children and their Families*. Edinburgh: HMSO.

Seagull, E. and Scheurer, S. (1986) Neglected and Abused Children of Mentally Retarded Mothers. *Child Abuse and Neglect*, 10: p493–500.

Seal, H. (1998) *See the Adult, See the Child: The Needs of Children Living with Adults with Mental Health Problems in Swindon: An Exploratory Study*. Swindon Social Services Department/Wiltshire Health Authority.

Segal, J. and Simpkins, J. (1993) *My Mum Needs Me: Helping Children with Ill or Disabled Parents*. Harmondsworth: Penguin.

Segal, J. and Simpkins, J. (1996) *Helping Children with Ill or Disabled Parents: A Guide for Parents and Professionals*. London: Jessica Kingsley.

Selbourne, D. (1994) *The Principle of Duty*. London: Sinclair Stephenson.

Seligman, M. (1975) *Helplessness: On Depression, Development and Death*. San Francisco: W.H. Freeman.

Seligman, M. (1987) Adaptation of Children to a Chronically Ill or Mentally Handicapped Sibling. *CMAJ*, 136(12): p1249–52.

Seligman, M. (1998) *Learned Optimism*. New York: Pocket Books.

Shah, R. and Hatton, C. (1999) *Caring Alone: Young Carers in South Asian Communities*. Ilford: Barnardo's.

Sheldon, B. (1984) A Critical Appraisal of the Medical Model in Psychiatry. In Olsen, M.R. (Ed.) *Social Work and Mental Health: A Guide for the Approved Social Worker*. London: Tavistock Publications.

Sheldon, B. and Macdonald, G. (1999) *Research and Practice in Social Care: Mind the Gap*. Exeter: Centre for Evidence Based Social Services.

Sheppard, M. (1997) Social Work Practice in Child and Family Care: A Study of Maternal Depression. *British Journal of Social Work*, 27: p815–45.

Shifren, K. (2001) Early Caregiving and Adult Depression: Good News for Young Caregivers. *Gerontologist*, 41(2): p188–90.

Shorter, E. (1992) *From Paralysis to Fatigue: A History of Psychosomatic Illness in the Modern Era*. New York: Free Press.

Showalter, E. (1998) *Hystories: Hysterical Epidemics and Modern Culture*. London: Picador.

Silberg, J., Rutter, M., Meyer, J., Maes, H., Hewitt, J., Simonoff, E., Pickles, A., Loeber, R. and Eaves, L. (1996) Genetic and Environmental Influences on the Covariation Between Hyperactivity and Conduct Problems in Juvenile Twins. *Journal of Child Psychology and Psychiatry*, 37(7): p803–16.

Smith, C. and Carlson, B. (1997) Stress, Coping and Resilience in Children and Youth. *Social Service Review*, 71(2): p231–56.

Smith, D.J. and Rutter, M. (1995) Time Trends in Psychosocial Disorders of Youth. In Rutter, M. and Smith, D.J. (Eds.) *Psychosocial Disorders in Young People*. Chichester: John Wiley.

Smith, P.K. and Sharp, S. (Eds.) (1994) *School Bullying: Insights and Perspectives*. London: Routledge.

Spaccerelli, S. and Kim, S. (1994) Resilience Criteria and Factors Associated with Resilience in Sexually Abused Girls. *Child Abuse and Neglect*, 19(9): p1171–82.

Sroufe, L.A. and Walsh, J.J. (1980) Seductive Behaviors of Mothers and Toddlers: Occurrence, Correlates and Family Origins. *Child Development*, 51: p1222–9.

Stables, J. and Smith, F. (1999) 'Caught in the Cinderella Trap': Narratives of Disabled Parents and Young Carers. In Butler, R. and Parr, H. (Eds.) *Mind and Body Spaces: Geographies of Illness, Impairment and Disability*. London: Routledge.

Stanford, P. (2000) 'You Poor Old Soul'. *Independent* (Colour Magazine Supplement), 25th Nov.: p31–5.

Stawski, M., Auerbach, JG., Barasch, M., Lerner, Y. and Zimin, R. (1997) Behavioural Problems of Children with Chronic Physical Illness and their Siblings. *European Child and Adolescent Psychiatry*, 6(1): p20–5.

Stein, J.A., Riedel, M. and Rotheram-Borus, M.J. (1999) Parentification and its Impact on Adolescent Children of Parents with AIDS. *Family Process*, 38(2): p193–208.

Steinhausen, H.C. (1995) Children of Alcoholic Parents: A Review. *European Journal of Adolescent Psychiatry*, 4(3): p143–52.

Stewart, R.B. (1983) Sibling Interaction: The Role of the Older Child as Teacher for the Younger. *Merrill-Palmer Quarterly*, 29: p47–68.

Stewart-Brown, S. (1998) Public Health Implications of Childhood Behaviour Problems and Parenting Programmes. in Buchanan, A. and Hudson, B. (Eds.) *Parenting, Schooling and Children's Behaviour.* Aldershot: Ashgate.

Stoleru, S., Nottelmann, E.D., Belmont, B. and Ronsaville, D. (1997) Sleep Problems in Children of Affectively Ill Mothers. *Journal of Child Psychology and Psychiatry*, 38(7): p831–41.

Stott, F.M., Musick, J.S., Cohler, B.J., Spencer, K.K., Goldman, J., Clark, R. and Dincin, J. (1984) Intervention for the Severely Disturbed Mother. In Cohler, B.J. and Musick, J.S. (Eds.) Intervention Among Psychiatrically Impaired Parents and their Young Children. *New Directions for Mental Health Services*, No. 24. San Francisco: Jossey-Bass Inc.

Summerfield, D. (2000) Post-traumatic Stress Disorder in Doctors Involved in the Omagh Bombing. *British Medical Journal*, 320: p1276.

Summerfield, D. (2002) ICD and DSM are Contemporary Cultural Documents. *British Medical Journal*, 324: p914.

Taggart, L. (1999) *An Examination of the Effectiveness of an Education Programme in Addressing the Psychological Needs of Young Carers in Northern Ireland* (Unpublished BSc Dissertation) Jordanstown: University of Ulster, Department of Applied Psychology.

Tanner, D. (2000) Crossing Bridges Over Troubled Waters? Working with Children of Parents Experiencing Mental Distress. *Social Work Education*, 19(3): p287–97.

Tardieu, M., Mayaux, M.J., Seibel, N., Funck-Brentano, I., Straub, E., Teglas, J.P. and Blanche, S. (1995) Cognitive Assessment of School-Age Children Infected with Maternally Transmitted HIV Infection: A Descriptive Study. *Journal of Pediatrics*, 126: p375–9.

Tatum, C. and Tucker, S. (1998) The Concealed Consequences of Caring: An Examination of the Experiences of Young Carers in the Community. *Youth and Family Policy*, 61: Autumn; p12–27.

Taylor, V., Fuggle, P. and Charman, T. (2001) Well Sibling Psychological Adjustment to Chronic Physical Disorder in a Sibling: How Important is Maternal Awareness of their Illness Attitudes and Perceptions? *Journal of Child Psychology and Psychiatry*, 42(7): p953–62.

Thomas, D.N. (1997) *When the Time Comes: Children and Young People in Wales Living with HIV/AIDS.* Cardiff: Children in Wales.

Thompson, S. (1991) The Search for Meaning Following a Stroke. *Basic and Applied Social Psychology*, 12: p81–96.

Thyer, B. and Wodarski, J. (1998) *Handbook of Empirical Social Work Practice, Vol. 1: Mental Disorders.* New York: John Wiley and Sons, Inc.

Tozer, C. (1998) *'I Need My Mum and My Mum Needs Me'*

A Preliminary Report on Young Carers in Dorset. Dorset Social Services Department.

Traynor, T. (1999) *Hopscotch is a Good Friend: An Evaluation of the Befriending Service at Barnardo's Hopscotch Project in Arbroath.* Ilford: Barnardo's.

Trevino, F. (1979) Siblings of Handicapped Children: Identifying those at Risk. *Social Casework*, 60: p488–93.

Tritt, S.G. and Esses, L.M. (1988) Psychosocial Adaptation of Siblings of Children with Chronic Medical Illnesses. *American Journal of Orthopsychiatry*, 58(2): p211–20.

Tsaltas, M. (1976) Children of Home Dialysis Patients. *Journal of the American Medical Association*, 236: p2764–6.

Tucker, S. and Liddiard, P. (1998) Young Carers. In Brechin, A., Walmsley, J., Katz, J. and Peace, S. (Eds.) *Care Matters: Concepts, Practice and Research Health and Social Care.* London: Sage.

Twigg, J., Atkin, K. and Perring, C. (1990) *Carers and Services: A Review of Research.* Social Policy Research Unit/HMSO.

Twyford, K. (1999) Risk Management and Risk Assessment. *Care*, 7(2): p42–52.

Tymchuk, A. (1992) Predicting Adequacy of Parenting by People with Mental Retardation. *Child Abuse and Neglect*, 16(2): p165–78.

Tymchuk, A. and Andron, L. (1990) Mothers with Mental Retardation who do or do not Abuse or Neglect their Children. *Child Abuse and Neglect*, 14: p313–23.

United Nations Development Programme/UNICEF (2002) *The Human Consequences of The Chernobyl Nuclear Accident: A Strategy for Recovery.* [www.grs.de/chernobyl/gb/ipsn-gb.pdf]

Wagner, A. (2001) *Young People Affected by Parental HIV: An Investigation from the Perspective of Service Users and Provider.* Monograph 190. Norwich: Department of Social Work and Psychosocial Studies, University of East Anglia.

Waiton, S. (2000) Parental Paranoia is Ruining Children's Lives. *Independent*, 22nd August.

Wake, M., Hesketh, K. and Cameron, F. (2000) The Child Health Questionnaire in Children with Diabetes: Cross Sectional Survey of Parent and Adolescent-Reported Functional Health Status. *Diabetic Medicine*, 17(10): p700–7.

Walker, A. (1996) *Young Carers and their Families.* London: The Stationery Office.

Walker, S. (1998) Wait Not, Want Not? *Health Service Journal*, 4th June: p32–33.

Wallender, J. and Varni, J. (1998) Effects of Pediatric Chronic Physical Disorders on Child and Family Adjustment. *Journal of Child Psychology and Psychiatry*, 39(1): p29–46.

Walsh, F.W. (1979) Breaching of Family Generation Boundaries by Schizophrenics, Disturbed and Normals. *International Journal of Family Therapy*, 1: p254–75.

Walsh-Burke, K. (1992) Family Communication and Coping With Cancer: Impact of the 'We Can Weekend'. *Journal of Psychosocial Oncology*, 10: p63–81.

Ward, C. (1994) Opportunities for Childhoods in Late Twentieth Century Britain. In Mayall, B. (Ed.) *Children's Childhoods: Observed and Experienced.* London: Falmer Press.

Ward, L. (1997) *Seen and Heard: Involving Disabled Children and Young People in Research and Development Projects.* York: Joseph Rowntree Foundation.

Waters, E., Salmon, L., Wakes, M., Wright, M. and Hesketh, K. (2001) The Health and wellbeing of Adolescents: A School Based Population Study of the Self-Report Child Health Questionnaire. *Journal of Adolescent Health*, 29: p140–9.

Wates, M. (1997) *Disabled Parents: Dispelling the Myths.* Cambridge: National Childbirth Trust in association with Radcliffe Medical Press.

Wates, M. (2002) *Supporting Disabled Parents in their Parenting Role.* Joseph Rowntree Foundation, York: York Publishing.

Watson, A. and Jones, D. (2002) The Impact of Fostering on Foster Carers' Own Children. *Adoption and Fostering*, 26(1): p49–55.

Webb, A. and Wistow, G. (1987) *Social Work, Social Care and Social Planning: The Personal Social Services Since Seebohm.* London: Longman.

Weiner, B., Frieze, I.H., Kukla, A., Reed, L., Rest, S. and Rosenbaum, R.M. (1971) *Perceiving the Causes of Success and Failure.* New York: General Learning Press.

Weinrott, M.R. (1974) A Training Programme in Behavior Modification for Siblings of the Retarded. *American Journal of Orthopsychiatry*, 44: p362–75.

Weir, A. and Douglas, A. (Eds.) (1999) *Child Protection and Adult Mental Health.* Oxford: Butterworth-Heinemann.

Weisner, T.S. and Gallimore, R. (1977) My Brother's Keeper: Child and Sibling Caretaking. *Current Anthropology*, 18(2): p169–90.

Welner, Z. and Rice, J. (1988) School-aged Children of Depressed Parents: A Blind Controlled Study. *Journal of Affective Disorders*, 15(3): p291–302.

Welsh Office (1996) *Digest of Welsh Local Area Statistics* (Provisional Edition) Pontypool: Government Statistical Service.

Werbner, P. (1990) *The Migration Process: Capital, Gifts and Offerings Among British Pakistanis.* London: Berg.

Werner, E. and Smith, R. (1982) *Vulnerable But Invincible: A Longitudinal Study of Resilient Children.* New York: McGraw-Hill.

Werner, E. and Smith, R. (1992) *Overcoming the Odds.* New York: Cornell University Press.

West, M.L. and Keller, A.E. (1991) Parentification of the Child: A Study of Bowlby's Compulsive Care-Giving Attachment Pattern. *American Journal of Psychotherapy*, 45(3): p425–31.

White, P. (1989) Caring for the Caring. *Young People Now.* June: p23.

White, S. (1996) Regulating Mental Health and Motherhood in Contemporary Welfare Services: Anxious Attachments or Attachment Anxiety? *Critical Social Policy*, 46(16): p13–20.

Wiesel, E. (1960) *Night.* Harmondsworth: Penguin.

Wilkinson, R. (1996) *Unhealthy Societies: The Afflictions of Inequality.* London: Routledge.

Wilkomirski, B. (1997) *Fragments: Memories of a Childhood, 1939–48.* London: Picador.

Williams, O.B. and Corrigan, P.W. (1992) The Differential Effects of Parental Alcoholism and Mental Illness on their Adult Children. *Journal of Clinical Psychology*, 48(3): p406–14.

Williams, P.D. (1997) Siblings and Pediatric Illness: A Review of the Literature. *International Journal of Nursing Studies*, 34(4): p312–23.

Williams, P.D., Hanson, S., Karlin, R., Ridder, L., Liebergen, A., Olson, J., Barnard, M.U. and Tobin-Rommelhart, S. (1997) Outcomes of a Nursing Intervention for Siblings of Chronically Ill Children: A Pilot Study. *Journal of The Society of Pediatric Nurses*, 2(3): p127–37.

Willow, C. (1997) *Hear! Hear! Promoting Children and Young People's Democratic Participation in Local Government.* London: National Children's Bureau.

Wilson, E.O. (1998) *Consilience: The Unity of Knowledge.* London: Little, Brown and Co.

Wilson, J. (1980) *How Many Disabled People Are There?* London: Disability Alliance.

Wilson, S. (1985) Risk and Resilience in Early Mental Development. *Developmental Psychology*, 21(5): p795–805.

Winn, M. (1983) *Children Without Childhood.* New York: Pantheon Books.

Winnicott, D. (1964) *The Child, the Family and the Outside World.* Harmondsworth: Penguin.

De Winter, M., Baerveldt, C. and Kooistra, J. (1999) Enabling Children: Participation as a New Perspective on Child-Health Promotion. *Child: Health, Care and Development*, 25(1): p15–25.

Wolkind, S. (1985) The First Years: Pre-school Children and their Families in the Inner City. In Stevenson, J. (Ed.) *Recent Research in Developmental Pathology.* Oxford: Pergamon.

Wong, D.F. (2000) Stress Factors and Mental Health of Carers with Relatives Suffering from Schizophrenia in Hong Kong: Implications for Culturally Sensitive Practices. *British Journal of Social Work*, 30: p365–82.

World Health Organisation (1948) World Health Organisation Constitution. In *Basic Documents.* Geneva: World Health Organisation.

Worsham, N.L., Compas, B.E. and Ey, S. (1997) Children's Coping with Parental Illness. In Wolchik, S.A. and Sandler, I.N. (Eds.) *Handbook of Children's Coping: Linking Theory and Intervention.* New York: Plenum Press.

Young, S., Young, B. and Ford, D. (1997) Parents with a Learning Disability: Research Issues and Informed Practice. *Disability and Society*, 12(1): p57–68.

Zeitlin, H. (1994) Children with Alcohol Misusing Parents. *British Medical Bulletin*, 50(1): p139–51.

Zelizer, V. (1994) *Pricing the Priceless Child: The Changing Social Value of Children*. Princeton, NJ: Princeton University Press.

Zeltzer, L.K., Dolgin, M.J., Sahler, O.J., Roghmann, K., Barbarin, O.A., Carpenter, P.J., Copeland, D.R., Mulhern, R.K. and Sargent, J.R. (1996) Sibling Adaptation to Childhood Cancer Collaborative Study: Health Outcomes of Siblings of Children with Cancer. *Medical and Pediatric Oncology*, 27(2): p98-107.